Maharaja Ranjit Singh

THE RISE OF THE SIKH EMPIRE AND THE MILITARY HISTORY OF THE PUNJAB

RNP SINGH

Vitasta

Published by
Renu Kaul Verma
Vitasta Publishing Pvt Ltd
2/15, Ansari Road, Daryaganj
New Delhi-110 002
info@vitastapublishing.com

ISBN 978-93-90961-69-6

First Edition 2022
2nd Reprint 2024

MRP ₹ 795

Cover and layout by Somesh Kumar Mishra
Printed by Chaman Enterprises, New Delhi

Sikh Empire under Maharaja Ranjit Singh 1838AD

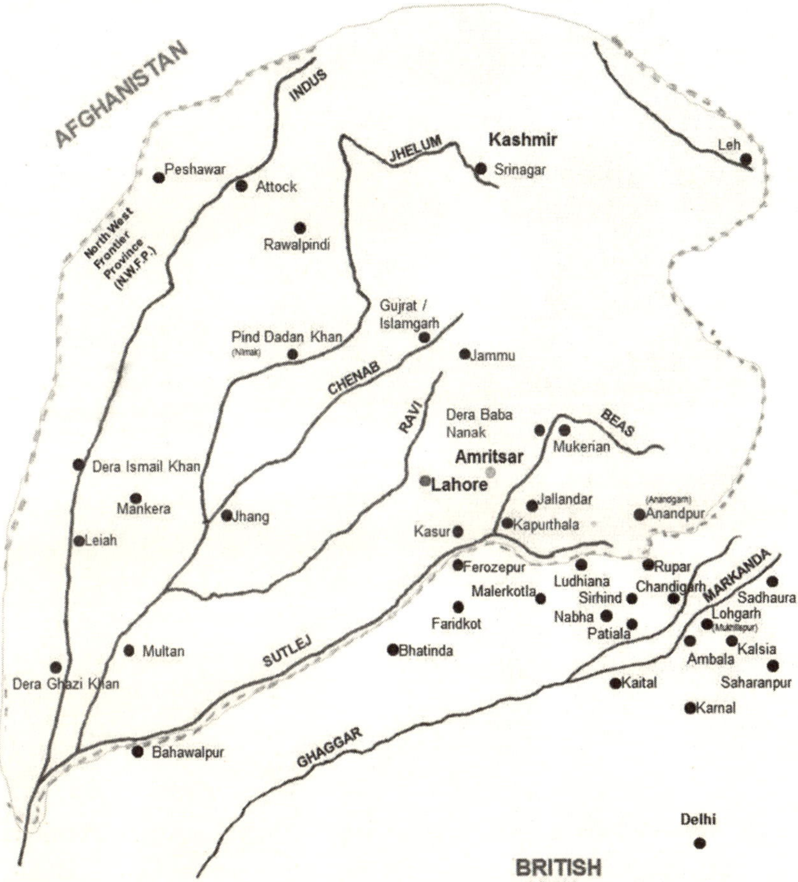

PUNJAB under Maharaja Ranjit Singh
Area : 260,124 sq.km (100,436 sq.miles)
Map not to scale

sikhcoin.blogspot.com

A Painting at the Maharaja Ranjit Singh Museum in Amritsar.

CONTENTS

He who regards all men as equals is religious

Guru Nanak

Asceticism doesn't lie in ascetic robes or in walking staff nor in the ashes. Asceticism doesn't lie in the earring nor in the shaven head nor blowing a conch. Asceticism lies in remaining pure amidst impurities

Gurbaani

There is but One God. His name is Truth...
He was True when the ages commenced and has ever been True.
He is also True now

Gurbaani

PREFACE

There is, perhaps no more notable and memorable figure among the chiefs who rose to power on the ruins of the Mughal Empire than Maharaja Ranjit Singh, the founder of the short-*lived Sikh Kingdom of Lahore. In the stormy days in the* second half of the eighteenth century, amid a fierce conflict of races and creeds, he found his opportunity, and seizing it with energy, swiftness, and genius, he welded the turbulent and warlike followers of the teaching of Guru Gobind Singh into a homogeneous nation. Under his strong and remorseless rule, the Sikhs, trained and disciplined on a military system more perfect than there had ever been before in the native States of India, were rapidly converted into a formidable fighting machine which only broke into pieces when the great Maharaja's successors persuaded them to use it against the English.

The Sikh monarchy was Napoleonic in the suddenness of its rise, the brilliancy of its success and the completeness of its overthrow due to the folly and weakness of Ranjit Singh's successors. Like his contemporary, Napoleon Bonaparte, the Maharaja of Lahore failed to found a lasting dynasty on the ruins of petty States, Rajputs, Mohammedan and Sikh, which he in turn had attacked and destroyed. His victories had no permanent result; his possessions, bound together during his lifetime by force of his commanding will, fell apart the moment the restraining band was severed. His throne and the tradition of power and greatness passed into the hands of incompetent successors, who allowed the ship of the state to drift on to the rocks of Raj Britain in irremediable wreck.

The downfall of the Sikh monarchy was chiefly due to the fact that the authority of Ranjit Singh was personal and drew no part of its strength from the inherent respect of the people for an ancient house. Sprung from the people and an outcome of the democratic principles of Sikhism, the one chance of the survival of his dynasty was that his successors should have inherited his character and ability. But this was not the case. His only son Kharak Singh was incompetent; his grandson, Nau Nihal Singh, a youth of promise, died a violent death and a period of anarchy set in, which the men who succeeded had no power to subdue or control.

There were several who claimed the throne as sons of the great Maharaja but there was not one whose legitimacy the Sikhs accepted as proved. Then came the wars with the English, in which the Sikhs, badly led, mainly because of treachery and traitorous commanders, displayed the utmost gallantry in vain; ending in the occupation of the Punjab by a foreigner's army, dismemberment, and finally annexation.

Ranjit Singh was unquestionably a great man. He went by instinct and though young, ruled with sagacity. As he swept through the Punjab, bringing more and more of it under his own control, he showed his understanding of men who obeyed him just on the basis of personal authority, building a team of exceptional administrators to become either his ministers or the holders of key positions, such as the governorship of newly won territories.

Himself an outstanding military commander who had learnt the art of war on the battlefield from an early age, he created the Sikh Khalsa Army which the British would come to acknowledge as the best in India, an accolade that would become widely accepted after the two Sikh Wars of 1845 and 1848. General Sir Charles Gough and Arthur Innes wrote in the introduction to *The Sikh Wars*: '... in the Sikhs we found the most stubborn foe we ever faced on Indian soil since the French were beaten at Wandewash'. That army made possible the remarkable military success which characterised the forty-two years of Ranjit Singh's reign.

No man is perfect and, as history frequently reveals, it is often apparent that the greater a man's merit and talents, the greater his failings and weaknesses. If that were not so he would be less than human. Ranjit Singh was no exception. He too had certain qualities which were unworthy of his greatness. Though illiterate, he was highly intelligent and extremely able, and at times showed himself to be cunning, treacherous and quite ruthless. Yet, with one or two particular exceptions, he took no life except in battle, and rehabilitated all those he vanquished. When it came to acquisition of treasure, such as the great Koh-i-noor diamond, or possession of some object that had seized his imagination, such as the beautiful Persian horse, Leili, or even less desirable objects, he would cheat and even steal, if need be. If he had decided that he wanted something, he took it, regardless of the means or cost.

As a political figure, Ranjit Singh was in every way as remarkable a man as his two famous contemporaries, Napoleon Bonaparte of France and Mohammad Ali of Egypt. He rose from the status of petty chieftain to become the most powerful ruler of his time. He was the first Indian in a thousand years to stem the tides of invasions that had come across the North-West frontiers of Hindustan. Although he dispossessed hundreds of feudal land holders to consolidate his kingdom, he succeeded in winning their affections and converting them into faithful courtiers.

In the history of the world, it would be hard to find another dictator who never took life in cold blood yet built as large an empire as Ranjit Singh's. He persuaded the turbulent Sikhs and Muslims of the Punjab to become willing instruments of his expansionist policy which brought the Kashmiris and the Pathans of the North-West frontier under his subjugation and extended his sphere of influence from the borders of Tibet and Afghanistan in the North to the deserts of Sindh in the South. His success was undoubtedly due to his ability to arouse the growing sense of nationalism amongst his people and make them conscious that more important than being Muslim, Hindu or Sikh was the fact of being Punjabi. His Sikh and Hindu troops subdued the Sikh and Hindu Rajas of the Punjab. His Mussalman *najib*s rejected the appeals of their Hindustani, Afghan and Pathan co-religionists to crusade against an 'infidel', and instead, helped to liquidate the crusaders.

Ranjit Singh's most compelling quality was his total commitment to the religious faith into which he was born. If in Sikhism secularity – or equal respect for other religions – was its founding principle, then he was determined never to deviate from it. Proof of this was the fact that no other ruler in the sprawling subcontinent had ever had in his cabinet as many men owing allegiance to other religions as Ranjit Singh had. In that sense, he was the most cosmopolitan among his contemporaries. At the peak of his power, there were only seven Sikhs in his cabinet of fifteen ministers and the rest were Hindus and Muslims. Many others of different religions, such as Jains, Buddhists, Christians and the bewildering sub-divisions of these faiths from different countries, were accommodated according to their talents. He had Napoleon's generals like Jean-Francois Allard and Jean-Baptiste Ventura as well as the canon-maker, Auguste Court, in his service.

How was this leader able to achieve the seemingly impossible goals he set himself? The answer lies in his reverence for the ten founding fathers of the Sikh faith and the ethos of decency and discipline they preached. A part of the answer also lies in the fact that at the age of nine he had to assume the chieftainship of his father's *misl*, or Confederacy, which was one of the more powerful in the Punj-ab (the land of the five rivers or the Indus delta). To take on the Chief's position was an awesome responsibility. But Ranjit Singh, by handling it with energy and enthusiasm, gained the self-confidence that never left him.

The achievements of his grandfather and father before him (his mother Raj Kaur was the daughter of Sikh Raja Gajpat Singh of Jind and his father was Mahan Singh of Gujranwala), who were warriors and leaders of great repute, were of fundamental importance to his own career. But the distinctive qualities that made Ranjit Singh truly exceptional were his humanitarianism, his respect for other faiths and his total disgust for the inhumane treatment that rulers of the day inflicted on their defeated adversaries. As the British historian Sir Lepel Griffin rightly observed: 'Ranjit Singh was not cruel or blood thirsty. After a victory or the capture of a fortress he treated the vanquished with leniency and kindness, however stout their resistance might have been, and there were at his court many despoiled of their estates but to whom he had given suitable employment....'[1]

He was great because he possessed in an extraordinary degree the qualities without which the highest success cannot be attained. 'He was a born ruler, with the natural genius of Command. Men obeyed him by instruct and because they had no power to disobey. The control which he exercised, even in the closing years of his life, over the whole Sikh people, nobles, priests and people, was the measure of his greatness.'[2]

Griffin describes Ranjit Singh as: 'He possessed the faculty – which is one of the highest attributes of genius, and for lack of which many brilliantly gifted men have suffered shipwreck

– the faculty of choosing his subordinates well and wisely. He knew men, and he selected each servant for the special work which he could best perform....'[3]

The personal life of Ranjit Singh was as colourful as his political career. Although an ugly man himself (pock-marked on his face), he loved to surround himself with handsome men and beautiful women. The Maharaja was a hard drinker, and it was his indulgence in frequent and heavy drinking which killed him, as it has killed a large number of Indian princes in whose States there was no public opinion sufficiently strong to restrain them from excessive drinking. However, his habitual and excessive drinking did not deter Ranjit Singh from going to the battlefield. He was small of stature and slight of build, but he was full of daring. In many campaigns, he led his troops himself and fought sword in hand. He lived a life of a soldier, and a soldier drank hard. But after the parties were over, he sat up till the early hours of dawn, dictating letters and memoranda to a relay of writers.

It is his commitment to the faith and reverence of the Gurus that even after he had wrested control of Amritsar from the chiefs of the Bhangi misl in 1802, Ranjit Singh arrived at the Harmandir, the Golden Temple, not as a victorious military leader or the monarch of a Sikh State, but as a devotee – amongst countless others – who had come to pray at the holiest of Sikh shrines. This was the way of demonstrating his conviction that within the sacrosanct precincts of the Durbar Sahib, there was no place for the self-important or the arrogant.

The story of the ten years following the death of Ranjit Singh is truly tragic. As the story unfolds and the underlying treachery on the part of the Lahore Durbar and the Sikh generals emerges, so does the clear evidence of the gallantry and determination of the solders of the Khalsa Army. How else could it have been that the British were so nearly defeated at

Ferozeshahar and Chillianwala and again were given such a bloody nose at Ramnagar and Sobraon? Gujrat was indeed a famous British victory in the end. Treachery and intrigue apart, at no time did the Sikh generals bow their heads before the British. This extraordinary story calls for the most relentless research until at last, the whole truth finally emerges.

The story ends with the annexation of the Punjab in 1849 and the final demise of the Sukerchakia dynasty, founded by Ranjit Singh's paternal grandfather, Charhat Singh, and brought to further greatness by his father Mahan Singh before Ranjit Singh himself created a kingdom which finally embraced not only the entire Punjab in present-day Pakistan but territories to the north and west which even included Jammu and Kashmir, extending up to the Tibetan frontier and Afghanistan, and what is now known as the Northern Areas in Pakistan. To these were also added the eastern areas of the present Indian Punjab and Himachal Pradesh, the entire west of the river Sutlej. This extraordinary empire, built up over a period of seventy years, finally collapsed with the exile of Maharaja Dalip Singh.

Was it destiny that brought about that downfall or did the prophecy of Guru Gobind Singh come true? Guru Gobind had said at Hazoor Sahib, at Nanded, just before his death in 1708, that whosoever built a memorial to him would die and his dynasty fade out of history. Ranjit Singh did build such a memorial and at the end of his glorious reign of half a century, the dynasty collapsed due to lack of worthy successors. His grandson, Maharaja Kharak Singh's son, Maharaja Nau Nihal Singh died in an accident without leaving an heir, and the following maharajas, Sher Singh and his son Partap Singh, were assassinated. Dalip Singh, the last of Ranjit Singh's children (the son of Jind Kaur), was exiled from the Punjab as a ten-year-old boy, never to return and, though married twice with nine children of his own, Dalip never saw his grandchildren, as none of the nine, though some were married, had a child. Whatever the reason, it is beyond doubt that the collapse of the dynasty finally paved the way for the complete annexation of the Punjab and the Indian subcontinent into the British Empire.

Even though many books have been written on Ranjit Singh, I chose to write on this legendary figure of India because I felt that the vast range of this man's characteristics and strategies still require to be studied. The rare qualities of Ranjit Singh are not only confined to his military achievements but his secular behaviour among fellow men, liberal and kind attitude towards the vanquished and the humane rule he provided during the turbulent times when barbarism was the order of the day – this makes him a ruler rarest among the rare.

The present book cannot be said to be a complete study of this man from the Punjab. Mainland India is indebted to this great warrior who could deter and stop the inflow of invaders into India, who mostly found their way through the North-West frontier, for at least forty years before the advent of the British. So, this work is more in the nature of a tribute to a great leader of men who liberated North-West India from brutal invasions, establishing a rule in which all people, without distinction of caste, class or creed, were co-sharers.

References

1. Sir Lepel Griffin, Rulers of India: Ranjit Singh, Oxford, London, 1892, p-98.
2. Ibid, pp-91-92.
3. Ibid, p-92.

SIKH CONSOLIDATION AND THE MARTYR GURUS

MAHARAJA RANJIT SINGH was so completely a product of the Sikh theocracy, and so embodied the spirit of the Khalsa, that no account of his character and career would be complete without a description of the religious system which had so powerful an effect upon the Jat cultivators of the Punjab in the eighteenth and the first half of the nineteenth century.

The *Adi Granth* derives its chief authority from Guru Nanak, the founder of the religious order of the Sikhs, who provided the spoken words that form large portions of his *Granth* sometime in the late sixteenth century. It was collected in its present state by Arjan Deb, the fifth Guru of the Sikhs, who added the writings of the successor Gurus and other older mystical Hindu authors to that of Nanak's original compositions.

More important than the *Adi Granth*, the military and political constitution of later-day Sikhdom were determined by the writings of the tenth and greatest of the Sikh Gurus, Gobind Singh, who, in 1696 composed a voluminous extended and extant work, which he partly wrote himself and had it partly written by the local language poets attached to him. Guru Gobind Singh did not, however, change the mystical doctrine of Guru Nanak in any essential particulars, although his teaching and practice were more distinctly pantheistic.

Guru Nanak

Nanak, the founder of the Sikh faith, was born on 15 April 1469 at a village called Talwandi on the bank of the river Ravi, near the city of Lahore. Later, the village Talwandi was called Nankana Sahib in honour of the Guru. Born into a Hindu family, there are a number of miraculous stories of his childhood frozen around him. When he asked his parents, or the family's Brahmin priest, Pandit Hardyal some forthright questions or made some profound observations, their astonishment was beyond belief. For example, when he announced, 'There is no Hindu, there is no Mussalman'.[1]

Pandit Hardyal was further baffled when at the age of eleven, amidst a gathering of relatives and friends, Nanak refused to wear the *janeu* or the sacred thread of the Hindus, which all male Brahmin offspring are required to wear from that age onwards. The janeu consists of strands of cotton thread woven into a thin cord, in the form of a circle, which is then looped from the left shoulder around the right hip. After declining to wear it, Nanak asked the Brahmin priest presiding over the ceremony to explain to him what difference wearing the thread would make to his life. If he was not convinced that it could make any real difference, he would prefer not to be a party to the ceremony. As if this had not shaken the priest enough, he then recited his own composition to him and to the assembled guests:

> Out of the cotton of compassion, Spin the thread of contentment;
> Tie the knot of continence, and the twist of virtue;
> Make such a sacred thread, O Pandit, for your inner Self.
>
> Guru Granth Sahib
> Rag Asa, p-471.

Pandit Hardyal predicted in the horoscope, which he drew up for Nanak, that he would be looked up to in the years to come as a scholar and philosopher by both Hindus and Muslims and he would not make any distinction between them. His second teacher, who taught him Sanskrit, is quoted as saying, 'He is the blessed one... he grasps instantly what he hears once'.[2] His teachers were thoroughly impressed by his potential for scholarship, spiritual quest and by his tendency to question the rationale behind traditional practices, as by his inquiring mind and contemplative nature.

At the age of 16, on the persuasion of his adoring sister Nanki, he moved to the town of Sultanpur, a hundred miles away from his parental home. He began living with her and her husband, who worked for Nawab Daulat Khan Lodhi, the region's powerful governor and a relative of the ruler Bahlol Khan at Delhi. A refined and scholarly man, Daulat Khan was so impressed by Nanak that he offered him a job, which Nanak accepted, even though this wasn't exactly what he was looking for.

During his eight-year stay in Sultanpur, Nanak married Sulakhani at 19 and subsequently became father of two sons, Srichand and Lakhminda. When he was barely in his twenties, word spread about his saintliness and scholarly insights into the purpose and meaning of life and the code by which it should be lived. These attributes drew people – even from distant places – towards him, and they listened to him with a growing reverence. But Nanak knew, intuitively, and because of his intellectual honesty, that he still had much to probe and question, learn and absorb before he could meaningfully communicate with the disciples who had begun to gravitate towards him.

During this period Nanak appears to have lived a commonplace life with wife and two sons. It is said that, 'going one day to bathe in the river, he was taken up by angels and carried to the Divine Presence where he received the gift of prophecy and orders to preach the doctrine of the True God on the Earth'. This incident changed the course of his life. In obedience to this divine mission, Nanak abandoned his wife and family and, with just one follower named Mardana, he assumed the garb of an ascetic and 'roamed the land preaching the new faith'.[3]

He visited all the centres of religious learning in the country that he could, and travelled to several far-off countries as well, to understand the essence of their beliefs and what helped to sustain them. He himself believed in the concept of One God. He was increasingly of the view that only this could help a war-ridden, conflict-prone and totally fragmented world, in which millions of weak and demoralised victims of aggression suffered. He wished to meet the scholars and sages at the great religious centres of the world and hear their views on these critical human concerns.

His journeys were a remarkable feat for those times. The troublesome paths and difficult situations did not deter his iron will. Starting in 1496, Nanak's travels lasted for twenty-eight years. The first phase of his travels in India took him from Hardwar to Banaras, Kamrup (Assam), Puri Jaganath (Orissa) and to Southern India and Ceylon. In the next phase, he visited foreign lands and distant places such as Tibet, Kabul, Baghdad and Mecca. He put his visits to these places to good use in that he undertook extensive exchanges of views and beliefs with men of learning and those with the philosophical bent of mind. Thus, Nanak became a global citizen, an inheritor of universal philosophies. Each new encounter helped him to define more sharply the contours of faith he was giving shape to in a number of hymns that he was composing. Nanak composed 974 hymns to his one God during this period.

Emperor Babur, sitting on Kabul's throne at the time and eyeing the Lodhi throne in India, met Nanak in his outward journey and is described to have 'received Nanak with kindness and courtesy'. Towards the close of his life, Nanak returned to his family at Kartarpur, now in Pakistan and commonly known as Kartarpur Sahib, where he died on 7 September 1539. His life had been uneventful, much resembling that of any much-travelled Buddhist or Hindu or Sufi saint from this subcontinent, and the influence he left behind him was enshrined in his compositions in the oral tradition and a few written texts which were subsequently collected. He named as his successor, his disciple Angad, passing over his two sons.

Sikh, the Forever Learner

The word 'Sikh' comes from the Sanskrit word *sishya* which means a devoted follower or a disciple – a learner – a word very much in tune with the new faith Nanak was professing. Nanak, the Guru or the teacher, was as much the founder of the Sikh faith as he was the father of Punjabi nationalism. Consequently, Nanak's faith was comprehensive, comprising the teaching of the Hindu *bhaktas* who had rebelled against the rigid caste system, ritualism and the intolerance of Brahminical Hinduism and the teachings of Muslim Sufis who believed in converting non-believers by persuasion and not by the sword of Islam.

Nanak's pronouncement: 'There is no Hindu, there is no Mussalman' does not seem very startling at first glance but as Nanak proceeded to elucidate it in sermons and to put it into practice, its revolutionary implications became clearer to societies and religious heads of different communities as well as to all students of theology and philosophy at the time. For those seeking religious guidance, it meant that the (advaitya) God of the Hindus and (the Allah) of the Muslims was one and the same God; what really mattered was not in the form but the spirit of worship.

Nanak set an example by taking as companion a Muslim musician and by going to Hindu holy places as well as making a pilgrimage to Mecca. He joined Hindus in their temples and chanted hymns from the Vedas; he stood in line with the Muslims in their mosques and knelt down in prayer facing the Kaaba. He, thus, started a religious movement which ignored sectarian differences between the two communities by emphasising what they had in common. The secular implications of his simple statement were far-reaching and momentous because he proclaimed more emphatically than any one before him that it was *not necessary* to look upon one's neighbours as either Hindu or Muslim; that the people who lived in the wide plains intersected by rivers which had given the land its name, Punjab – land of five rivers – were one people because their interests were common. Nanak's was a global vision of a universal philosophy and a religion of tolerance.

The Second Guru, Angad

Guru Nanak was succeeded by Guru Angad, who had been chosen by Nanak in preference to his two sons. Guru Angad proved to be a worthy successor, giving further push to this new world vision. He began the task of collating all of Guru Nanak's hymns and took 62 of his own compositions and put them together in the form of a book. The script he chose was Gurumukhi, the hymns were composed in medieval Punjabi, Hindi and other languages of the time. This book, known as Nanak's *baani*, would be the precursor (the first text format of the *Adi Granth* or the *Gurbaani)* of the *Guru Granth Sahib*, the present-day holy scripture of the Sikhs.

When time came for Guru Angad to name his successor, he installed Guru Amar Das, one of his devotees, as the next Guru. Angad's two sons had their own ambitions and were up in arms against Amar Das. Guru Angad told them that among his followers and devotees of their Sikh faith, 'the honour must go to the one who deserved it most'.[4] Guru Angad died on 29 March 1552.

The Third Guru, Amar Das

Guru Amar Das was 73 when he became the successor of Guru Angad. A mere devotee who prided himself on being the humblest servant of the Guru, living where the Guru desired him to live, doing what the Guru asked him to do, he was all of a sudden raised to the supreme status of the master to provide leadership to innumerable followers far and near.

Guru Amar Das gave priority to organise and strengthen the Sikh faith by fulfilling the needs of the *sangat*s, or assemblies, of Sikhs which were first set up by Guru Nanak. Guru Nanak had laid stress on the sangat, which meant a congregation of Sikhs, both in the morning and evening, in order to sing praises of the Almighty. Guru Amar Das strengthened the institution of sangat by setting up 22 *manji*s (dioceses) formally presided over by devout Sikhs. With a view to spreading Guru Nanak's message, he trained a band of 146 high priests of whom 52 were women, to go to various parts of the country and attend to the spiritual needs of the Guru's followers. He also institutionalised the concept of *langar*, a community kitchen, open to all, no matter what their religion was. Every Sikh Gurudwara, a deeply venerated place of worship that houses the Sikh scriptures, has a langar attached to it. The Guru himself made it a point to eat there every day along with the others. On a historical note, the countryside of northern India was ravaged at the time by successive invasions and wars and people were poor. This provision of community food kitchens meant a great deal for people then as it does now. By this time, the Mughals had entrenched themselves on the throne in Delhi.

The story goes, during one of his visits to Lahore in 1567, the emperor, Akbar, was crossing the river Beas. He decided to make a slight diversion in his route to visit Goindwal (in India's Taran Taran district) to pay homage to Guru Amar Das about whose godliness he had heard a great deal. To see the Guru, even the emperor had to partake of food in the langar like any other visitor. It is said that the emperor sat with the lowest of the low and ate with them and then had audience with the Guru. Akbar was highly impressed at the meeting and wished to grant a *jaagir* to the Guru for maintenance of the langar. The Guru did not agree to take this, saying, 'we start afresh every morning. Nothing is saved for the next day. The rations are brought by the devotees daily and are distributed among them every day'.

The emperor nevertheless insisted on making the grant in appreciation of the great humanitarian work being done by the Guru. Since the Guru would not accept any favour from the emperor, Akbar, a great alliance-maker, thought of a method. 'I can, at least, present a few villages to your daughter, Bhani, who is as much my daughter, as a wedding gift.' In good grace, Guru Amar Das could not decline this offer. It is believed that it was on this land gifted by Emperor Akbar that Amritsar, the renowned Sikh centre of faith and doctrine, came to be established.[5]

Guru Amar Das took the first steps in building of the holiest of all Sikh shrines (the Harmandir Sahib, which later came be known as the Golden Temple), by choosing a site in the gifted estate with a beautiful clear pool (Amrit Sarovar or a pool of elixir) surrounded by a grove of trees, and a variety of flora and fauna. The actual construction of the temple destined to become the emblematic core of Sikhism would take several decades, and owed much to the fourth and fifth Gurus, Ram Das and Arjan Dev, but it was Guru Amar Das who conceptualised it all during his short tenure.

The Fourth Guru, Ram Das

When Amar Das died on 1 September 1574, the leadership of the faith passed on to the fourth Guru, Ram Das, who had created a lasting impression on the third Guru by totally identifying himself with the principles and purposes of Sikhism. He personally directed the development of the Golden Temple's Amritsar site. In the construction of the Harmandir and the development of its surroundings, Sikhism's enduring principles of voluntary labour and self-reliance were considered sacrosanct. Guru Ram Das wanted to provide the community with a nucleus but he could neither complete the work on the holy tank nor start the actual construction of the Harmandir as he left this world rather early in life, handing over the stewardship of the community to his youngest son, Guru Arjan Dev, a sensitive poet and scholar of eminence. Thus, while the next six Guru positions were inherited, there was no concept yet of kingship or any inherited kingdom or inherited rulership until after the Tenth Guru, among the Sikhs. However, it is during Arjan Dev's leadership of the faith that the Sikhs entered into conflict with the Mughals on their east.

The Fifth Guru, Arjan Dev

What Guru Arjan Dev, born on 15 April 1563, achieved in twenty-five years of his stewardship proved to be of lasting significance to the future course of Sikhism; he played a pivotal role in strengthening the vigor of the faith. In keeping with the basic Sikh belief that there are no Hindus or Muslims, all being one in the eyes of God, he invited an eminent Muslim saint, Mian Mir (belonging to a Sufi sect) from Lahore to lay the foundation stone of the Harmandir which was in most likelihood in 1588 (most written records were destroyed in the conflicts between the Sikhs, the Afghans, the Mughals and the English), and construction work began in 1589.

The Sikhs desired that it should be the tallest building in the rapidly growing town. The Guru, however, thought otherwise. He reminded his followers that there was no virtue like humility. The temple was, therefore, built on as low an elevation as possible. He also decided to have the new temple open on all the four sides; anyone could enter it from any side. This was contrary to extant mosque and Hindu temple architecture and there could not be a better way to send forth the message of Guru Nanak's philosophical percept – all gods were equal, all religions are to be respected and no one should be discriminated against. All people are equal.

In addition to the creation of the Darbar Sahib (Golden Temple) and the holy city of Amritsar, Guru Arjan Dev's contribution to the faith was in compiling the Sikh scripture in the form of *Adi Granth*, later known as the *Granth Sahib*. (This original edition was known as *Adi Granth* while the final edition as the *Guru Granth*. This was given its final form by the tenth and last Guru, Gobind Singh, who added the hymns of the ninth Guru, Tegh Bahadur, to it.)

This compilation contained the thoughts, verses, hymns and teachings not only of the first five Sikh Gurus but also of those Hindu and Muslim scholars and saints like Kabir, Namdev, Ravidas, Sheikh Farid, Jaidev and Surdas. The *Granth Sahib* also enshrines the secular principle enunciated by Nanak, that is, that all great faiths must be respected for their nobility of purpose, which will always remain a faith's cornerstone.

Guru Arjan Dev's monumental efforts produced an *Adi Granth* of 1,948 pages containing more than 7,000 hymns, 2,218 of them being his own. The scriptures are set to 31 *raga*s (the basic modes in Indian classical music), so that the rationality of thought is rendered lyrically in a musical framework of symphonies. All this could not have been done without the meticulous editing standards Arjan Dev set himself and the minutest attention he paid to style, syntax and rhythm to ensure a natural flow of the text.

The *Adi Granth* was installed in the Harmandir Sahib in 1604, thereby fulfilling Guru Arjan Dev's aim of providing those who visited the holy shrine with a profound sense of fulfilment they could never get from an empty structure. The reverence and sanctity accorded to the Harmandir Sahib are focused on the *Granth Sahib* installed in it. It became the practice for passages to be read from the *Granth Sahib* at particular times every day (and nowadays throughout the day), alternating with verses sung to the sound of music played on traditional instruments for the edification of those coming to listen to the words, thoughts and wisdom of the various other sages.

Martyrdom of Guru Arjan Dev

It has been common throughout history for individuals of saintly character to be viewed with disfavour, if not hostility, by those resentful of their spiritual stature and authority. Guru Arjan Dev was no exception. Unfortunately, Akbar, the monarch with a wide vision, did not live long. He was followed by his son Jehangir on the throne. Jehangir was pleasure loving; eat, drink and be merry was his motto. He left the administration of his kingdom to his Queen and courtiers. Under the influence of the *ulema* and courtiers of the fundamentalist school, it was Emperor Jehangir who became the perpetrator of a brutal act that changed the course of Indian history forever.

Unlike his father who had been greatly impressed by observing for himself what the Sikh religion stood for, the shallow and self-indulgent Jehangir listened to the advice of envious and bigoted men who wanted to put an end not only to the Guru, but to all Sikhs and the faith itself. These envious men were alarmed at the rate at which the Sikh community was growing day by day, with large numbers of both Hindus and Muslims deciding to become followers of the new faith.

Within two years of the first copy of the *Granth* being reverently placed in the Harmandir and the electrifying effect this historic event had on Sikhs everywhere, the fanatics who had Jehangir's ear made their first move. 'This group included Sheikh Ahmad, the head of the revivalist *Naqshbandi*s; Sheikh Farid Bukhari; Chandu Shah, an influential Brahmin in the service of the Mughals; and the majority of the ulema; along with a Brahmin lobby deeply resentful of the independent ways of the Sikhs.'[6] They were all convinced that Sikhism was antithetical to their faiths.

It was a liberal Sikh worldview and the entrenched fundamentalism feared it. It was not too difficult to convince Jehangir that the Sikhs posed a threat to his rule. He finally moved to act when the news was conveyed to him that his eldest son Khusrau had been sympathetically received by Guru Arjan Dev at Taran Taran. Khusrau had been Emperor Akbar's favourite. He was a liberal and scholarly, and the exact opposite of Jehangir. When Akbar died in 1605, in an attempt to replace Jehangir as emperor, Khusrau pretended to visit Akbar's tomb at Sikandra at the time, waged battle with his father at Panipat and dug in, in Lahore. Jehangir amassed a mighty troop against his own son, defeated him and captured Khusrau and his supporters and took them to Agra. He killed the followers one by one. (Jehangir blinded and imprisoned Khusrau at Agra until 1622, when he was killed by brother Khurram, who became emperor Shah Jehan.)

Jehangir turned on Guru Arjan Dev in demonic fury, and in his own memoir he records: 'I ordered my men to produce him and hand over his houses, dwelling places and children to Murtaza Khan, and having confiscated his property commanded that he should be put to death with torture.'[7]

The emperor's anger had been further fueled when Guru Arjan Dev had brushed aside his offer of commuting his death sentence if he paid a fine of Rs 200,000 and deleted certain verses from the *Granth Sahib*. The treatment of Guru Arjan Dev was exceptionally brutal. He was made to sit on a red hot iron sheet, and burning sand was poured over him. After that, he was immersed in boiling water. Later, his burnt body was thrown into the river Ravi. Thus, he was killed on 30 May 1606. The Sikh-Mughal antipathy thus began with Jehangir.

Guru Arjan Dev's last words to his disciple, Mian Mir, were: 'I bear all this torture to set an example to the teachers of the True Name, that they may not lose patience or rile at God in affliction.'[8] To his son Hargobind, he sent this massage: 'Not to mourn or indulge in unmanly lamentations, but to sing God's praises.'[9] He also advised him 'to sit fully armed on his throne and maintain an army to the best of his ability'.[10]

With Guru Arjan Dev's martyrdom, the Sikhs' attitude to life changed. Emulating their Guru, they would readily give their lives for any cause dear to them, whether it was protection of their faith, the freedom of the country or the integrity of the motherland.

In Guru Arjan Dev, the Sikhs had the culmination of all that Guru Nanak and the three Gurus following him stood for. They combined in themselves the best of Islam and the best of Hinduism. Rather than alienate any section of society on the Indian subcontinent, they strove for mutual understanding. Revered equally by Hindus and Muslims, they promoted love and harmony and they devoted themselves to meditation and prayer and to the service of their fellow beings.

Guru Arjan Dev's martyrdom gave a new direction to Sikh history and polity. While Guru Arjan Dev's non-violence and the way he made the supreme sacrifice reflect the best in Guru Nanak, the training he gave to his son and successor, Hargobind, was a signpost to future trends, culminating in Guru Gobind Singh's career of resistance to tyranny and injustice.

The example set by each Guru in his lifetime has influenced successive generations of Sikhs, helping to weld them together and strengthen their willpower and valour. Their determination was particularly enhanced by the bravery of the saintly Guru Arjan Dev during his terrible torture and killing, which became a touchstone for the Sikhs to test their courage. This senseless deed also sent the Sikhs into a towering rage, which carried them into bitter battles with Mughal and other Islamic forces for over 150 years, and by bringing them face to face with the concept of martyrdom, Guru Arjan Dev's courageous act left an unforgettable impression on Sikh minds and strengthened their resolve to take an unbending stand against tyrants.

The Sixth Guru, Hargobind

Born on 19 June 1595, Hargobind donned Guru Arjan Dev's mantle in 1606. His father's phenomenal contributions to the Sikh faith had made a profound impression on the son from a young age. Accepting the will of God, Guru Arjan Dev had given up his life, suffering inhuman atrocities in a calm manner. Yet, the last massage he sent to his son was to arm himself fully and prepare for what was going to be a long-drawn-out campaign against tyranny and intolerance. The father's message steered the heart of his youthful son, Hargobind, who had succeeded his father as the Sixth Guru of the Sikhs.

The first of the far-reaching consequences of Guru Arjan Dev's martyrdom was the effect on eleven-year-old Hargobind who, despite his young age, rose to the occasion with remarkable self-assurance. Challenging though the task was – of converting a community conditioned from the beginning to peaceful and spiritual goals into one now confronted with the harsh reality of war with the Mughals and Islam – Hargobind was, nevertheless, able to succeed. One of the important reasons for his success was because Sikh rage would not be contained until Guru Arjan Dev's martyrdom was avenged. This is when a small religious sect decided to confront a mighty empire.

It is said that when Bhai Budha, the grand old man of Sikh

brotherhood, brought him *seli*, the holy man's thread worn round the headgear that Guru Nanak had passed on to his successor and which the succeeding Gurus had inherited, Guru Hargobind had put it aside respectfully and asked for a sword instead. Bhai Budha brought out one. The new young Guru then said, 'I shall wear two swords – one that of *shakti* (power) and the other that of *bhakti* (devotion)'.[11]

Guru Hargobind combined in himself *piri* (saintliness) and *miri* (sovereignty). Henceforth, the Guru's Sikhs were to carry arms and ride horses. This gave rise to the new concept of the soldier-saint. As the numbers of volunteers willing to join his battle increased, Hargobind's plans took shape. He sent men far and wide to buy outstanding breeds of horses and also new and effective weapons that had been developed and battle-tested elsewhere. He also opened military training camps that taught archery, horsemanship, swordsmanship, hand-to-hand fighting, spearing, physical fitness and other techniques of combat.

The impact of the concept of *miri* and *piri* on the Sikhs was immediate, as it offered a way of following their faith and its ideals with dignity. It helped them to spiritually reconcile to always being prepared to take on religious fanatics who opposed them in armed conflicts. For those disinclined to accept people who prayed to a different God, the Sikhs now had an answer. If *piri* was attacked, they would hit back with the razor keen edge of *miri*. The distinction between *miri* and *piri* would ensure that the supreme authority of the Harmandir would never be compromised by worldly concerns. And the Sikhs were willing to sacrifice their lives for the source of their inspiration.

To help deal with these worldly matters, representatives of the Sikhs started meeting at the Akal Takht – the literal translation being the Almighty's Throne. The temporal power of the Sikhs now began to be exercised from here and not from the spiritual sanctity of the Harmandir. The Akal Takht, in its present form, was built much later. In the beginning it was merely a raised platform of bricks built on an earthen embankment across a wide-open space facing the thoroughfare to the Harmandir. Guru Hargobind would usually sit on the platform as Sikhs from far and near came to him. They talked to him about their aspirations, preoccupations and pressing concerns, apart from their factional feuds and other distractions. They also sought the guidance of their Guru in the elevating environment of their beloved Darbar Sahib. The mirror of the tradition of the faith was clearly evident here as no decisions were imposed on those assembled but accepted only after reaching a consensus. Advice and suggestions of all were welcomed.

Clashes with the Mughals

The practice of reaching a collective agreement, especially on the actions to be taken in the confrontations with the Mughals, was a wise step, since increasingly bloody encounters with them soon began. Disquieted by reports of the methodical manner in which Guru Hargobind was raising and equipping a body of men to fight against the Mughals, Emperor Jehangir ordered his arrest in 1609 and confined him in the Gwalior fort, now in Madhya Pradesh, for the next two years.

Guru Hargobind was, however, set free after some time. It is generally believed that Jehangir 'was highly impressed' with the saint Mian Mir. He tried to please the saint in every way and showed him his highest regard and respect. 'It seems probable, that on this occasion Guru Hargobind was released from the Gwalior fort jail on Mian Mir's recommendation.'[12] Mian Mir, a great friend of Arjan Dev, had laid the foundation of Harmandir and his intervention mattered. 'The Guru's imprisonment does not seem to have dampened his (Hargobind's) military ardour in any way, and there is evidence to show that he continued the same old policy which he had adopted at the beginning of his preaching.'[13]

After Jehangir's death in 1627, his successor Shah Jehan proved no less hostile towards the Sikhs. Within a year of his ascending the throne, he precipitated the first clash with the Sikhs. The cause was a rare white hawk. Not far from Amritsar, where they were hunting on the same day, Shah Jehan's and Guru Hargobind's followers clashed over the hawk that had been shot down, to which each side laid claim. When told of this incident, the irate Emperor sent a contingent of troops under Mukhlis Khan to arrest the Guru. In the armed encounter, which lasted two days, Mukhlis Khan was killed and his force defeated. Accurately assessing the consequences of this defeat of the Mughals, Hargobind decided to move away from Amritsar because he did not want to provide opportunity to Shah Jehan to destroy Harmandir on the pretext of attacking the Guru.

Three years later, the two antagonists were again joined in battle, the first time at Lahira (near Bhatinda in 1631) and then at Kartarpur in 1634. In both these encounters, the Mughal forces were defeated with heavy casualties. Their general, Painda Khan, was killed in a hand-to-hand combat with the Guru. The casualties in the Sikh ranks were also high, but their morale was even higher, as they had proved that the Mughal writ could not only be successfully opposed, but also that its dominance could be halted in the battlefield in the peak of their power. The limitations of Mughal power had been demonstrated, and a defiant force created within the empire.

Guru Hargobind's greatest contribution is that he gave a new direction to the Sikh way of life. He turned saints into soldiers and yet remained a Man of God. He believed that non-violence is cowardice if resorted to out of helplessness or fear. It is the brave and heroic who can be truly nonviolent. Guru Hargobind, the soldier saint who gave Sikhs the reputation of being among the world's best fighters, died on 3 March 1644. In his short lifespan, he had considerably strengthened the Sikh's self-esteem and gave them a wholly new identity. He had exercised his leadership through deeds and ignited a spark in the Indian character, which would, in time, remove the passivity drilled into it by centuries of brutal invasions. His achievements, like those of Guru Nanak, his father Guru Arjan Dev and later, Guru Gobind Singh, went into formation of a legacy that was to give Ranjit Singh his confidence and his inspiration.

Seventh Guru, Har Rai & Eighth Guru, Har Krishan

The Seventh Guru, Har Rai, succeeded his grandfather Hargobind at the age of fourteen. Of a different disposition from Hargobind, he was scholarly, meditative, immersed in the scriptures. But he had a core of steel as well, and was unflinchingly opposed to anything which seemed to him as violating human decencies. This is illustrated by an incident in which this man took an inflexible stand against the Mughal emperor, Aurangzeb, who would soon attempt to bring the entire Indian subcontinent under his rule. Aurangzeb was a cruel, iron-fisted man, incapable of forgiving anyone who stood up to him. To secure the throne for himself, he had shown no compunction in finishing off his brothers and imprisoning his father, Emperor Shah Jehan.

The clash of wills between Har Rai and Aurangzeb occurred when Dara Shikoh, Shah Jehan's scholar and secular son, was being pursued by the emperor's troops in order to eliminate him as a contestant to the imperial throne. The Guru, who liked Dara for his liberalism and philosophic bent, sent a Sikh contingent to divert the imperial troops so that Dara could escape, which he did, although he was captured soon afterwards and put to death on Aurangzeb's orders.

An irate Aurangzeb, now securely installed on his throne,

ordered Har Rai to meet him. Har Rai refused the invitation in these words: 'I am not a king who payeth thee tribute, nor do I desire to receive anything from thee, nor do we stand in the relation of priest and disciple to each other, so where for hast thou summoned me?'[14] Rather than go himself, he sent his son Ram Rai to meet Aurangzeb but told him, 'he should, under no circumstances, acknowledge any objections the emperor might raise to the writings in the *Guru Granth Sahib*. Unfortunately, Ram Rai faltered. When reading passages to the emperor, he knowingly misinterpreted a passage he felt would be seen as derogatory to Islam. When his father came to known of this, he refused ever to see his son again for his audacity in altering a verse written by Guru Nanak'.[15]

Even though Ram Rai was his eldest son, Guru Har Rai chose a younger son, Har Krishan, aged five, to succeed him when he died on 6 October 1661 at Kartarpur. Tragically, Har Krishan too died about three years later, on 30 March 1664.[16] The brief stewardships of Guru Har Rai and Guru Har Krishan marked a tenure of peace in the life of the Sikh community, free from any major conflict with the ruling authority.

The Ninth Guru, Tegh Bahadur

The Ninth Guru, Tegh Bahadur, who now succeeded Har Krishan, was born on 1 April 1621. He was the youngest of Guru Hargobind's five sons. Tegh Bahadur was essentially of meditative temperament. But the conditions in the Punjab and the rest of the country were such that would not allow him peace. Like Nanak, Tegh Bahadur was also a traveller. For the purpose of rallying round the people of the Sikh faith, he travelled to different parts of the country, including Delhi, Mathura, Banaras, Allahabad, Gaya, Patna and Dhubri in Assam. It was in Patna, where during the course of his travel that his son Gobind – the tenth and last Guru – was born.

His return to Chak Nanaki in Punjab in 1672 saw the end of his travels. Chak Nanaki was later known as Anandpur where Tegh Bahadur established his stronghold. Guru Tegh Bahadur, however, was not destined to remain in peace for a longer period because by then, the outlines of a major tragedy were beginning to unfold in the subcontinent because of Aurangzeb's religious intolerance.

In April 1669, Aurangzeb issued orders to the governors of all Mughal provinces 'to demolish the schools and temples of the infidels and with utmost urgency put down the teachings and public practice of the religion of these disbelievers'.[17]

His governor in Kashmir initiated a severe campaign of conversion. Driven to dire consequences, the Brahmins of the valley decided to make a pilgrimage to Amarnath and seek help of the deity. It is said that while at the Amarnath temple, a member of the group of worshippers, Pandit Kirpa Ram dreamt that they could be protected only by Guru Tegh Bahadur, the ninth in succession to Guru Nanak, the saviour in the *Kaliyug*.[18]

Immediately, a group of Kashmiri Hindus left for the Punjab and reached Anandpur to meet the Guru. They explained their plight to him. The Guru heard their tale of woe and was lost within himself when Gobind, his young son, walked in. 'What keeps you thus preoccupied, dear father?' he asked. The Guru explained the situation to him. 'They can be saved only if a great soul can offer himself for martyrdom.' 'Then who is greater than you?' remarked the future prophet-preceptor of the Sikhs. The father was assured that Gobind was ready to take over. He advised the visiting supplicants to return and inform their tormentors that they would be willing to accept Islam if Guru Tegh Bahadur could first be persuaded to do so.[19]

While the Pandits of Kashmir were deeply moved by the

Guru's decision to risk his own life for their cause, Aurangzeb was enraged. On being told of the Guru's stand, he ordered the Lahore governor to fetter and detain him. Tegh Bahadur had already left for Delhi of his own free will, but was arrested near Ropar and brought to Delhi in an iron cage on 5 November 1675. His message to the Mughal did little to calm Aurangzeb as it appeared to trivialise the emperor's authority as well as his faith: 'The Prophet of Mecca who founded your religion could not impose one religion on the world, so how can you? It is not God's will', Tegh Bahadur had told him.[20]

Aurangzeb responded by ordering that for the next five days, Guru Tegh Bahadur's treatment should alternate between inducement to convert to Islam and torture if he refused. The Guru's three close companions were put to death in his presence: One was sawn in two, one placed in a boiler and boiled to death and the third burnt alive. Since Guru Tegh Bahadur was unmoving in his stand, he was publicly beheaded the same day. On the very spot of his beheading, the Sikhs, when they captured Delhi a century later, built Gurudwara Sis Ganj to commemorate his sacrifice.

During the stormy night that followed the beheading, a loyal follower, Bhai Jaita, recovered the Guru's head and carried it all the way to Anandpur where his nine-year old son Gobind received it. It was cremated on a sandalwood pyre amidst mixed emotions of the assembled Sikhs; immense pride at the Guru's resolute character and a burning hatred for those responsible for his killing. In Delhi, on the very same night, in an extraordinary expression of admiration and devotion to the Guru, a man called Lakhi Shah Lubana, with his companions, carried off his body and cremated it in Rakabganj, on the outskirts of Delhi. Because an open air cremation would have invited suspicion, Lakhi Shah placed the body in his own house and set it on fire. On the cremation site, the Sikhs later built a magnificent Gurudwara, Rakabganj Sahib.

Thus, while Guru Nanak refused to wear the janeu (sacred thread), Guru Tegh Bahadur laid down his life so that the right of the people to wear sacred thread and practice their faith were protected. This makes Guru Tegh Bahadur's martyrdom unique in history. People have given their lives for principles dear to them, for ideals cherished by them and for their faiths. There is hardly anyone who has staked his life for other people's faith. The supreme sacrifice made by Guru Tegh Bahadur stemmed the tide of intolerance in the subcontinent and inculcated in the people respect for other religions.

A more detailed study of the tenth and the last Guru, Gobind Singh, who prepared the ground for the Sikh kingdom, has been made in the next chapter.

GOBIND SINGH WELDS THE SIKHS INTO A NATION

GURU TEGH BAHADUR'S execution, in Delhi in public, outraged the conscience of the entire Sikh brotherhood. After Guru Arjan Dev's martyrdom in Lahore, the slaughtering of another peace-loving, non-violent man of God like Guru Tegh Bahadur gave a rude shock to the young community. The Sikhs streamed towards Anandpur from far and near to be with their young Guru.

Born in Patna on 22 December 1666, and brought up for the grim struggle ahead, the young Gobind Rai, rather than being overcome by his tragic loss, evinced firm determination and tenacity of will to fight the forces of evil and bigotry in defence of the poor and the *dharma*. The dejected Sikhs, who flocked the Anandpur, saw in their child Guru the promised saviour and the man of the hour.

A soldier of destiny, the tenth Guru started consolidating his resources and preparing himself and his people for the struggle that would last until the poison that had permeated the body-politic of the country had been completely rooted out. Guru Gobind realised the need to give the new religion a distinct identity. Islam under rulers like Aurangzeb had become rigid, narrow-minded and uncompromising and Hinduism had been crippled by its rituals.

No one has written more eloquently on Gobind Singh's chosen emblem of steel than Edmund Candler, a soldier-turned writer. 'When Guru Gobind Singh inaugurated the sacrament of steel he proved himself a wise and far-sighted leader. For, of all material things which genius has inspired with spiritual significance, steel is the truest and most uncompromising... it welded the Sikhs into a nation; and in the dark days of Muslim rules in the middle of the eighteenth century, when the Sikh was at sight and no quarter was given, it drove them on to those gallant crusades in which they rode to Amritsar in the dead of night, leapt into the sacred tank and out again, and galloped back through the enemy's line, purified. Hundreds were slain, but no one adjured his faith or perjured his soul to preserve his muddy vesture of decay.'[1]

Gobind Singh, the tenth and last of the Gurus, was fifteen years old when his father was tortured and killed as a martyr by the bigoted emperor, Aurangzeb. The boy fled to the hills where he remained for some years completing his education, in which he was superior to his predecessors, knowing Persian, Hindi and a little of Sanskrit, which at times he attempted to introduce into his later compositions. This remarkable man who in intelligence, capacity and fixed purpose was superior to all his predecessors did not undertake the mission of his life to unite the scattered Sikhs until he was well advanced in manhood; certainly over thirty years of age. Till then he devoted himself to study and a preparation for his self-imposed duties.

At the same time, not neglecting the accomplishments of a well-born youth of his age, he became a keen sportsman and skilled in all feats of arms. When he emerged from seclusion he was at once accepted by the Sikh people as their natural and hereditary leader and they were quite ready to follow him to avenge the murder of his father and kill the Muslim oppressors. Before commencing his work, he obtained the blessing of the

Hindu Goddess Durga, whose shrine on the hill of Naina Devi was near his home at Anandpur.

Guru Gobind now assembled his followers and assured them of the sacred character of his mission and its success. He began boldly to preach the new doctrine which was to supersede that of Nanak as a political creed and unite the Sikhs, in the manner which Guru Arjan Dev and Guru Hargobind had suggested, into a military nation. The old Sikh faith had a baptismal rite which had fallen into disuse. This was restored by Gobind Singh as *Pahul* (necessary initiatory ceremony of Sikhism). He administered to all his disciples present this pahul. The ceremony involved dissolving sugar-candy in pure water which was stirred by a dagger. During this process, certain verses from the *Granth* were recited and the pledged drank a portion, the rest being sprinkled on his head and body, while the baptiser and the disciple shouted, '*Wah Guruji Ka Khalsa* (victory to the Khalsa of the Guru)'. This mixture of sweetness and steel, which the Guru called *Amrit,* could be administrated to any person wishing to join the Khalsa fellowship.

By creating the fellowship of the Khalsa or 'purified ones', Guru Gobind Singh gave the Sikhs a distinctiveness, which no other followers of no other religion in India had until then. The first requirement was this baptism. The second was that the members of the Khalsa brotherhood should be easily identifiable through five distinctive symbols they would always wear. Each of the five personal symbols emblematic of the Sikh faith would start with the letter K – as in Khalsa – and would provide a forthright statement of Khalsa beliefs: *Kesh* (long hair), *Kanga* (comb), *Kara* (steel band around the wrist), *Kachh* (short breeches) and *Kirpan* (short sword).

All these distinctive symbols had a special significance and purpose. *Kesh* set the tone for the other four by making the Khalsa instantly recognisable. It was forbidden to cut *Kesh* including the beard. The long hair was meant to put iron in the spine. Since a Sikh's life was constantly in danger and there was usually a price on his head, Gobind Singh wanted his Khalsa to stand up with pride and be counted – not to tremble or run away from the danger. The confidence that their appearance instilled in people was vital for a person whose courage and conviction would be repeatedly tested in the battles ahead. The *Kanga* or comb emphasised the importance of cleanliness, which should start with keeping the hair tidy. In the same vein the *Kachh*, or short breeches, stressed the need for celibacy and moral restraint. The *Kara* or circular steel band safeguarded the wrist, which wielded the sword, while the *Kirpan*, or short sword, symbolised the Khalsa's commitment to giving wrong-doers an appropriate punishment.

To make the psychological impact of these distinctive characteristics still more powerful, the *Pagdi* or turban – six yards of muslin cloth tide around the head in an impressive manner – would become another distinguishing feature of Sikh men. It would set them apart from all others. Choice of colour and style would be a matter of personal preference. The final inspired move announced by Gobind Singh was that, in the brotherhood of Khalsa each man, without exception, would use the surname Singh or lion, while women would have the surname Kaur, or princess.

Creation of the Khalsa: A Turning Point

The creation and the baptism of the Khalsa brotherhood on Baisakhi Day, 30 March 1699, had all the emotional power and drama befitting such an event. For the Baisakhi fair, Guru Gobind Singh issued a general invitation to Sikhs throughout the length and breadth of the country to visit Anandpur. He advised them to come with unshaven hair. It is estimated that around 80,000 Sikhs came to participate in the fair in response to the Guru's call. On the morning of the main fair day, after the hymn-singing had concluded, the Guru appeared on the dais with a naked sword dazzling in his hand and spoke to the audience: 'My sword is thirsty. It needs the blood of a Sikh to quench the thirst. Is there anyone in the audience who is willing to offer his head?'[2] There was shock amongst those present.

'Is there no one who is willing to present his head to satisfy my sword?' The Guru repeated. The gathering grew more uneasy. 'Do I take it that there is none amongst my Sikhs who is willing to sacrifice his life for his Guru?'[3] The shocked audience was at a loss as to how to respond and some quietly slipped away. But one Sikh man named Daya Ram, a Khatri from Lahore, about 30 years of age, rose from the crowd to offer his head. The Guru took him into the tent pitched adjacent to the dais. The Guru emerged a few minutes later with his sword dripping blood. The same exercise was repeated with four more volunteers, and each time the Guru emerged from the tent amidst incredible suspense and with still more blood on his sword.

The terrible suspense ended in an unexpected turn of the events as the Guru walked out of the tent with five Sikhs, each now attired in saffron-coloured robes and turbans – smilingly driving home the point that what the Guru had been testing was the courage and resoluteness of the assembled Sikhs, which he had found lacking in those who had fled in fear. It is said that the Guru had killed only goats. Every time he took a Sikh inside the tent, he had beheaded a goat and come out with its blood dripping from the blade on his sword.

It was fiber he was looking for in his Khalsa, not fear. The new martial community that emerged that day on India's multi-religious landscape would be a race apart. It would be sustained by its religious faith, its strong convictions and its fearlessness. The bedrock of its beliefs would be equality among all and an unbreakable commitment to the secular principles defined by the nine Sikh Gurus who had preceded Gobind Singh.

His message to the assembled Sikhs was to the point: 'You will love man as man, making no distinction of caste or creed… you will never worship stock, stone, idol or tomb…. In each of you the whole brotherhood shall be reincarnated. You are my sons, both in flesh and spirt.'[4] The proof of Gobind Singh's own commitment to 'making no distinction of caste or creed' was provided by the Hindu caste composition of the first five *Panj Piyare* or the five loved ones, as the Guru called them. One was Daya Ram from Lahore, who was Khatri of a higher caste, the second was a Jat from present-day Haryana, a step lower, and the remaining three were Mokham Chand (a Sikh from far-off Dwarka), Himmat Chand (from Jagannathpuri in Orissa), and Sahib Chand (of Bidar in the South), all were Sudras, untouchables, or those belonging to a low Hindu caste hierarchy.

The most convincing proof of the Guru's opposition to the caste system became obvious to the assembled gathering when he first baptised each of the five himself, then knelt before them and asked them to baptise him. By taking Amrit from them, the Guru put an end to detrimental hierarchical customs that had annoyed the Sikhs just as other societies. As Guru Gobind Singh put it on that Baisakhi Day: 'Your previous race, name, genealogy, country, nation, religion, customs, beliefs and sub-conscious memories are completely burnt and annihilated. Believe this to be so without a doubt for you now start a New Birth in the House of Guru – Akalpurakh.'[5]

The creation of the Khalsa proved to be a turning point for Sikhism because of the dynamism injected into the faith by making every individual Sikh feel responsible for upholding Sikhism's stature and practice. The Guru was aware that the need of the hour was an army of saint-soldiers who could effectively fight the forces of evil, and fight against exploitation of the poor and injustice in Indian society. The anointed Sikh is not to smoke or take any other intoxicants. All Sikhs are equal: there would be no high or low caste amongst the Khalsa. The Khalsa believes in one God, says the prescribed prayers daily and does not worship idols or images. He must help the needy and protect the poor. The Sikhs who adopt the prescribed way of life become the very image of the Guru. The Guru is Khalsa and the Khalsa is the Guru.

After the grand baptism, the Guru declared that all Sikhs be known as Singhs. The baptism had turned jackals into tigers. One single Sikh considered himself equal to a lakh and a quarter (125,000) of its enemies. If a man in a turban and wearing the other symbols of his faith disgraced himself, he would be disgracing all Sikhs. So, it was obligatory for him to conduct himself in a manner conducive to the principles that the Sikhs had pledged to uphold. With his sensitive awareness of human nature and the many pitfalls that lay in its way, Guru Gobind Singh was determined that Sikhs should possess those qualities which would equip them for facing the exacting and turbulent times ahead. His foresight inspired the leaders, of subsequent generations, like Ranjit Singh, Hari Singh Nalwa, Jassa Singh Ahluwalia and others to perform spectacular deeds and come out victorious even though the Sikhs were so few in numbers when compared to their enemies.

When the coming generations of Sikhs planted their roots in remote corners of the earth, it was in no small measure due to their pioneering spirit, mandatory virtues and qualities the Gurus had defined and instilled in them. Their commitment to the secular principle, for instance, came from the same source, as also the democratic underpinnings of the Sikh faith. It was to drive home this point that Guru Gobind Singh had inducted men belonging to different castes as his first Panj Piyare on the momentous day in 1699. And when he had knelt before them, it was to stress yet again the republican spirit of the faith.

Guru Gobind's Army takes on Aurangzeb

Reports of the historic success of the Anandpur conclave, where about 50,000 people were baptised, alarmed the incumbent Mughal emperor. At the same time, the chieftains of the hilly tribes in the region, who were passing their time peacefully under the patronage and protection of the Mughal rule, also felt nervous at the rising power of the Sikhs, and therefore they alerted and sent messages to Aurangzeb which said: 'The Guru has established a new sect distinct from the Hindus and Mohammedans, to which he has given the name of Khalsa. He has united the four castes into one and made many followers… he suggested to us that if we rose in rebellion against the emperor, he would assist us with all his forces… we cannot restrain him and have accordingly come to crave the protection of this just government against him. If the government considers us its subjects, we pray for its assistance to expel the Guru from Anandpur. Should you delay his punishment, his next expedition will be against the capital of your empire.'[6]

Such archived notes from the chieftains of the hills is illustrative of the moral decay of the protectorates around the Punjab, who behaved like slaves of the Mughals, although they had often come to the Sikh Gurus for help. Their allegiances could not be relied upon. Now they were not averse to betraying Guru Gobind Singh when it suited them. After receiving the complaint, Aurangzeb, who was then camping in the Deccan, ordered his two commanders, Painda Khan and Din Beg, to go and settle the Sikh problem. Aurangzeb and his two commanders had underestimated the strength and valour of the Sikh Guru and his forces, with the result that Painda Khan was killed in a hand-to-hand combat with Gobind Singh; another commander, Din Beg, was seriously injured and was carried off the field, the hill chiefs fled and the Mughal force faced an humiliating defeat.

Betrayed by Aurangzeb

Armed clashes between the Sikhs and Mughal forces continued for the next three years. Meanwhile, another delegation of hill chieftains met Aurangzeb, who was still camping in the South, for intervention. This time the emperor sent a larger and more organised force under the command of Nawab Wazir Khan of Sirhind. This time, the Mughals adopted a different strategy. They laid siege to the entire Anandpur area, cut off food and other essentials supply and diverted the main stream which was the only source of drinking water. As a part of this strategy, Aurangzeb offered the Guru and his party a safe passage if they promised to vacate Anandpur for good. In order to save the lives of the hundreds of his people, Guru Gobind Singh accepted the proposal in good faith.

But, despite their pledge of ensuring safe passage, the Mughals attacked the Sikhs as soon as they reached the plains to cross the river Sirsa. During this attack many lives were lost. Besides, the flooded river also washed away many men and women as they tried to reach the opposite bank. Many more though were able to cross the river but were separated from each other, and among them were Guru Gobind Singh's mother, Mata Gujri and his two younger sons Zorawar Singh, aged eight and Fateh Singh, aged six. There was heavy loss to the Sikh contingent of 500 men. Gobind Singh was now left with just about forty fighting men, which included the Guru's two older sons, Ajit Singh, aged 17 and Jujhar Singh, aged 15, who somehow found their way to Chamkaur village, with a sizeable Mughal force close on their heels.

In an uneven fight with the Mughals at Chamkaur, Guru Gobind Singh lost his two older sons, Ajit Singh and Jujhar Singh. Out of the valiant forty, now only four survived, which included Guru Gobind Singh himself. With no food or shelter, he spent the cold winter night in the forest with the thoughts of his two sons and comrades and the Mughal betrayal which had brought him to this pass.

Gobind Singh's two younger sons Zorawar Singh and Fateh Singh who were separated due to the flooded river Sirsa had fallen into the hands of Aurangzeb's governor of Sirhind, Nawab Wazir Khan. Having no consideration of their tender ages, Wazir Khan bricked them alive, burying them up to their necks, then beheaded the two children when they refused to convert to Islam.

He who lived like a prince in royal splendour was rendered homeless. He was chased by enemy forces from town to town, from wilderness to wilderness. Even then, he was not demoralised. While camping at Dinga village, the Guru wrote a letter to Aurangzeb. This was an open letter to him in Persian and bluntly accused him of deceit: of first guaranteeing the Sikhs safe passage if they vacated Anandpur and then ordering his troops to attack the men, women and children after they had left their citadel. The Guru's letter is known as *Zafar Nama* (letter of victory). The Guru told the emperor that he had taken up arms because he had exhausted all other means of redress. The Guru continued:

> If I had not believed your word and your oath on the Quran, I wouldn't have left my town. If I had known that you are deceitful and crafty like a fox, I wouldn't have been here today. Every soldier of your army who left his defences to attack us was slaughtered. Many were done to death on either side with arrows and bullets showered on them. The whole earth was smeared with red blood. Heads and legs lay in heaps. The arrows flew and bows twanged and the clamour all over reached the heavens. My heroic soldiers fought like lions. But how could forty men, even the bravest of soldiers, succeed against countless odds?
>
> You are faithless and irreligious. You neither know God

> nor Mohammed. A religious man never breaks his promise. Had the Prophet been here, I would make it a point to tell him about your treachery.
>
> What if my four sons have been killed? I live to take revenge. It's no heroism to extinguish a few sparks. You have only excited a devastating fire.
>
> You have the pride of your empire, while I am proud of the kingdom of God. You must not forget that this world is like a caravanserai, and one must leave it sooner or later....[7]

The emperor received the Guru's letter and was struck with remorse. He removed all restrictions on the movement of the Guru and gave orders that Guru Gobind Singh and the Sikhs should no more be harassed. Aurangzeb's conscience seemed to prick him for the cruelties inflicted on the Guru and his Sikhs.

After Aurangzeb's death, in 1707, there was scramble for succession to the throne. His eldest son Bahadur Shah being in Peshawar, the younger son, Mohammad Azam, proclaimed himself emperor. Bahadur Shah sought the Guru's assistance. Since he was the rightful successor to the Peacock throne, the Guru helped him and placed a detachment at his disposal. Bahadur Shah was victorious and invited Guru Gobind Singh for his coronation at which he presented him a robe of honour and several precious gifts.

They became such good friends that Bahadur Shah I persuaded Gobind Singh to accompany him to the South on his tour. From numerous conversations during their journey, Gobind Singh realised that the emperor's statements lacked substance and that he had little intention of doing anything decisive to end the tyrannical ways of Mughal rule. The Guru, therefore, felt that it was pointless to convince the emperor and continue his journey with him. He, therefore, parted ways with him in Nanded on the banks of the Godavari river in September 1708.

Gobind Singh Converts Banda Singh Bairagi

During the short stay at Nanded, Guru Gobind Singh converted a Hindu ascetic known as Madho Das Bairagi to the Sikh faith. The man was born at Rajauri in Poonch. A Rajput of the Dogra tribe, his real name was Lachhman Dev. Bairagi was also locally known as Banda Singh Bahadur. He met Guru Gobind Singh in Nanded in 1708 and endeared himself to him. Bairagi, who was assertive and had strong views on most subjects, was a man of standing in the area with a following of his own. The Guru and Bairagi had assessed each other's worth correctly and Madho Das' initiation into the Sikh faith was to prove to be of profound significance in the times to come. After initiation into Sikh faith, Banda Singh Bahadur was called Banda Singh Bairagi. Guru Gobind Singh then assigned Banda with the conduct of his campaign for the deliverance of the people from the despotic rule of the Mughals, who had beheaded his saintly father, Guru Tegh Bahadur and martyred his four sons.

Guru Gobind Singh is Killed

In the meantime, however, a catastrophic event took place which shook the Sikh camp at Nanded. Two Pathans assassins sent by Wazir Khan of Sirhind stabbed the Guru in the chest as he lay on his bed after evening prayers. The ruthless Wazir Khan, who had already brutally put to death Guru Gobind Singh's two younger sons, feared Emperor Bahadur Shah's closeness to the Guru and thought this might adversely affect his own fortunes. Therefore, he sent two Pathans to kill him. While his injury seemed to be healing well and his recovery appeared certain, but his over-exertions reopened the wound and the excessive bleeding ended the life of the tenth Sikh Guru, Gobind Singh on 7 October 1708, at the age of 42.

End of Tradition of a Living Guru

Before the end of his life, Guru Gobind Singh called upon his followers, who had assembled in large numbers around him, and told them that the tradition of *living Gurus* would end with him and after his death the *Granth Sahib* would be the Guru of the Sikhs for all time. Guru Gobind Singh declared unequivocally that those who wished to seek God would find Him in the Scripture. Since then, the Sikhs came to give the same esteem, the same reverence to the *Holy Grantha* as they had done to the living Gurus. They bow down before it every morning, make offerings, and seek guidance from it by reading, reciting and singing the holy hymns.

GOBIND SINGH PREPARED GROUND FOR SIKH KINGDOM

GURU GOBIND SINGH had announced to his disciples that he was their last Guru. With his death, the work of forming the Sikhs into a proud, ambitious and warlike people, inspired with deadly hatred of Muslim conquerors and invaders was complete. The Khalsa, fully armed and equipped for victory, was the brainchild of the great Guru. But it was strong only in organisation, in martial spirit and in picking up of the sword. They had faith in their belief but were few in numbers when compared to the big volumes of their enemies. They were poor in terms of resources. With nothing but their faith, their brave hearts and their swords, they engaged in a death-struggle with the Mughal empire. Fortunately for the Sikhs, they had an ally in the bigotry of the rulers which created enemies to his throne in every feudatory Hindu State, and eventually brought the magnificent fabric of the Mughal empire to the ground.

As for the Sikhs, their persecution strengthened their unbending attachment to their faith, and the threat of death and torture never came in the way of their commitment. The blood of martyrs and the unsuccessful attempts to crush the Sikhs only succeeded in infusing its spirit into fresh disciples and in inspiring the Sikh people with hatred of the Muslims.

Guru Gobind Singh had prepared his people well for the

ninety years of strife with the Mughals and their satraps, the Afghans, the Persians and other marauders from the North, who regularly invaded India between his death in 1708 and the founding of the Sikh kingdom by Ranjit Singh in 1801. Just before his death Guru Gobind Singh, with his unerring instinct, had sensed in Banda Singh Bahadur the capabilities of a future leader. In converting this seemingly calm and quiet *sadhu* to the Sikh faith, Guru Gobind Singh released his red-hot feelings for a worthy cause.

Burning with hatred for those who had perpetrated such dreadful crimes against a noble and courageous leader like Guru Gobind Singh and his family, Banda was determined on vengeance. From Nanded, he set out for Punjab, almost 1,500 miles away, with only 25 armed followers. But he was armed with Gobind Singh's *hukumnama* (directive) to all Sikh sangats (places of congregation) to rally round his banner. The Guru had given him five arrows from his own bucket, a *Nishan Sahib* (flag) and a *Nagara* (war drum) as symbol of authority. Banda's tiny force soon swelled with the addition of warriors eager to strike back at their Mughal tormentors.

Reaching Punjab after a journey of several months and after many armed clashes on the way, Banda and his men arrived at the gates of Samana (near Patiala), home of Sayyed Jamaluddin, Guru Tegh Bahadur's executioner, and Sahal Beg, who had executed Guru Gobind Singh's two sons. Banda ransacked the town, killing Wazir Khan, the Mughal *fauzdar* (governor), and annihilated his formidable force equipped with field guns, superior armaments and a host of elephants. Wazir Khan's well-equipped army of 20,000 men fought a far smaller Sikh force, but he was killed and a Muslim historiographer thus described the outcome. 'Not a man of the army of Islam escaped with more than his life and clothes he stood in.'[1]

Banda continued to fight and in six years he had sweeping

victories. After Sirhind, he captured Raj Kot, Saharanpur, Jalalabad, Ludhiana, Jullundur (Jalandhar), Hoshiarpur, Batala, Kalanaur and Pathankot. He, thus, brought the Sikhs to the gates of Lahore, a city symbolic of Mughal and Afghan authority in India. In one of his most audacious campaigns, Banda captured the fortress of Mukhlispur built on the ridges of the lower reaches of the Himalayas, renamed it as Lohgarh and hoisted the Khalsa flag over it.

The campaign continued until the Khalsa held sway over the entire country from Lahore to Panipat. Banda's conquest brought back the Sikhs' long-sought prestige and power. Further, it showed the Hindus, suffering from centuries of subjugation, that they could throw off the bondage of enslavement; they could fight and conquer. Thus, Banda Singh Bahadur, military successor of Guru Gobind Singh, showed great energy and military talent by defeating the Mughal troops on more than one occasion. This was Banda's most conspicuous contribution. He gave the Hindus of northern India the self-confidence which they had lost long, long ago. He knit the Sikhs into a community of devoted heroes. It is amazing to find that during the period of fierce persecution that ensued, not one Sikh among thousands renounced his faith. They gave their lives with exemplary valour, holding dear the tenets of Guru Gobind Singh, the tenth Guru.

Banda Captured, Brutally Killed

Banda had to pay heavily for his crusade. Banda's continuous victory, particularly the capture of Lohgarh, infuriated Emperor Bahadur Shah I, who, with a force of 60,000 horsemen, laid a siege to Lohgarh. On this occasion, the Sikh forces consisted of only about 3,000 horsemen and foot soldiers combined. The Sikhs could not continue this uneven fight for long and eventually, Banda, along with a large number of his men, was captured in Gurdas-Nangal on 17 December 1715. 'Banda was brought to Delhi in an iron cage along with 780 followers in chains. Leading them were 2,000 Sikh heads hoisted on spears. On their arrival in Delhi, the Sikhs were executed in batches of one hundred daily. Then came Banda's turn. His son was placed on his lap, and he was asked to slice his throat with a dagger himself. As if that were not enough, his own flesh was torn away with red-hot pincers.'[2]

Gobind Singh's Slogan 'Raj Karega Khalsa'

The execution of Banda Singh Bahadur and liquidation of the Sikh force ushered in a period of about fifty years when the Sikhs, as a community, were persecuted mercilessly. It was a life-and-death struggle for them. The more they were harassed, the more determined they appeared to be to wrest power from the dwindling Mughal authority in Delhi. There was a price on every Sikh head. Their homes were the horseback. They were hounded from pillar to post. With the death of Bahadur Shah I in 1712, and the accession of Farrukh Siyar to the throne in 1713, the Mughal empire came to be headed by a man who outstripped all his predecessors in exhibiting unwarranted cruelty. His commanders and governors rushed to curry favour with him by sending him severed Sikh heads 'for pleasure'.[3]

When once, Zakaria Khan (who was later to become governor of Lahore under him) presented Emperor Farrukh Siyar in Delhi with a particularly large number of Sikh heads, the overjoyed emperor raised Zakariya's rank and loaded him with presents. Zakariya vowed to leave no Sikh alive in the Mughal empire and ordered his men to arrest the Sikhs wherever they saw them and bring them to Lahore for daily public executions. He also announced a reward of 50 rupees for every Sikh head brought to him.[4]

Emperor Farrukh Siyar and the successive governors of

Lahore, Abdus Samad Khan, Zakariya Khan, Yahiya Khan and Mir Mannu were determined to put an end to the Sikh menace, as they put it. But the Sikhs were getting bolder and more determined. The provincial governors had made up their minds to exterminate the Sikhs as a community. The Sikhs fled to the jungles and lived on leaves and roots, but they continued with their guerrilla warfare. They had to achieve what, according to Guru Gobind Singh, 'they were destined for'. *Raj Karega Khalsa* – the Khalsa shall rule, the Guru had prophesied.

The witchhunt was thorough and relentless. It has few parallels in history. Some of their most revered leaders like Bhai Man Singh and Bhai Taru Singh were tortured to death. Bhai Man Singh was a companion of Guru Gobind Singh. He was hacked to pieces alive, limb by limb. Zakariya Khan had laid siege to Amritsar, plundered the Harmandir Sahib, filled the pool with slaughtered animals and desecrated its relics. The Harmandir Sahib was, however, liberated by Jassa Singh Ahluwalia from Mughal control and he restored the shrine to its former glory.

The Sikhs and the Afghan Invaders

In the meanwhile, finding the Mughal hold loosening, foreign invaders – Nadir Shah and Ahmad Shah Abdali – attacked India successively. This was both a misfortune as well as an opportunity for the Sikhs. Punjab now became the setting for a triangular struggle among the Afghans, Sikhs and Mughals. Abdali and the Mughals wanted to see the end of the Sikhs, but the Khalsa was willing to take on both adversaries. While the intruders persecuted them no less, the Sikhs reorganised themselves in the disturbed conditions in the country and started retaliating. They did not spare even Nadir Shah. While he was returning home, they pounced upon his rear and relieved him of a good deal of the booty that he was carrying with him along with beautiful young Indian women who were recovered and restored to their parents.

Ahmad Shah Abdali, the founder of the Durrani dynasty from Afghanistan, invaded India eight times between 1748 and 1768, and while he brought the harassed Mughals to their knees, his attempts to destroy the Sikhs did not succeed despite his best efforts. To irk the Mughals, in 1748, he audaciously declared Punjab to be a territory of a new Afghanistan after decisively defeating their Lahore governor. In 1752, the new governor of Lahore, Mir Mannu, a duplicitous and barbaric man who had defected from the Mughals to the Afghans and was keen to gain favour with Abdali, now officially proclaimed Punjab to be an Afghan province.

This act was in defiance of the declared Sikh sovereignty over several regions and towns of Punjab, dating from Banda Singh's time and also of their plans to annex more territory. The Sikhs' independent stand was unbearable for Abdali. Abdali told his son, Timur Shah, to eliminate the infidels and their Golden Temple once and for all.

Attack and counter attacks between the Sikhs and forces of Abdali had become a routine affair in Punjab but for a disastrous fight on 5 February 1762 in which Abdali's army massacred around 10,000 to 30,000 (estimates vary) Sikhs at village Kup near Sirhind.

A few days later, Abdali headed for the Golden Temple and attacked it on 10 April 1762, at a time when thousands had gathered there for Baisakhi celebrations. The blood bath was horrific. The Harmandir Sahib was blown apart with gun powder. The pool was filled with the debris of destroyed buildings, mutilated human bodies, carcasses of cows and much else. Topping it all, a pyramid of Sikh heads was erected. However, a man called Charhat Singh, head of the Sukerchakia misl or confederacy, managed to soon wrest back control of the Golden Temple.

Abdali again struck the Sikh shrine next year, and once again demolished and defiled it. This time, the determined Sikhs, in a swift military action, not only annexed Lahore on 16 April 1765, but also declared their sovereignty over the whole of Punjab. With a view to making their declaration firm and clear – that political power in the region rested with them – they struck coins and declared Lahore the mint city, *Dar-ul-Sultanate* (Seat of Sikh Power).

After having a firm grip over the entire region of Punjab, representatives of all 12 misls under the leadership of Jassa Singh Ahluwalia, together approached the then Mughal emperor, Shah Alam II at Red Fort in Delhi, to fix an annual tribute to be paid by them. The broke emperor agreed. The emperor also agreed to the construction of eight gurudwaras, each built on a site with a special significance for the Sikhs, one of them being the Gurudwara Sis Ganj (1783), on the spot where Aurangzeb had Guru Tegh Bahadur, father of Guru Gobind Singh, tortured and beheaded in November 1675.

Sikh Sacrifices

The eighteenth century was a costly one for the Sikhs. It has been estimated that Guru Gobind Singh, in his battles with the Mughals, lost about 5,000 men; and Banda Singh at least 25,000. After Banda Singh's execution, Abdus Samad Khan, governor of Punjab (1713-26), killed not less than 20,000 Sikhs and his son and successor Zakaria Khan (1726-45), an equal number. Yahiya Khan (1746-47) accounted for some 10,000 Sikhs in a single campaign. His brother Shah Nawaz Khan assassinated nearly 1,000 Sikhs in 1747 and his brother-in-law Muin-ul-Mulk, between 1748 and 1753 more than 30,000. Muin-ul-Malik, commonly known as Mir Mannu, earned no laurels in the battlefield but applied his barbarous instincts during his tenure as governor of Punjab. This period is held to be the darkest in the history of Punjab. The price of every Sikh head brought to this governor ten rupees, a huge sum in those days, and his inhuman treatment of those brought to him alive was legendary. Ahmad Shah Abdali and his Afghan governors killed around 60,000 Sikhs between 1753 and 1763. Abdali's deputy Najib-ud-Daulah, also an Afghan, slew nearly 20,000. Petty officials and others might have killed around 4,000 more.[5]

Institutionalisation of the Sikh Solidarity

The head-hunt policy of the Mughals and Afghans made the Sikhs even more determined to counter their misdeeds. Because of the unending plunder of the Mughal treasuries and arsenals and loss of number of men, Zakaria Khan, governor of Lahore, with a view to appeasing the Sikhs, offered them a large jaagir (assigned land). The Sikhs willingly accepted. The Sikhs found this appeasement as an opportunity for consolidating and institutionalising their activities relating to the larger purpose of safeguarding the faith and its followers from genocidal Mughal attacks. Kapur Singh was the man chosen to head this programme. A tough, self-assured and an experienced warrior, he was also deeply devout, and dedicated to building solid institutions that would protect Sikhs.

Kapur Singh organised the Sikh solidarity into an army of veterans called *Buddha Dal* and an army of youthful elements known as *Taruna Dal.* Buddha Dal was to look after the places of pilgrimage and maintain the spiritual health of the community. Taruna Dal remained in readiness to fight when needed. Kapur Singh was an integral link between the two wings of the *Dal Khalsa.*

The Taruna Dal gained considerable strength and also it multiplied numerically. In order to maintain discipline, Kapur Singh split the mass of Sikh solidarity into five well-demarcated divisions. They were led by eminent commanders like Baba

Dip Singh, Karam Singh, Kahn Singh, Dasaundha Singh and Jiwan Singh. Each one of them had separate identity with an individual flag and drum. They had their respective areas of activity which, in due course, emerged as political States. A careful recode of territories (misls) conquered by them was maintained centrally at the Akal Takht. These principalities came to be known as misls. In due course of time, the Khalsa carved out for themselves seven more such States. Thus, by the beginning of the eighteen century, there were in all 12 principalities called misls in the Punjab.

The Misls and Sikh States in Punjab

The term misl (principality, diocese) was first used by Guru Gobind Singh in 1688 during the battle of Bhangani (now in Himachal Pradesh) against the hill rajas, when he organised the Sikhs into groups, each under their own leader with equal power and authority. The word misl in Arabic means 'equal'. The misl chiefs, who have been compared to the barons of medieval times, had complete control over their territories and their own cavalry and infantry units, essentially to discourage any defiance of their authority. They had absolute autonomy, but in times of war, they pooled their resources to take on the enemy. In times of peace, they often fought each other.

The system of misls, if it can be called a system, was obviously a makeshift arrangement suited to meet the challenge of foreign invasions. Twice a year, the Sardars used to meet at Amritsar to discuss problems of defence and when there were no such problems, to deal with frictions that had begun to take place between them. In later years, these meeting of *Sarbat Khalsa* (All-Khalsa Assembly) were little more than noisy sessions where the Sardars were with difficulty restrained from coming to blows. It was obvious that if the Punjab was to be saved from being splintered into little kingdoms and to be unified and made strong, one of the misls would have to absorb the others.

The following were the 12 misls:

1. Phulkian
2. Ahluwalia
3. Bhangi
4. Kanhaya
5. Ramgarhia
6. Singhpuria
7. Kora Singhia
8. Nishania
9. Sukerchakia
10. Dulewala
11. Nakkais
12. Shahids

of these 2, 3, 4, 5, 9 and 11 held lands north of the Sutlej river and the remaining sat south of that river.

The contest was really between the most powerful five misls; of these Sukerchakias gradually forced their way to pre-eminence. These most powerful misls were:

Bhangis – who were in possession of Lahore, Amritsar, and most of Western Punjab; Kanhayas – who held the Himalayan foot hills; the Phulkias – spread themselves around Patiala and Sirhind; the Ahluwalias – took the land between the Ravi and Bias; the Sukerchakias – owned the town of Gujranwala (forty miles north-west of Lahore) and the neighbouring villages.

Phulkian Misl

The Phulkian misl was composed of a group of chiefs descended from a common ancestor and represented at the present day by their descendants, the Maharaja of Patiala, the Raja of Jind and Nabha, the Sirdars of Bhadour, Malod and many others of less importance. It played a very important part in early Sikh history. The founder of the Phulkian misl was one Phul, of the Sindhu tribe. The most powerful ruler of this misl was Ala Singh. He was sought even by the Mughal emperor, Muhammad Shah, who bestowed upon him the title of Raja, for his helping him in the management of Sirhind. He had a frightful skirmish with Ahmad Shah Durrani when thousands of Sikhs were massacred at Kup, near Malerkotla. 'The Phulkian principalities came into prominence when the British, fearing an attack on India by Napoleon, took them under their influence as per the Minto-Metcalfe treaty, signed with Maharaja Ranjit Singh on 30 May 1809.'[6]

Ahluwalia Misl

The Ahluwalia misl was founded by Jassa Singh. He belonged to the village Ahlu which lent its name to the misl. Jassa Singh Ahluwalia was a man of remarkable military talent and ambition. He organised a formal Khalsa force. He is said to have struck a coin in his own name, which modern research has established, was taken by the mullahs to Ahmad Shah Abdali to incite Abdali against him. He was bold enough to attack Ahmad Shah Abdali's force on its return path and rescued a large number of abducted Indian women being taken away by the invader. He was called *Badshah*, i.e. King, by his followers.

He had reconstructed the holy temple at Amritsar after it had been desecrated and demolished by Abdali. Jassa Singh died in 1783. One of his successors, by the name of Fateh Singh, earned a great name as a warrior and diplomat. Ranjit Singh befriended him by exchanging turbans with him, a symbol of eternal brotherhood. He represented Ranjit Singh in signing the first treaty of friendship between the East India Company and the kingdoms of Lahore and Kapurthala in 1806.

Bhangi Misl

Bhangi was one of the most powerful misls, who were in possession of Lahore, Amritsar and most of western Punjab. The Bhangi misl derived its name from Bhima Singh, one of the founders who was addicted to *bhang* (cannabis). He was succeeded by Hari Singh, a great soldier who rose to considerable eminence. He commanded an army of 20,000 men and emerged as the most powerful chieftain of his time. He annexed Sialkot and Jhang, looted the ammunition of the governor of Lahore, stored at Kot Khwaja, near Lahore. He took Rawalpindi, vanquished Majha and Malwa (Punjab) and sacked Jammu. In the east, his influence extended up to the river Jamuna.

Hari Singh was succeeded by his son, Jhanda Singh, who led an expedition to Multan and then Bahawalpur. He attacked Ram Nagar and took into his possession Zamzama, the celebrated gun that came to be known as *Tope Bhangian.* He built a fort in Amritsar called *Qila-i-Bhangian.* Jhanda Singh was assassinated at the instance of the Kanhayas and Charhat Singh of the Sukerchakias. Soon thereafter, the misl started disintegrating.

One of its rulers, Gulab Singh, entered into a conspiracy with Sahib Singh, Jassa Singh and Nizamuddin to assassinate Ranjit Singh who had just then occupied Lahore. While Ranjit Singh was too clever for them to allow any harm to come to him, Gulab Singh died of over drinking in a party. Gulab Singh was succeeded by his minor son, Gurdit Singh. A little while later, Ranjit Singh asked for Tope Bhangian, which the mother of the minor ruler refused to part with. Ranjit Singh attacked Amritsar and took charge of the city as well as of the famous gun within five hours.

Gujar Singh was another powerful chieftain of a branch of

the Bhangi misl. He conquered Lahore, then annexed Gujrat and penetrated up to Poonch.

Kanhaya Misl

Kanhaya misl was founded by Jai Singh who played a considerable role in Ranjit Singh's career. The Kanhayas were as powerful as the Bhangis and retained their possessions longer, owing to their connection by marriage with Maharaja Ranjit Singh. Their chief, Jai Singh, married his infant granddaughter Mehtab Kaur, in 1786, to Ranjit Singh, who was himself only six years old. When Jai Singh died in 1789, his daughter-in-law Sada Kaur, the mother of Mehtab Kaur, a widow of great ability and highly conniving temperament, took command of the principality, and wielded great influence on Maharaja Ranjit Singh until he fell out with her and annexed her estates in 1820.

Ramgarhia Misl

One Jassa Singh, a carpenter by caste, was the founder of the Ramgarhia misl. It shared with the Kanhayas the sacred city of Amritsar and the neighbouring districts. It could, at the height of its power, put eight thousand fighting men into the field. Sirdar Jassa Sing, one of the most distinguished captains, succeeded to its leadership in 1758. He first fortified Amritsar, a portion of which he surrounded with a high mud wall, calling it Ram Rowni or the fort of God. It was soon attacked and destroyed by Adina Beg, imperial governor of the Jalandhar Doab; but on his death, Jassa Singh rebuilt it, and renamed it Ramgarh, from which the principality took its name.

He was a famous fighting baron and made long expeditions, plundering up to the walls of Delhi. On one occasion, he penetrated into the heart of the city and carried off four guns from the Mughal quarter. The governor of Meerut paid him tribute.

Singhpuria Misl

The Singhpuria principality was at one time very powerful and before the days of Jassa Singh Ahluwalia and Ala Singh of Patiala, its founder, Sardar Kapur Singh was perhaps the most renowned of the barons. He was known as Nawab, one of the few instances of a Sikh taking a distinctively Muhammedan title. He seized the village and district of Faizullapur near Amritsar from Faizullah Khan, and gave it the name of Singhpuria, from where the title of the misl was derived, though it is often known as Faizullapura. Kapur Singh died in 1753 and Jassa Singh Ahluwalia held a great part of Kapur Singh's territory, though his nephew Kushal Singh and his descendants kept possession of a part of the territory. This principality held portions of Ludhiana, Nurpur, Jalandhar, and the north-western portion of the Ambala district.

Krora Singhia Misl

The Krora Singhias, who took their name from Sardar Krora Singh, had possessions between the Jamuna and Makanda rivers. The powerful family of Kalsia was the principal member of this misl, who continued to be a ruling house in the Cis-Sutlej for a long time.

Nishania Misl

The Nishanias, who took their names from the Nishan or banner of the Khalsa, were never of much consequence. Sirdar Jai Singh, the most important leader of the principality, obtained his estates after the conquest of Sirhind in 1763. Members of this misl held Ambala, Liddran, Shahabad, Amloh and other districts.

Sukerchakia Misl

The Sukerchakia misl owes its name to Sukerchak, a village in

Amritsar district. The founder of the misl, Budha Singh, was a formidable warrior who is said to have been wounded 40 times during his career. He died in 1718, leaving two enterprising sons, Chanda Singh and Naudh Singh, who was the direct ancestor of Maharaja Ranjit Singh. Naudh Singh was killed fighting the Afghans. He was survived by his son Charhat Singh, who, in due course, became a powerful commander. With the help of the Ahluwalias and the Bhangi Sardars, he drove away the Afghan governor, Ubed Khan, capturing his guns. He led an expedition to Jammu where he was killed by his own gun which exploded accidently.

Charhat Singh was succeeded by his son Mahan Singh who was married to Raj Kaur, a princess from Sangrur. She gave birth to Maharaja Ranjit Singh in 1780, six years after her marriage. Other details of this misl will be dealt with in the context of Maharaja Ranjit Singh.

Dulelwala Misl

The Dulelwala misl took its name from the village of Sardar Tara Singh, who was its principal leader, and who, with his followers, held a great portion of the upper Jalandhar Doab and the northern portions of Ambala and Ludhiana, with some estates in Firozpur.

Nakkai Misl

The Nakkais inhabited what was known as the Nakka area lying between Lahore and Gogaira in the direction of Multan. It was never a powerful principality but could bring into the field some two thousand horsemen, camels and guns. The Jats of this part of the Punjab were notoriously brave and under Sardar Hira Singh and Ram Singh, they acquired territory worth nine lakh of rupees per annum in Gogaira, Kasur and Sharakpur.

Shaheed Misl

The Shaheeds, the last of the principalities, was more of a religious than a military body, though the priests fought in those days as well as the laymen. The founder of the Shaheed misl was Sudda Singh, the *mahant* or head of the shrine at Talwandi, which was Guru Gobind Singh's resting place (Damdama). Sudda Singh was killed fighting against the Muslim governor of Jalandhar, and his head having been struck off, he is reported to have ridden some distance and killed several of the enemy before he fell from his horse. Hence, he was known as the Shaheed (martyr), and his followers took his name. This principality used to join itself to others rather than fight on its own account. Its representatives still hold charge of the sacred shrine of Damdama.

Such is a sketch of the fighting principalities of the Sikhs during the eighteenth century and the first part of the nineteenth century. But their composition was always changing, and their possessions passed from one hand to another very rapidly. They fought against each other more often than against the common enemy, the Muslims, and their mutual destructive war was only ended by Maharaja Ranjit Singh crushing all who were not shielded by the British guarantee. Even within the borders of each principality itself, the barons were always quarrelling, and first one chief and then another took the lead. 'This was due to the constitution of Sikhism, under which no such thing as feudal superiority was acknowledged. The principle of the creed was fraternity, and the Sikhs boasted of being communities of independent soldiers.'[7]

While the Khalsa was still young and enthusiastic, and the power of no individual chief was excessively great, this idea of independence represented a state of things not far removed from the truth; but as the more important chiefships gradually increased in power, their smaller neighbours were compelled, either for protection against others, or to avoid absorption altogether, also to place themselves under the protection of some able leader to defend them, redesigning in return, service in the field. A sort of mercenary service with whosoever suited the group's purpose evolved.

All that a Sikh chief asked in those days from a follower was a horse and matchlock (shot gun). All that a follower sought was protection and permission to plunder in the name of God and the Guru under the banner of the chief. All Sikhs were theoretically equal and those like Amar Singh Majithia, who could pierce a tree through with an arrow or like Hari Singh Nalwa, who could kill a tiger with a blow of his sword, might soon ride with followers behind him and call himself a Sardar.

But all the great families, north and south of the Sutlej river, have the same origin: the law of force, the keen sword and strong hands were the foundations upon which Sikh society, as indeed every other powerful society in the world, was founded. To attract followers by his power and success was the main desire of every Sikh chief. Who they were, and what were their antecedents, were matters of no consequence if only they could fight and ride, which almost every Sikh could do. In those days, every village became a fort, built on a high mound to overlook plain country, with one entrance, and narrow lanes in which two men could hardly walk together.

The Sikh army was known as the *Dal Khalsa*, the army of God, sometimes the Buddha Dal or veteran army. It consisted for the most part of cavalry called *Kattiawand*, comprising men who found their own horses and received a double share of the prize money. Each chief, in proportion to his means, furnished horses and arms to his retainers who were called *Birgirs*; and as the first tribute exacted from a conquered district was horses, the infantry soldier was, after a successful campaign, generally transformed into a regular serviceman. The infantry was considered an inferior branch of the service and was only used for garrison and sentry duty. The battles of the Sikhs were invariably cavalry actions.

The only infantry who enjoyed any respect were the Akalis. These were a fanatical body of devotees, who dressed in dark blue and wore round their turbans a steel disc, partly for show and partly as weapons, though they were not very effective. The other distinctive signs were a knife stuck in the turban, and a sword slung round their neck. These men, excited by hemp, were generally the first to storm a town, and often did excellent service; but they were lawless and uncertain, and, in peaceful times enjoyed a privileged life.

The Sikh weapon was the sword, with which the cavalry was very skillful. Bows and arrows were used by the infantry, and a few matchlocks; but the powder was scarce and its use little liked by the Sikhs, who were never at ease with a musket in their hands. For the same reasons they possessed scarcely any artillery; although Ranjit Singh, with the aid of French and Italian officers, formed a very powerful and well-appointed artillery.

The prize money taken in a campaign was equally shared among the combatants. If a soldier was wounded, he invariable received compensation, and if he was killed, his son or nearest male relative was entertained in his place. The chiefs or barons were known by some nickname or surname which specially distinguished them. Hindu names were few in number and the suffix Singh was universal. Generally, this addition was taken from their birthplace or from a town they had conquered, like Jassa Singh, Ahluwalia; sometimes from a personal peculiarity or attribute, good or bad. As examples of these may be quoted Nidhan Singh Panjhathah (the five-handed, from his great prowess in battle); Lehna Singh, Chimi (from his short stature); Mohr Singh, Lamba (the tall); Sher Singh, Kamla (the fool); Karm Singh, Nirmala (the spotless) and there are a hundred more with which Sikh history is dotted, and of which many have descended to the present-day as an honoured part of the family title.

However, Sukerchakia is not a name commonly found in the Punjab today, though their clan name, the Sandhu is used both, in Pakistan as well as Indian Punjab.

Sandhanwalias were a Jat Sikh group from Sandhanwala village, now in Pakistan, who rose to importance during the last years of Ranjit Singh's rule. Some scholars connect Ranjit Singh himself with this group too.

THE STATE OF PUNJAB AND RISE OF RANJIT SINGH

His Ancestors

THE MOST COLOURFUL of Ranjit Singh's ancestors was a figure from the seventeenth century, Desu, a cultivator, his father's great-grandfather. Desu's earthly possessions consisted of 25 acres of land, a well, three ploughs, two houses for his family and cattle. The Sukerchakia misl took its name from that of his village, Sukerchak, which was located near the town of Gujranwala, about 40 miles north of Lahore.

Desu was a fearless fighter, known for his courage and daring action and also an expert cattle lifter. Desu, at the age of 50, personally met Guru Gobind Singh at Anand with a request to get baptised by him. After the baptism, his name was changed to Budha Singh. He was greatly inspired by the Guru, he stayed with him to participate in the many battles fought by the Khalsa.

When Budha Singh died in 1718, his body was found to be riddled with scars of sword and musket wounds. He left his two sons Naudh Singh and Chanda Singh a few villages they could call their own and many others in the neighbourhood which paid them protection tax – *rakhi*.

Budha Singh's son, Naudh Singh, fortified the village Sukerchak and raised a body of men who came thereafter to be called Sukerchakias. The Sukerchakias joined forces with other misls and fought in several engagements with Ahmad Shah Abdali. As the Afghans retreated, they took possession of parts of the land between the Ravi and the Jhelum rivers.

Naudh Singh was killed fighting Afghans in 1752. He was survived by his son Charhat Singh who, in due course, became a powerful commander. He moved his headquarters from the village, Sukerchak, to Gujranwala and fortified the entire town. The region's Afghan governor, Ubed Khan, came with a small force to apprehend Charhat Singh but he was driven away by the latter, with the help of Ahluwalia and Bhangi Sardars, leaving behind his guns and stocks of grains. Emboldened by this success, Charhat Singh extended his domains by capturing the towns of Wazirabad, Ahmedabad and Rohtas.

Charhat Singh also brought many other territories under his control, such as parts of Rawalpindi, but in some cases, he was content merely to receive revenue. By means of such arrangements and many other related ones, he established his suzerainty, in the form of the Sukerchakia misl, with influence over a considerable area. His power was won and consolidated not only by force of arms but also through alliances entered into by marrying his sons, sisters and daughters into families of consequence; the broad base he created was without doubt the springboard which was to enable his grandson to establish an empire of the Sikhs. Had it not been for his untimely death at the age of 45, caused by accidental firing of his own gun, this energetic man would have achieved more.

Out of Charhat Singh's three children, his two sons Mahan Singh and Sahaj Singh and their sister Raj Kaur, it was Mahan Singh, born in 1760, who proved a worthy successor to his father, who had died when he was just ten. Till he took formal charge of the misl just five years later, his able mother, Mai Dessan, handled its affairs and its extensive territories with exemplary skill, self-confidence and courage. She provided Mahan Singh with invaluable lessons in the management of his complex inheritance, lessons which he put to good use. The problems she dealt with ranged from a revolt by senior officials appointed by the misl to winning the army's support of her stewardship and rebuilding the Gujranwala fort, which had been destroyed by Abdali.

Mai Dessan befittingly exemplified the tradition by which Sikh women took on crucial responsibilities in critical times. Mahan Singh married a daughter of Gajpat Singh, the Chief of Jind, and thereby strengthened his own position amongst the *misldar*s. Within the walled town of Gujranwala, he built a fort which he named after himself as 'Garhi Mahan Singh'. He increased the number of his horsemen to 6,000 and resumed the ancestral occupation of acquiring territory. He captured Rasoolnagar from a Muslim tribe, the Chatthas; he took Alipur, Pindi, Bhattian, Sahiwal, Isakhel and Sialkot. Then, like his father, he proceeded to Jammu. Its Hindu Dogra ruler fled leaving the rich city to the mercies of the acquisitive Sukerchakia.

With the loot of Jammu, Mahan Singh raised Sukerchakia from a position of comparative dimness to that of being one of the leaders of the misl confederacy. The Kanhayas, who had replaced the Bhangis as the most powerful misl, disputed Mahan Singh's right to plunder Jammu, and in one of the many skirmishes between the two misls, Gurbaksh Singh, the only son of the head of the Kanhayas, was killed. The Kanhaya Chief's pride was humbled and he agreed to marry his granddaughter, Mehtab Kaur, to Mahan Singh's son Ranjit Singh. The Kanhaya Chief, Jai Singh, died in 1789 leaving his estates to his widowed daughter-in-law, Sada Kaur, the mother of Mehtab Kaur.

Mahan Singh died in 1792. The legacy which Budha Singh, Naudh Singh, Charhat Singh and Mahan Singh left to young Ranjit consisted of a sizeable estate in north-western Punjab, a band of fearless horse-and-matchlock men, and an ambition that knew no bounds. His child bride too came with considerable properties.

Birth of Ranjit Singh

Ranjit Singh was born on a Tuesday, 13 November 1780, in the small fortress town of Badrukhan not far from Jind. Badrukhan was the home of his mother, Raj Kaur, the daughter of Rajah Gajpat Singh of Jind, known in her husband's home as Mai Malwain, the lady of Malwa. She had, as was customary in the Punjab, come to her parental house for her first delivery.

There is a difference of opinion among academics about the place and date of Ranjit Singh's birth. An old house in Gujranwala bears two plaques outside one of the rooms, stating that to be Ranjit Singh's place of birth and mentioning the date as 2 November 1780. These plaques have been accepted as authentic evidence by many historians including McGregor, Griffin and Prem Singh. It is quite clear that the plaques were put up many years after the annexation of Punjab by the British – the legend is in Urdu, Punjabi and English – and at the instance of some civil servant who did not go into the historical evidence. Both Sohan Lal Suri and Diwan Amar Nath refer to Ranjit Singh's birth-day celebrations which confirm the date as the 13th and not the 2nd of November. They also state that the place of birth was Badrukhan.[1]

Whilst there are differing views about Ranjit Singh's date of birth and birthplace, there is agreement among numerous accounts of the wild rejoicings that followed the news of the heir's arrival; spectacular feasts and distribution of large sums of money amongst the poor continued for days in the city, festooned with lights and alive as never before.

The child was named Buddha Singh, the wise one. News

of the birth of a son was sent to Gujranwala. But Mahan Singh was out with his band of horsemen, subduing the Chatthas living along the Jhelum. The dispatch rider met Mahan Singh returning from his victories against the Chatthas and broke the news of the birth of Buddha Singh. With prophetic insight Mahan Singh changed his son's name from Buddha Singh to Ranjit Singh (Victor of Battles). He wanted his son to be a conqueror. True to his name, Ranjit Singh rose to be a renowned warrior.

Early Years

Little is known about Ranjit Singh's early years except that he had no formal education. He could hardly sign his name, though he had a fair proficiency in Punjabi and Persian and could modify drafts of important documents read out to him by his courtiers.

He was sent to the Bhagu Singh Dharamsala (centre of learning) in Gujranwala where he learned no more than a few numerals and acquired some knowledge of how to use maps and charts, which were to stand him in good stead throughout his life. He showed no interest in the arts, mathematics or bookkeeping, but was instinctively drawn to agriculture and other disciplines that required physical inputs. Just after one year, he left Bhagu Dharamsala and engaged himself in learning the martial arts – especially how to fight with the sword and the spear. He also loved to swim, wrestle, shoot and hunt.

In his childhood, at the age of six, Ranjit Singh was taken ill with smallpox, the accursed disease of those days. While his life was saved, he lost his left eye to the pox and also had a face pock-marked all over. This disfigured the youthful warrior considerably, who was otherwise short-statured and not very impressive either. However, it is said, the moment he sat on horseback, his ill-looking appearance was completely transformed. Every muscle of his body seemed to vibrate. There was a glow on his face and a sparkle in his eyes.

There are many contemporary descriptions of him. This, by Baron Charles von Hügel, is as vivid as any:

> In person he is short and mean looking, and had he not distinguished himself by his great talents, he would be passed by without being thought worthy of observation. Without exaggeration I must call him the most ugly and unprepossessing man I saw throughout the Punjab. His left eye, which is quite closed, disfigures him less than the other, which is always rolling about wide open and is much distorted by disease. The scars of the small-pox on his face do not run into one another but form so many dark pits in his greyish-brown skin; his short straight nose is swollen at the tip; the skinny lips are stretched tight over his teeth which are still good; his grizzled beard, very thin on the cheeks and upper lip, meets under the chin in matted confusion, his head, which is sunk very deep on his broad shoulders, is too large for his height, and does not seem to move easily.
>
> He has a thick muscular neck, thin arms and legs, the left foot and left arm drooping, and small well-formed hands. He will sometimes hold a stranger's hand fast within his own for half-an-hour, and the nervous irritation of his wind is shown by the continual pressure on one's fingers. His costume always contributes to increase his ugliness, being in winter the colour of gamboge from the *Pagri* (the turban) down to his very socks and slippers. When he seats himself in a common English chair with his feet drawn under him, the position is one particularly unfavourable to him, but as soon as he mounts his horse and with his black shield at his back (which) puts him on his mettle, his whole form seems animated by the spirit within, and assumes a

> certain grace of which nobody could believe susceptible. In spite of the paralysis affecting one side, he manages his horse with utmost ease.[2]
>
> As excellent horseman, he would remain the whole day in the saddle without showing any sign of fatigue. His love for horses amounted to a passion, and for his personal use he kept only those selected horses which were collected from India, Arabia and Persia. He was also a keen sportsman and an accomplished swordsman. It was strange indeed to observe how complete was his ascendency, even when he had become feeble, blind and paralysed, over his brilliant court of fierce and turbulent chiefs.

Once, when Fakir Aziz-ud-Din was asked by the British Governor General of which eye the Maharaja was blind, the devoted courtier replied, 'the awe and the grandeur of his royalty is such that no one dares look our noble Sarkar in the face, your Excellency. I have never dared to cast my eyes at his face'. It is said that Lord William Bentinck so appreciated the reply that he took out his gold watch and presented it to Fakir Aziz-ud-Din. The watch is still preserved in the Fakir family at Lahore as stated by Syed Waheeduddin, who wrote the book, *The Real Ranjit Singh*.[3]

He was great because he possessed an extraordinary degree of qualities without which the highest success cannot be attained; and the absence of the commonplace virtues which belong to the average citizen neither diminished nor affected in any way the distinction of his character. He was a born ruler, with the natural genius of command. Men obeyed him by instinct and because they had no power to disobey. The control which he exercised, even in the closing years of his life, over the whole Sikh community, nobles, priests and people, was the measure of his greatness.

To the highest courage he added a perseverance which no obstacles could exhaust, and he did not fail in his undertakings because he never admitted the possibility of failure. His political sagacity was great and was demonstrated in nothing more convincingly than in his determined friendship with the English, when he realised that they were safe friends and very dangerous enemies. He possessed the faculty of choosing his subordinates well and wisely. He knew men and he selected each servant for the special work which he could best perform.

The age of six seemed to have a special significance in Ranjit Singh's life because his first marriage also took place in 1786, soon after he recovered from his illness. His bride Mehtab Kaur was five. The dating of this event too is a matter of controversy, some records suggest that he was married at age of 26. Most of the historical evidence, however, points to the earlier date.

Marriages in those days were usually arranged for political or dynastic reasons, and the practice was to book the bride and groom early, lest other parents with similar concerns steal a march in the marriage market. The Sukerchakia and Kanhaya misl being among foremost of the twelve, Ranjit Singh's marriage to the daughter of the Kanhayas was decided in order to forge an advantageous alliance. It was, in fact, at the initiative of Sada Kaur, mother of Mehtab Kaur, that the marriage between these two (Ranjit Singh and Mehtab Kaur) materialised. Sada Kaur had taken over the leadership of the Kanhayas in 1789, after the death of her father-in-law Jai Singh. Her husband Gurbaksh Singh had been killed earlier in a battle with the Ramgarhia misl in 1785, when she was only 22.

However, Ranjit Singh's marriage to Mehtab Kaur was a complete failure, not only because of his abiding interest in other women, but because of his wife Mehtab Kaur's deep and continuing conviction that Ranjit Singh's father Mahan Singh had a hand in her father Gurbaksh Singh's death in battle, although he had died in a clash with the Ramgarhias. Sada Kaur's view was more pragmatic. She hoped to repair the rift between the two misls through this marriage, with the aim of creating a grand alliance with far bigger goals in mind. Ranjit Singh later went on to have twenty wives in all, besides a very sizeable harem.

The special nature of the boy Ranjit Singh may be grasped from the fact that within three years of the smallpox attack, he took over the siege of Sodhran in 1789, at the age of nine, when his father was suddenly stricken by serious illness. It was an amazingly young age to take on such a task. The town of Sodhran, lying some 40 kilometers south-east of Gujranwala, belonged to the Bhangi Chief's son, Sahib Singh. Ranjit Singh's father Mahan Singh had demanded tribute from Sahib Singh Bhangi, and on the latter's refusal to comply, ejected him from his principality. Sahib Singh took refuge in the fort of Sodhran and appealed to his kinsmen in Lahore to come to his help. In what was to be his first experience of military campaign, his father Mahan Singh took Ranjit Singh with him to Sodhran and laid siege to the fort.

The siege dragged on through the winter months. Mahan Singh was suddenly taken very ill, and fearing that he might not recover, invested Ranjit Singh as the head of the Sukerchakia misl by putting saffron paste on the boy's forehead and then returned to Gujranwala. When the Bhangi Sardars of Lahore heard of Mahan Singh's illness and of the plight of the Sukerchakias under the command of a nine-year-old, they hurried to the relief of Sodhran. Ranjit Singh ambushed the Bhangi force coming from Lahore many miles from Sodhran and routed it. Mahan Singh heard of his son's victory before he died. Ranjit Singh was just able to get back in time for his father's funeral.

Intrigues and Ranjit's Visions of Power

Ranjit Singh was too young and temperamental to bother about the day-to-day management of the estate and let his father's manager, Lakhpat Rai, continue in charge. His mother had confidence in Lakhpat Rai's integrity but her brother Dal Singh, who wished to take the administration into his own hands, found an ally in Sada Kaur, Ranjit's mother-in-law. The intrigues and counter-intrigues that went on between his mother, mother-in-law, uncle and other relations and friends made Ranjit heartily sick of the atmosphere at home and he began to spend most of his time out hunting and in the company of servants. These were impressionable years; the experience made him forever suspicious of people who professed affection for him, and he developed an acute aversion to quarrelsome people. He spent most of his time in the chase, he learnt to ride and shoot well. And since a day's hunting was followed by a drinking party, he was introduced to alcohol early in life.

A murderous assault was made on Ranjit Singh during one of his hunting expeditions. He had ridden off alone in pursuit of game when Hashmat Khan, a chief who had suffered many humiliating defeats at the hands of Ranjit's father, Mahan Singh, attacked him. Ranjit's horse smelt threat of danger and fell back when the Khan made an attempt to hit Ranjit with his sword. Before the assailant could make a second move, Ranjit pierced him with his own sword. He cut off Hashmat Khan's head and rode back to his companions with the blood-soaked trophy stuck on his spear. He was then barely thirteen.

As mentioned earlier, Ranjit Singh's marriage with Mehtab Kaur was not a very happy one. It is not unlikely that Mehtab Kaur felt somewhat inhibited in giving her affections to a man whose father had slain her father; and Ranjit Singh's reaction to her reservation was to withdraw into himself. It soon became a marriage of convenience. Sada Kaur did not seem particularly disturbed at the prospect of her daughter occasionally sharing a bed with a man for whom she had little use: that sort of thing was common enough; the important thing was for her to produce sons who could be heirs to Sukerchakia domains. Meanwhile, she could utilise the alliance to safeguard and even advance the interests of the Kanhayas.

To Ranjit Singh, who was undoubtedly conscious of his own plainness, the disillusionment was great enough to change his values. Instead of trying to win affections, he began to want to command loyalties – which he could only do by becoming powerful. The Kanhaya, thus, became a means towards this end. A curious love-hate relationship developed between Sada Kaur and Ranjit Singh. Both of them were ambitious and respected the other's ambition; they could be dishonest and consequently willing to overlook the other's concern; in short, being very much alike, they began to understand each other perfectly.

Sada Kaur was the first to ask for help. In the summer of 1797, her possessions were threatened by the Ramgarhias and Ranjit Singh had to besiege a Ramgarhia fortress to relieve the pressure on the Kanhayas. On his way back to Gujranwala, Ranjit Singh stayed at Lahore for three days as the guest of the Bhangi Sardars and acquired valuable information on the state of affairs in the city and its defenses.

Ranjit Singhs' mind was now completely obsessed with visions of power. Experience of the previous campaign had proved to him that the Kanhayas were not as strong as he had believed. His chances would be brighter if he could draw some other misl on his side. He made overtures to the chief of the Nakkais and early in 1798, took a second wife who was the sister of the Nakkai Sardar. This marriage proved to be more successful than the first. The new wife bore the same name as his mother, Raj Kaur, and had the same maternal gentleness and understanding in dealing with the headstrong Ranjit Singh.

Although many other women came into his life, for no one did he have greater respect than for Ravi Raj Kaur (renamed Datar Kaur), but affectionately known as Mai Nakkain.

The second marriage gave Mehtab Kaur an excuse to return to Batala and thereafter, she only made occasional appearances at her husband's home. This saddened Sada Kaur, Mehtab's mother, but she reconciled herself to Ranjit's polygamous venture because she had set her heart on bigger things and was determined to see that for her own sake and the sake of her only child (and her progeny if she had any), Ranjit Singh carried out the plans that she had made for him.

Two Power Camps around Ranjit Singh

Sada Kaur played a major role in Ranjit Singh's life. Her role was, however, preceded by his mother's more modest but, nevertheless, significant contribution. Raj Kaur was only 24 years old when Mahan Singh died in 1790 but, despite her young age, she was of considerable help in holding the misl together for seven years through a form of regency, which included Diwan Lakhpat Rai, who was Mahan Singh's maternal uncle and the Chief of Analgarh. But her regency was the cause of friction between the two power camps around Ranjit Singh, with Raj Kaur and Diwan Lakhpat Rai bitterly opposed to Sada Kaur and Dal Singh, who was Raj Kaur's brother, each camp trying to bring young Ranjit Singh under its influence.

In this situation, Sada Kaur and Dal Singh, the more aggressive supporters, were determined not only to undermine Raj Kaur's effectiveness as an administrator but also to tarnish her personal reputation. Besides launching a defaming campaign against her over her alleged relationship with Lakhpat Rai, many intrigues well beyond the bounds of decency were hatched to destroy her image in the eyes of the public.

Meanwhile, Raj Kaur died mysteriously. The mysterious

and controversial incident gave rise to vicious rumours suggesting that Ranjit Singh himself had a hand in the killing of his mother. One British army officer, writing nearly half a century later, gave a distinctly sugar-coated version of the incident. Ranjit Singh, his story goes, entered his mother's chamber early one morning and, finding a man there, quietly left, summoned some followers, took up a sword, and returned to his mother's room where he now found her alone. In an increasingly heated argument, Raj Kaur is said to have rebuked her son for casting a slur on her moral character and Ranjit Singh, 'stung to madness by her reproaches, is believed to have killed her' as she was sitting up on her bed 'half naked, with disheveled hair'.[4]

The historian, Hari Ram Gupta, a specialist in the history of that period, later wrote, '…Some writers accuse Ranjit Singh of having killed his mother with his own hands…. Kushwaqt Rae, Sohan Lal, Amar Nath and Bute Shah (writers and chroniclers of distinction whose accounts are based on first-hand observation or on a serious study of events of the period) do not mention this event. Kushwaqt Rae wrote his book in 1811, and he was not in Ranjit Singh's service. Bute Shah was an employee of the British in Ludhiana. He says that Ranjit Singh took charge of his misl in consultation with his mother. N K Sinha says the story is based on "gossip". Sita Ram Kohli considers the charge entirely false and baseless. In our view, by any stretch of imagination, Ranjit Singh cannot be called a killer of his mother. The story is purely malicious and absolutely unfair and unjust'.[5]

There would seem to be no justification for the charge of mother-killer against a man whose patent decency throughout his life is especially striking, when it is seen in a historical context so replete with the most extreme examples of cruelty and bloodthirstiness on the part of the rulers not only towards persons defeated by them but also towards the innocent. To repeat the British historian Lepel Griffin's comments: 'With all his rapacity, Ranjit Singh was not cruel or bloodthirsty. After a victory or the capture of a fortress, he treated the vanquished with leniency and kindness, however stout their resistance might have been, and there were at his court many chiefs despoiled of their estates but to whom he had given suitable employment....'[6] Eventually, it came to be accepted that Raj Kaur had been poisoned at the instigation of her adversaries.

Ranjit Singh Consolidates his Position

In spite of family intrigues and Sada Kaur's great ambitions, Ranjit Singh came to his own and started taking decisions independently, Dal Singh continued to be his chief advisor and Sada Kaur his political mentor who helped him consolidate his position as *the* Sikh Chief.

Though Ranjit Singh's mother Raj Kaur and his mother-in-law Sada Kaur were both highly ambitious women, the latter's ambition was on a higher scale and, in comparison to the former, she possessed a higher degree of courage and ability in abundance. On several occasions, she proved herself a valuable ally to her son-in-law. Lepel Griffin describes her as 'a widow of great ability and unscrupulousness who took command of the confederacy and her own against her son-in-law successfully till 1820'.[7]

Soon after Raj Kaur's death, Diwan Lakhpat Rai was also killed during an expedition against Chattha Pathans, and with both of her rivals removed from the field, Sada had ample scope to pursue her ambitions. It was a fact that the combined strength of the Sukerchakia and the Kanhayas had made these two misls as the most powerful among the existing 12 misls. Sada Kaur had, therefore, made her own plan to establish her writ over the entire Punjab. Here she failed to gauge the vision and ambition of her son-in-law, Ranjit Singh, who had already envisioned a larger plan of capturing not only all of Punjab, but also the entire territories well beyond India's boundaries which had been barbarously captured by others for centuries. He was, therefore, clear in his mind that to achieve his objective he would have to bring different misls under his control to create a sound power base.

The Sikh misls were torn with intrigues and conspiracies. They were ever-ready to attack one another. The religious fervour and idealism that Guru Gobind Singh had instilled in his followers seemed to have faded away. The Dal Khalsa no longer existed. Rather than adhere to the republican principles introduced by Guru Gobind Singh, the Sikh confederacy had brought about a feudal structure. It had the seeds of disintegration in it.

The existing behaviour of the misls was not favourable for Ranjit Singh. However, the sizeable estate that had been bequeathed to Ranjit Singh was an advantage for him. Besides, the courage, vision and thirst for creating a kingdom was a favourable entreprise for the young chief. Bikrama Jit Hasrat pinpoints the political situation in the Punjab at the time when Ranjit Singh took over the Sukerchakia misl in 1797 as: 'The misl system, born out of a sense of national unity to combat foreign aggression, had foundered on the rock of personal ambition and lust for power. The carving out of several principalities by the powerful Bhangis, the Ramgarhias, the Ahluwalias and the Phulkians had struck a blow at the mystic ideal of the Commonwealth of Guru Gobind Singh.... The unity of action or concerted will in the name of Khalsa had become a thing of the past.'[8] However, in spite of such deplorable conditions of the misls, Ranjit Singh's vision ended up in creating a kingdom, which was beyond Sada Kaur's powers of conception.

As regards leadership among the misls, there was hardly any towering personality with whom Ranjit Singh had to contend. The decline of the Durrani power had created a regional vacuum which needed a man of Ranjit Singh's ambition to fill.

THE MAHARAJA

PUNJAB WAS IN great turmoil during the period when Ranjit Singh was born (1780s). It was divided into fourteen pieces of landmasses and bombarded with arrows of fire from different sides. Twelve of these fourteen pieces were the Sikh misls and the other two, the Pathan controlled district of Kasur in the neighbourhood of Lahore and Hansi in the south-east under the English adventurer, George Thomas. The five arrows were: the Afghans in the north-west; the Rajputs of Kangra in the north; the Gurkhas in the north-east with connection with Nepal; the British in the east and the Marathas in the south-east.

The misl system had failed and it had lost the purpose of the *Khalsa Panth,* for which it was formed fifty years before. The misls had ceased to be the united fraternity they were created to be, and instead of giving united fight against foreign aggressors, they started hobnobbing with them. When Ahmed Shah Abdali had started his incursions into India, they had fought as one under the leadership of Jassa Singh Ahluwalia. The first to default were the Phulkias of Patiala. Ala Singh had submitted to Abdali and later on, the Phulkias had become collaborators. Sahib Singh of Patiala was in communication with Abdali's grandson, Shah Zaman, who was planning to re-establish Afghan dominion over northern India.

Capturing Sikh Power

In view of the prevailing situation, it was very necessary for Ranjit Singh to move cautiously and to break important misls and make the other misldars subservient to his wishes. The misls that mattered were the Kanhayas, the Nakkais, the Ahluwalias and the Bhangi. Ranjit Singh had matrimonial ties with the first two (the Kanhayas and the Nakkais) and they could be counted on to help him, provided this cooperation did not hurt their own interests. The Ahluwalias were led by Fateh Singh, who was an able leader, and because he was Jassa Singh's successor, held in great esteem by the Sikhs. Ranjit Singh decided to befriend Fateh Singh. The other important misl was those of the Bhangis, who held Lahore, Amritsar, Gujrat, and large portion of northern Punjab. Since Ranjit Singh could not reconcile his interests with the Bhangis, he decided to break it.

Another urgent problem to be solved before Ranjit Singh was to tackle Nizamuddin Khan, a Pathan ruler of Kasur, which was thirty miles from Lahore. This Pathan ruling family's loyalties were more to the land of their forefathers than to the Punjab. The rise of Sikh misls had made them nervous. Each time Abdali had come to the Punjab, they had joined him to plunder their own neighbours. When Abdali's grandson, Shah Zaman expressed the desire to establish an Afghan empire in India, among the first to promise him assistance was Nizamuddin Khan of Kasur.

Sada Kaur's Decisiveness Helped Ranjit

In the first years after Raj Kaur's untimely end, Ranjit Singh gained a good deal from Sada Kaur's decisiveness. For example, when Zaman Shah appeared in Punjab on his fourth invasion of India in September 1798 and crossed the river Indus at Attock, Ranjit Singh prepared to oppose him at Ramnagar on the river Chenab but had to head back for the Amritsar-Lahore region. This was because some of the Muslim landlords of the area along with the Afghan governor of Kasur, Nizamuuddin, had prepared to occupy some of the Sikh forts. In the ensuing action, a wounded Nizamuddin had to be removed along with the dead Afghan soldiers who were more than twice the number of Sikh soldiers killed.

While Sikh contingents under Ranjit Singh continued to attack the Afghans, several chieftains and their men in Amritsar, at that time, were most reluctant to combine forces with him, despite his urging. Great panic spread in the Punjab at the time. At Amritsar, even the sacred shrine had only a handful of guards left to protect it. 'The timidity of the Sikhs', wrote Collins, who was the English Resident at the court of the then Mughal emperor at Delhi, 'is undeserving of credit'.[1] Sahib Singh Bhangi evacuated Gujrat and the Afghans plundered the town and massacred the inhabitants. Hindus and Sikhs had fled earlier, the Afghans' victims were Punjabi Muslims.[2] Gujranwala, which had been abandoned by Ranjit Singh, met the same fate.

At the meeting of the Sarbat Khalsa at Amritsar, the majority were again for fleeing to the hills. Sada Kaur, who was also then in Amritsar, promptly made her presence felt. She reminded the Sikh chieftains that they owed a duty to the people from whom they had been taking protection tax. And if the Sardars decided to flee, she would lead those Sikhs who were willing to follow her. She further said, 'If you are disposed to assist Ranjit Singh, advance and join him, if not, throw off that dress and take mine, give me your clothes and I will march against the enemy'.[3] Ranjit Singh supported his mother-in-law and made a passionate appeal that the holy city of Amritsar should not be left to the mercies of people who made desecration of shrines a point of honour. Ranjit Singh's uncle, Dal Singh, who was also present, told the story of his success in looting an armed caravan carrying fruits for Zaman Shah.

The Afghans, he reassured the assembled gathering, were vastly overrated as soldiers and the Sikhs would have no difficulty in beating them. This emboldened the other Sardars and they decided to take on the Afghans. They said, 'victory is the gift of God. Let us make one effort to oppose them'. Ranjit Singh was again chosen to be their leader.[4]

On 24 November 1798, Zaman Shah, temporarily in control of Lahore, which had been under Bhangi rule since the ousting of the Afghans in 1765, sent a force of 10,000 men to Amritsar to teach the Sikhs a lesson by occupying their holy city too. Ranjit Singh, with just 500 horsemen, waylaid the advance contingents of Zaman's army and after intense fighting – in which the Sardars from Amritsar with 2,000 of their men joined in – the Afghans retreated to Lahore. These were the same Sardars who had been addressed by Sada Kaur, and clearly her taunts had worked.

The following year provides another example of Sada Kaur's utility and capability. After Zaman Shah's departure and the vanquishing of his garrison stationed in Punjab, Lahore had the misfortune of being occupied by Chet Singh, Sahib Singh and Mohar Singh, three Bhangi Sardars. They exacted exorbitant taxes and made themselves unpopular by their misrule. The people were sick of them. They got together, Hindus, Sikhs and Muslims, and invited Ranjit Singh to take over Lahore.

The Prize, the City of Lahore

Ranjit Singh was waiting for such an opportunity, but he acted with restraint and caution. First of all, he sent Qazi Rahman, a trusted Muslim officer, to verify the genuineness of the invitation. After he had been fully satisfied, he sent word to his mother-in-law Sada Kaur to meet him. On the pretext of making a pilgrimage, he visited Amritsar to take stock of the situation personally.

The attack on Lahore was a masterpiece of planning. Ranjit Singh collected 25,000 soldiers under his own command and the command of his mother-in-law, Sada Kaur. The operation was fixed for the night following the tenth day of Muharram in 1799. After spending a night at Majitha, near Amritsar, they reached the outskirts of Lahore the next evening. Ranjit Singh had already split his army into two parts. It is said that the city gates were left unguarded for them. Ranjit Singh entered the city from the Lahore Gate and Sada Kaur from the Delhi Gate. The Bhangi Sardars, who were engaged in merrymaking, were taken by surprise. While Mohar Singh made good his escape, Chet Singh shut himself up in the fort.

Ranjit Singh wished to bombard the fort, but he was dissuaded from this by his shrewd mother-in-law Sada Kaur, who correctly guessed that Chet Singh did not have rations and would not be able to hold out for long. The Bhangi Chief, Chet Singh, surrendered the very next day and his stronghold was taken without bloodshed. Ranjit Singh treated him kindly and granted him a jaagir for his maintenance. On other occasions too, as Ranjit Singh fought on many fronts to consolidate his hold, Sada Kaur was there to lend him support.

Thus, nineteen-year-old Ranjit Singh became the master of Lahore on 7 July 1799. Lahore was the traditional capital of the Punjab. All the doors were now open for the young Ranjit to spread his influence. This became a landmark in Sikh history as well as in the life of Ranjit Singh.

Ranjit Singh's first move on occupying Lahore was to issue an order that his officers and troops were to treat the people of the city with courtesy and consideration, and that failure to obey this order, as also any attempt at plunder, would bring severe punishment. Ranjit Singh himself rode through Lahore's streets to assure the citizens of their personal safety and the safety of their property, and to leave no doubt in their mind that they would be in no danger under his rule.

Lahore – once the prized possession of the Mughals and then of Abdali, who, after his victories over the Mughals in 1748, had declared Punjab a territory of Afghanistan with Lahore as its capital – was now in the possession of Ranjit Singh. The 19-year-old conqueror was master of one of the most historic cities of India. Lying on the banks of the river Ravi, one of Punjab's living great rivers, the 2,000-year-old settlement of Lahore had not only borne wave after wave of Muslim invaders beginning with Mahmud of Ghazni in 1014 but had also been home to dynasties established by numerous invaders, including the Ghoris, Mongols, Tughlaks, Khiljis, Lodhis and Suris.

When Akbar moved his capital to Lahore in 1584, he had built a strong brick fortress with imposing towers that would intimidate his enemy, and, within its walls, he had constructed spacious villas for his harem and himself. His successors continued to fortify the walls of Lahore Fort until it was virtually unassailable. It had twelve gates, three of which opened on to the river. The elegant buildings inside were decorated with fine paintings, engravings and carved and lattice-worked marbles, some even finer than those in the Taj Mahal in Agra. The Badshahi Mosque and the Moti Masjid (Pearl Mosque) were just two of the imposing structures inside the fortress. Soon, Lahore Fort became Ranjit Singh's principal residence, work place, and the Durbar from which he ruled when he was in his capital.

According to legend, Lahore had been founded by Lav, the elder son of the Hindu avtaar Lord Rama (the name Lahore being a derivation of Lavpura – the city of Lav); at the same time Kasur was founded by his younger brother, Kush. Lahore had been in the hands of the Rajputs till 1002 AD, when the Muslims defeated and threw them out. Mahmud of Ghazni renamed it after him as Mahmudpura but the old name, Lahore, soon came back into circulation. The city was occupied in turn by different tribes of Muslim conquerors of the Punjab until Babar established Mughal rule in India. The Mughals built most of the city's fortifications, palaces, mosques, and gardens. While Delhi or Agra were the seats of the Mughal government, Lahore was the chief city of the Punjab and a sort of half-way house between the Indian capital and the territories beyond the North-West Frontier of India, from where the Muslim rulers recruited their best men.

For the Sikhs, Lahore was only second in importance to Amritsar. It was the birthplace of their fourth Guru, Ram Das, who founded the city of Amritsar and it was the site of the martyrdom of their fifth Guru, Arjan Dev, the compiler of their sacred book, the *Granth Sahib*. There were temples to mark these events and the visits of other Gurus. The capture of Lahore was consequently of the greatest significance to Ranjit Singh. The possession of the city made him the most powerful chieftain in northern India, and since it was known to have always been the capital of the province, it gave him a vague sort of title over the rest of Punjab.

Ranjit brings all Misls under Control

His acquisition of Lahore in 1799 was the first major step towards fulfilling his vision of the future. He was even more convinced now than ever before of the need to bring all the misls under his control. Or better still, do away with them altogether and merge their territories with the others he was acquiring. Some of the misl chiefs provided him with the excuses he needed. The first two, reckless enough to stick their necks out, were the Bhangis and Ramgarhias. Resentful of Ranjit Singh's growing power, they formed an alliance to take Lahore, even after he had dealt magnanimously with the defeated Bhangi Sardar when taking over the city.

These two misls, like other adversaries, misjudged Ranjit Singh. The Bhangis were the first to suffer one humiliating defeat after another until they not only lost their share of the sacred city of Amritsar, but in due course, all their other territories as well. Thus, they ceased to exist. The loss of their part of Amritsar and the fall of Bhangis was entirely a self-inflicted tragedy.

Sahib Singh and Mohar Singh, the two Bhangi Sardars who had escaped from Lahore, joined hands with Jassa Singh Ramgarhia, Jodh Singh of Wazirabad and Gulab Singh of Amritsar to wrest the city back from Ranjit Singh. Nizamuddin of Kasur also joined hands with them. Advancing towards Lahore, they encamped at Bhasin, about 10 miles east of Lahore. They invited Ranjit Singh for talks. They had conspired to kill him during the negotiations.

The young ruler, though barely 20, was well-versed in the ways of the world, and, coming to know of their plot, arrived at the venue with a formidable force of men. The would-be assassins, realising the folly of trying to kill him, abandoned their plan. But Ranjit Singh, by now fully informed of their intentions, would exact a heavy price for what they had planned to do. To legitimise his overthrow of the Bhangi misl, he first asked for the return of the Zamzama gun, the highly prestigious symbol that was now in their hands, but which the Sukerchakias had earlier acquired from the Afghans. Quite understandably, the Bhangis refused to return it, which was the excuse Ranjit Singh needed to attack and take over Amritsar.

By this bold move, Ranjit Singh became possessor of the two Sikh capitals, the political and the religious, and was well on his way to the execution of his grand strategy.

With the year 1800 almost entirely taken up by continuous campaigns, it was time for Ranjit Singh to return to Lahore, henceforth to be his home for the rest of his life. And here he announced the setting up of his rule; something he had thought of for quite some time and for which he had judiciously laid the groundwork by earning considerable good will in the conquered territories through the humane and generous treatment of his defeated foes.

From a very young age, Ranjit Singh clearly aimed at establishing his own state. But what was unique about him and makes his life story so different from most of the other rulers of the time, was that he drew his strength not from the brutal exercise of power but from his humanity, vision, vitality and tolerance, and that he never allowed irrational or primitive instincts to interfere with the affairs of state. The powerful impulse that drove Ranjit Singh to create a just, secular and cosmopolitan society for his people was his unshakeable faith in the religion into which he was born.

Ranjit Singh's goal was not to live in monarchical splendour but to make a just and civilised State out of a Punjab fractured with in-fighting, intrigue and instability, where power was dispersed among a large number of constituent factions.

In 1799, just before he established his rule over the Punjab, there were 68 territories quite independent of one another between the Indus and the Sutlej rivers: 25 Muslim States, 27 Hindu States and 16 Sikh States,[5] an amazing blend of chiefs and feudal lords, including some who owed allegiance to nations beyond India's borders. While, for instance, Kashmir, Peshawar and Multan belonged to the Afghans, Kasur, Kunjpura, Bahawalpur and Malerkotla also owed allegiance to Kabul, and some other Muslim territories were, again subsidiary of Afghanistan. A few ran their own fiefdom, like Jammu, Kangra, Pind Dadan Khan and Muzaffarabad, Jhang and Shahpur. The Hindu Chieftains were a divided lot, and the Sikhs – including the twelve misls – though far fewer in numbers, were as unruly as the rest.[6]

The complexity of Punjab, invasion's frontier footstep, whether in its religions or its demographic composition, posed problems in the way of even-handed governance. With Sikhs accounting for only 7 per cent of the population, as against 50 per cent Muslims and 42 per cent Hindus (based on the 1881 census figures which placed Punjab's population at 22 million), Ranjit Singh could neither deny Sikhs considerable authority under Sikh rule nor deny others a fair representation.

Ranjit Singh Proclaimed Maharaja of the Punjab

The winter of 1800 AD passed in apprehension of yet another invasion from the North-West. In the spring came the news of civil strife in Kabul and the advance of the Persians towards Afghanistan. The Punjabis heaved a sigh of relief, and Ranjit Singh's thoughts turned to giving himself a legal title over his possessions

Although Ranjit was acclaimed as the leader of the Punjab, he hesitated for some time to assume the formal title of maharaja, because he wished to avoid doing anything which would give the other chiefs yet another reason to conspire against him; their combined strength was not to be taken lightly. He was, however, conscious of the many advantages in investing himself with a legal title. He felt that the move would be welcomed by the masses, who had not a ruler and a government of their own for many centuries. It would induce the Punjabi Muslims and Hindus to recognise the compulsions of language, political and economic interests, and way of life and throw in their lot with the Sikhs who had been sighting an independent Punjab. The neighbouring powers would soon become accustomed to the idea that the Punjabis were a united people and Ranjit Singh was their Maharaja.

What perhaps persuaded Ranjit Singh to take the final step and risk the antagonisms of the Sardars was the birth of a son to the Nakkain, Ravi Raj Kaur, his second and favourite wife. The desire to make his infant son, Kharak Singh, the heir-apparent to a kingdom proved irresistible. Although Sada Kaur was somewhat put out by the failure of her own daughter to produce the first son, being a far-sighted woman, she reconciled herself to the idea of her daughter taking second place in a royal harem and encouraged Ranjit Singh in assuming the title of the Maharaja. She no doubt felt that if her daughter did have sons, they would at least inherit the Kanhaya estates, and if possible, also claim a part of their father's kingdom.

Ranjit Singh agreed to a formal investiture ceremony to install himself as the absolute ruler of Punjab on 12 April 1801. On the first day of Baisakh (12 April 1801), which was New Year's Day according to the Hindu calendar in use in northern India, Baba Sahib Singh Bedi, a descendant of Guru Nanak, applied saffron paste or *tilak* (which is a vermilion mark of a sacred significance) to Ranjit Singh's forehead and proclaimed him Maharaja of the Punjab, which in the past had been ruled by the Mughals, the Afghans and the countless intrudes and invaders. Now at the dawn of the Sikh Age, not only important Sikh Sardars but also Hindu and Muslim chiefs and notables witnessed the religious rites as Sardar Ranjit Singh was pronounced Maharaja, appointed as God's humble servant deputed for the service of the people of the region.

Historical distortions not only prevent an accurate assessment of persons whose contributions in the past were most significant, but they also confuse major milestones in a country's evolution. As a British chronicler of the times, General Sir John J H Gordon, rightly put it, the Sikhs 'had now reached nationhood… (and were) fully equipped with confidence and energy under Ranjit Singh, who by transforming the Khalsa into a territorial power, decided once and for all whether the Sikh or the Afghan was to rule the Punjab. Thus, after a hundred years of unflinching struggle, was fulfilled the prophecy of the martial Guru Gobind Singh'.[7]

Guru Gobind Singh, while forming the brotherhood of the Khalsa, had galvanised his people with the words: *Raj Karega Khalsa* or the 'Khalsa shall Rule'. And the time had come for the Khalsa to establish its rule over Punjab. So, it is no coincidence that the day of the Baisakhi festival, early in April 1801, was chosen by Ranjit Singh to be formally declared its ruler – the same Baisakhi day on which the fellowship of the Khalsa had been created by Guru Gobind Singh 102 years earlier. To the 80,000 or so who had assembled on that day in 1699 at Anandpur, his exhortation had been: 'You will love man as man, making no distinction of caste or creed.... In you the whole brotherhood shall be incarnated.'[8] This was the mission Ranjit Singh would now fulfil.

A SOVEREIGN AND SECULAR RULER

AFTER HIS CORONATION as Maharaja, in April 1801, a royal salute was fired from the Lahore Fort. Prayers were said in the mosques, temples and gurudwaras all over his domains. In the afternoon, the young Maharajah rode on the back of an elephant through cheering crowds of his subjects showering gold and silver coins. In the evening the city was illuminated with oil lamps and there was a rich display of fireworks.

Neither the flattery nor the pomp of the court turned Ranjit's mind from real facts. His political acumen is well illustrated in the compromise he made between becoming a Maharaja and remaining a peasant leader. Although crowned king of the Punjab, he refused to wear an emblem of royalty on his simple turban. He drew his authority not from titles, but from his qualities of leadership. No building or monument ever bore his name. The fort at Amritsar was called Gobindgarh, whilst the palace and gardens were named Ram Bagh.

He never possessed either a throne or a crown. In the words of von Hügel, 'The Maharaja has no throne. "My Sword" he observed, "procures me all the distinction I desire".[1] His strange oriental chair (*murha*) served him as throne, on which he often sat cross-legged, and his turban was his crown, which he proudly wore. Quite appropriately, his court was known as

Durbar Khalsaji. More often, he received visitors in the oriental fashion, reclining on cushions on a carpet. He ordered for coins which did not bear his image or his name but that of Guru Nanak and were named the *Nanakshahi* (of the Emperor Nanak) coins. The seal of the government, likewise, bore no reference to him. The government was not to be a personal affair, but *Sarkar Khalsaji* of the people who brought it into being; the court for the same reason came to be known as the Durbar Khalsaji. And with all the flatterers about him, the title by which he preferred to be addressed was the plain and simple *Singh Sahib*. These conventions were a complete departure from the accepted traditions of oriental courts, where protocol was rigidly observed to keep the monarch as far away from the masses as possible. Ranjit Singh did not want to, nor did, lose the common touch'.

The most important consequence of taking on the title of 'Maharaja of the Punjab' was that thereby, Ranjit Singh assumed the rights of sovereignty not only over all Sikhs (the government itself being Sarkar Khalsaji), but also over the people who lived within the ill-defined geographical limits of the Punjab. The title gave Ranjit Singh a legal right to demand that territories which had at any time paid revenue to Lahore – territories such as Jammu, Kashmir, the Rajput hill states, Multan, Bahawalpur, Dera Ismail Khan, Dera Ghazi Khan, Mankera and others – should pay tribute to him and owe allegiance to the Lahore Durbar.

Ranjit Singh's Secular Convictions

The young Ranjit Singh, as a misldar, had a small body of people to help him administer his misl. Its affairs were looked after by Diwan Lakhpat Rai, who was the treasury-keeper, or *toshania;* an accountant or *munim* and a few clerks or *munshis*. Ranjit Singh allocated the portfolios of civil and military affairs, revenue collection and expenditure to himself. After he became Maharaja, he built up his administrative department, which at one time consisted of 15 different offices of state.

Immediately after coronation, Ranjit Singh reorganised the administration of Lahore. He had the city walls and gates, which had suffered many sieges, repaired and posted pickets at all strategic points to check crime, which had increased enormously under the Bhangi misrule. The city was divided into different wards, each ward under a *Chaudhri* (headman), who was responsible for the peace of his locality and could call out the police when order was disturbed. He also reorganised the administration of justice in the city. Imam Baksh was designated the chief of police in Lahore and he, in turn, recommended appointments of headmen in the various parts of the town. A similar pattern was followed in the rest of the Punjab.

While Maharaja Ranjit Singh styled himself as a humble representative of the *Khalsa* who was going to rule in the name of Guru Nanak and Gobind Singh, he ensured that no community or group of people in his kingdom was discriminated against. He was aware that the vast majority of his subjects was Muslim by faith. In fact, the Sikhs were hardly 10 per cent. The Hindus were also no more than 10 per cent. The remaining 80 per cent were Muslims and he felt, he must not alienate them. And he never did.

In fact, on the day of his coronation itself, Maharaja Ranjit Singh proclaimed that the Muslims under his rule would be governed by the Muslim religious law (by the Sharia) as a majority of the population in this city was Muslim. He set up separate courts for Muslims, presided over by *Qazis* (judges) and judicial officers appointed by his Durbar. The Qazis who administered justice were paid from the state treasury.

He appointed *Muftis* as well. Mohammad Shahpuri and

Saidullah Chishti became the two Muftis. The important Muslim mosques continued to receive state support. In fact, the first thing the Maharaja did after taking over Lahore was to visit the local Shahi Mosque as a mark of respect, and also as a gesture of good will to the majority community of the town. A chain of dispensaries were opened in different parts of the city where *yunani* medicine was dispensed free of charge. Hakim Nur-ud-Din, the younger brother of Fakir Aziz-ud-Din, was appointed Chief Medical Officer.

*Panchayat*s were established in villages to settle disputes and look after the local administration. All the important officials were granted robes of honour.

Thus, from the very outset, Ranjit Singh left no doubt in anyone's mind about his adherence to the secular convictions that had been forcefully enunciated by Guru Gobind Singh when he established the Khalsa. The administration of Lahore was a model that Ranjit Singh replicated throughout his territories. He was determined to create an administrative system undiluted by religious prejudices, political affiliations, preference for family connections, regional and caste loyalties or countless other pulls and pressures that made a mockery of just governance. Despite the disparate and potentially destructive elements he had, he himself kept the administration in control. He was determined to strengthen his rule not through intimidation or state terror, but by providing good governance.

In contrast to the merciless treatment by fanatical rulers usually meted out to people of other faiths in those times, Ranjit Singh was determined to create a cohesive society out of erstwhile enemies. And in his own cabinet of ministers and in all positions of the highest responsibility, Hindus, Muslims and Dogras (hill Rajputs from the Jammu area) predominated. The Prime Minister's portfolio was given to a Hindu Dogra, Dhian Singh. Three of the most important portfolios were held by Muslims: Fakir Aziz-ud-Din was the foreign minister, Fakir Nur-ud Din the home minister and Fakir Imam-ud-Din the custodian of the Treasury at Amritsar.

That merit and suitability, rather than caste and creed, were the criteria for selection for government service is also evident from the greater representation of Hindus as compared to Sikhs.[2] An early cabinet under Ranjit Singh lists fifteen Hindu ministers and top officials compared to seven Sikhs. The former included the ministers of finance and revenue, besides the paymaster general, the accountant general and the governors of Multan and Kashmir, while the Sikhs were almost entirely generals, some of whom sometimes held additional posts as governors.

'Even Akbar, who was the most liberal of the Mughal emperors... did not go as far as Ranjit Singh did. Whereas Ranjit Singh gave the highest positions, such as prime ministership, foreign ministership etc., to members of other communities, Akbar could not go beyond associating one or two non-Muslim ministers with his court which, thus, predominantly remained Muslim in character and composition.'[3]

Non-Punjabis were not discriminated against in Punjab. More significantly, even though in 1606, Chandu Shah, an influential Brahmin in the service of the Mughals (along with a Brahmin lobby, deeply resentful of the independent ways of the Sikhs), had influenced Emperor Jehangir to cruelly put to death Guru Arjan Dev, builder of Harmandir and compiler of the *Guru Granth*, Ranjit Singh appointed Khushal Singh, a Brahmin, as the administrator of his court. He later converted to Sikhism. His nephew, Teza Singh from Meerut, was also taken into service and eventually became Commander-in-Chief of thc army after Ranjit Singh's death. He had also converted to Sikhism in 1816.[4]

His respect for Christianity again proved not only his

abiding interest in other faiths, but also his deep desire to know about the followers of those faiths. When he asked a European visitor to his court to tell him about the holy book of the Christians and was shown a Bible, he touched it to his forehead with reverence and had passages from it recited to him. He appointed many Christian officers to his army – Italians, Frenchmen, Englishmen, Greeks, Spaniards, Russians, a German and an Austrian, and even made some of them senior army commanders and governors of provinces. Their numbers have been put between 39 and 42.

Ranjit Singh's ongoing interest in other religious beliefs was born out of a genuine desire to broaden his mind and to deal effectively with the extraordinary mix of people under his rule, drawing on the wisdom of knowledgeable men of other faiths, with many of whom he enjoyed having discussions on the subject of divinity. Revering the *kalgi* (blue ribbon) of Guru Gobind Singh in his possession, he was respectful of the relics of others – and especially those held to be that of the Prophet Muhammed himself, which he found in some of the Muslim principalities conquered by him. These items included a copy of the Quran, a cloak and a pair of shoes kept in the Royal Toshakhana (Treasure House).

Within a short time, Ranjit Singh convinced the people of Lahore and neighbouring districts that he did not intend to set up a Sikh kingdom but a Punjabi state in which the Muslims, Hindus and Sikhs would be equal before the law and enjoy the same privileges and duties. He invited talented Muslims and Hindus to join his service and paid lively respect to their religious institutions by participating in their festivities. At *Dussehra,* he went through the ritual of the worship of arms like the Rajput warriors of old, and arranged mock battles between his troops to commemorate the battle of Rama against Ravana. At *Diwali* all public buildings, including the palace, were illuminated. During Holi, he went out along with a good number of his courtiers and followers and enjoyed the festival of colours, in a manner quite unbecoming of a monarch. On *Basant* he paid homage at the tomb of the two Sufi poets, Madho Lal and Hussain, of Lahore. On *Amavas* and *Baisakh* he joined his co-religionists in bathing at Amritsar or Taran Taran.

No Death Penalty

The one aspect of him that can be considered remarkable in those times is, that in his thirty-nine years at the helm of affairs, no death penalty was ever awarded, no matter how heinous the crime, in the civilian or military field. Alexander Burns, in his book *Travels into Bokhara,* writes about this: 'The most creditable trait in Ranjit's character is his humanity, he has never been known to punish a criminal with death since his accession to power... cunning and conciliation have been the two great weapons of his diplomacy.'[5]

When news reached Ranjit Singh that General Paolo Avitabile, his governor at Peshawar, had executed some Muslims who were attempting to foment trouble, he was soundly castigated. In another incident, when 'the Maharaja heard of the excesses carried out, also in Peshawar, by Sham Singh Peshoria, a leading landowner, he was summarily dismissed from the Durbar and put to chains'. Dr Honigberger, Ranjit Singh's doctor, recalls the Maharaja telling him: 'We punish but we will not take life.' In 1839, Captain La Font was warned by Ranjit Singh not to beat his sepoys.[6]

The punishments meted out in his army were dismissal or discharge; degradation, deduction of pay, confiscation of a jaagir, fines, extra duty; amputation of limbs, imprisonment, physical punishments; warnings and reprimands.

In the civilian field, justice covered a wide spectrum of judicial courts: the *Nazim*'s court, at the headquarters of a province; the *Adalat-e-Ala*, at Lahore which was an appellate high court; the ministers' courts, pertaining to their own departments; the *Jaagirdar*'s courts, a jaagirdar had certain civil and military authority to decide cases of his own jaagir; the Sharia courts, the courts of Qazis and Muftis, to decide cases of Muslims, according to the Quran and the Maharaja's court, to hear appeals from the lower courts. Ranjit Singh frequently censured guilty officials for having failed to decide cases honestly. The death penalty was banned.[7]

System of Administration

The Maharaja carried on with the existing system of administration, introducing reforms to make it more efficient. The welfare of the people was never lost sight of. The revenue system and the method of its collection were not interfered with. The government was *malik-i-ala* (Master) of all the land. The cultivator was *malik-i-adua* (under the Master), he, therefore, had to part with a portion of the produce. The Maharaja did not prescribe any uniform rules in this regard also. It was decided that the practices prevailing in various parts of the land would continue. There were, however, properly formulated laws about the rights and obligations of the labourer, cultivator and the jaagirdar. The government, at times, farmed out land on lump sum payment on yearly basis or in consideration of military service. Whether the rules were a prevailing practice or prescribed by the government afresh, the Maharaja ensured that they were generally benevolent and that no official, big or small, oppressed the poor.

A free hospital was established in the city of Lahore. It was placed under the charge of Hakim Nur-ud-Din who was the personal physician of the Maharaja. His father, Ghulam Mohiuddin, had earlier treated the Maharaja for his eye trouble and Ranjit Singh had very high regard for him. In fact, it was because of the high regard that the Maharaja had for Ghulam Mohiuddin that he invited his three sons to join the state service one after the other. The first to join the Maharaja was Aziz-ud-Din. He became the Minister of Foreign Affairs. Then came Imam-ud-Din who did not hold any office in the court but was entrusted with important administrative and military assignments.

Besides being a royal physician, Hakim Nur-ud-Din was also the Maharaja's Home Minister. He had a host of duties to perform. He looked after the upkeep of the palaces and royal gardens. He was the custodian of the key of the royal treasury, along with two other courtiers. He commanded the Maharaja's arsenal at the Fort. He also helped the Maharaja settle all judicial appeals made to him. There was a sort of spiritual bond between Fakir Nur-ud-Din and the Maharaja. At times, even the members of the royal family sought Fakir Nur-ud-Din's advice and intervention.

It is said that Prince Sher Singh had a fascination for the Maharaja's favourite horse, Dooloo. When he did not succeed in persuading his father to gift it to him, one day, not being able to resist the temptation, he went to the royal stables and rode away with the horse. When the Maharaja heard about it, he was furious. He ordered that the Prince be exiled and everything belonging to him be confiscated.

The Prince heard of this and approached Fakir Nur-ud-Din to speak on his behalf. When the Fakir was in audience with the Maharaja that evening, he said 'Sarkar, you have let off the delinquent Prince rather leniently. He rode away with the horse, as if it were his father's property.' The argument touched the Maharaja, and he pardoned the Prince.[8] The Maharaja had undeniable faith in him. The Maharaja never took any food unless it was tasted and approved by Fakir Nur-ud-din.

Fakir Imam-ud-Din was the custodian of Gobindgarh,

the Amritsar fort. He was also governor of the surrounding countryside. He held charge of the arsenals and the royal stables at Amritsar. He was sent on active service in a number of expeditions. Entrusting a Muslim with the charge of the main fort in the Holy City and appointing him governor of the area around it is indicative of the fact that Ranjit Singh made no distinction on grounds of religious faith while making appointments to the highest offices in the State administration, and that he trusted all alike.

The three Fakir brothers were, no doubt, closest to the Maharaja, and they never betrayed his confidence. The description of the loyalty of the Fakir family to the Sikh monarch is vividly found in the book entitled *The Real Ranjit Singh*, written by a descendant of the celebrated Fakir family at Lahore (Pakistan), in which the writer has paid glowing tributes to the Maharaja.

Ranjit Singh had an inborn quality of interacting convincingly with the people of different religions and races. He used diplomacy and treaties to deal with the British but bargained and battled against the Afghans. Military genius, empire builder, ladies' man – all this would have been of no account had he lacked the ability to consolidate his empire and keep it stable. This he managed to do for forty years through *just administration – no mean feat for an uneducated school* dropout. 'Governing' writes Sir Lepel Griffin, 'is an art which may no doubt be brilliantly practiced without special training by some men of exceptional genius, but, as an ordinary accomplishment, it must be painfully and laboriously acquired, while hereditary aptitude and the class and family traditions of rule are very important factors in its success.'[9]

Literary, there are hundreds of accounts by foreign writers on the Maharaja, his court, his army and his expeditions, victories and defeats. Indians were never known to be great raconteurs of the middle ages, but in the case of Ranjit Singh at the turn of the eighteenth century, there are many accounts by Indians as well, along with paintings, official documents of the Durbar and other records that tell a credible story.

Lahore was the headquarters of the Sarkar Khalsa or Central Government. Maharaja Ranjit Singh's system of governance reflected his strong personality and secular beliefs. He was the supreme head of the government and his orders were obeyed implicitly. All important matters and decisions were referred to him, particularly regarding military, civil or judicial matters. Everyone, including the army, diwans, generals, governors, foreign travellers, princes, treasurers, down to messengers reported directly to him. The power and authority of the Sikh empire rested solely with Ranjit Singh.

The administration, in its developed form, was divided into different *daftar*s or offices and officers of the state, such as: *Daftar-i-Toshakhana,* Treasury; *Daftar-i-Abab-ul-Mal,* Land Revenue; *Daftar-i-Darogha*, Excise and Octroi; *Daftar-i-Roznamcha*, Accounts and Audits; *Daftar-i-Moharyani*, Royal State Seals and Commissions, and so on. The names given to these departments were in Persian, and accounts, documents and records were also kept in the same language.[10]

Different Departments in Able Hands

Ranjit Singh was a good judge of men. His administration was filled with extremely able people, whom he brought in from all over. Maharaja Ranjit Singh chose each office-bearer very carefully, focusing only on the man's ability, character and loyalty. Religious beliefs or caste mattered little. Though Ranjit Singh himself had a tremendous capacity of remembering financial facts and figures, even then he appointed the most capable people to look after them. Bhawani Das of Peshawar, who was earlier Diwan to Shah Shuja, was inducted into Ranjit Singh's administration in 1808. He looked after land revenues, incomes and expenditure, and laid down the basis for their systemisation. Ganga Ram, a Kashmiri Pandit, who joined the Durbar in 1817, further developed the system laid down by Bhawani Das.

After the death of Ganga Ram, his grandson Dina Nath took over his post and also that of Keeper of the Royal Seal. The seal *Akal Sahai* (with God's help), Ranjit Singh's official endorsement, was affixed to all documents approved by the Maharaja; without the seal none was valid. For each seal affixed, the keeper of the Royal Seal charged a sum, which was deposited in the Treasury. Dina Nath was far-sighted, intelligent and well-educated, and proved to be hard working and loyal. He was called 'the Talleyrand of the Punjab.... He hated the English with a bitter hatred, for they were stronger than he or his country'.[11]

After becoming the finance minister in 1834, Dina Nath divided the finance department into various sections with separate officers to manage these independently. These sections included that of the revenue from customs, transit duties, tributes, gifts, forfeitures, registration fee and so on. There was a special cash keeper who looked after government funds. These included the Central Treasury funds, army funding and building expenses. Another section maintained records on the Durbar's daily purchases, robes of honour, rewards, charity, grants of land (jaagir), entertainment and the royal kitchen.

Another most trusted man was Raja Dhian Singh Dogra. Having gained Ranjit Singh's trust and confidence over the years as his Chamberlain, Dhian Singh Dogra was made Prime Minister. Raja Dhian Singh, the second of the three Jammu brothers, was given the title of Raja Kalhan in 1828, to distinguish him as the senior Raja in the Durbar.

In retrospect, bringing the Dogra brothers to the Durbar was, perhaps, the Maharaja's biggest mistake and they oversaw the destruction of Ranjit Singh's carefully crafted empire.

Over time, the size of the Maharaja's household and visitors to the Court had also increased enormously and necessitated the appointment of a Royal Chamberlin. The Maharaja's choice fell on a handsome Brahmin youth from Meerut named Khushal Chand, who was enlisted as a common soldier. Khushal Chand was promoted to the rank of *jamadar* in the palace bodyguard, and then appointed *deorhidar* – keeper of the royal palace. This post was of considerable importance, since anyone who wanted a personal interview with the Maharaja had first to approach the keeper of the deorhi. It gave the incumbent political power as well as handsome income from presents. Khushal Chand accepted Sikh faith and came thereafter to be known as Jamadar Khushal Singh. He introduced two of his relatives to the court; a nephew Tej Singh (who after Ranjit Singh's death, played a treacherous role as commander of the Sikh armies in the first Anglo-Sikh war), and a younger brother, Ram Chand. This family of Brahmins exerted a depressing influence on the court. It was one of the rare instances of Ranjit Singh misjudging the quality of the men he employed.

Fakir Aziz-ud-Din

Fakir Aziz-ud-Din, the eldest of the Fakir brothers, entered Ranjit Singh's service as early as 1799. Starting off as a physician to the young ruler and then serving in the army, he was over time rewarded with jaagirs by the Maharaja as he went from victory to victory. Ranjit Singh had unqualified trust in him; he was sent on various expeditions and campaigns: Gujrat in 1810, Attock in 1831, as envoy to the Bahawalpur court in 1819, Phillaur near Jalandhar in 1826 and Peshawar in 1835.

A fine looking, pleasant, well mannered, good-humoured and unassuming figure, a skillful negotiator and diplomat who spoke Persian beautifully, he played a major part in the signing of the Sutlej Treaty in 1809 and later became the Maharaja's foreign minister. He was personally in-charge of all dealings with the Afghans, British and other Europeans, and the Cis-Sutlej States. In April 1831, he accompanied Sardar Hari Singh Nalwa and Diwan Moti Ram, to Shimla for a meeting with the then British Governor-General, Lord Bentinck. He was a popular figure not only with the foreigners but with the Lahore Durbar as well.

Basti Ram, a Brahmin, was the first treasurer of Ranjit Singh's empire and after his death in 1816, his grandson Beli Ram, at the age of 19, succeeded him. The treasurer was also a keeper of records which included all treaties, royal *firmans* or orders, documents and important correspondences which were under his supervision. He was in-charge of the royal wardrobe.

Apart from silver and gold stock, the rarest of jewels, pearls, carved and chased saddles, *howdahs*, dishes and plates were kept at the treasury at Gobindgarh, Amritsar. All the rarities collected by Ranjit Singh were kept here, including the Kohinoor diamond and Guru Gobind Singh's kalgi. His personal treasury in the Lahore Fort, the Moti Masjid, had three keys to its gate, one of which was held by the treasurer, the second by the commander of the fort and the third by the *thanedar* or keeper. Captain William Murry, the British Political Agent at Ambala, reported in the 1830s 'that the wealth of Ranjit Singh stored at Gobindgarh Fort Treasury at Amritsar was valued at around Rs 10 crore or 10 million pounds sterling'.[12]

Administrative Division of Punjab

The Punjab had a population of 35 lakh (3.5 million) in 1831. Ranjit Singh divided Punjab into eight provinces. Each province was split into *Parganas* (districts), each *Pargana* into *Taluqas* and each Taluqa consisted of 50 to 100 villages. The eight provinces were Lahore, Jalandhar, Kangra Hills, Jammu,

Kashmir, Peshawar, Gujrat or Wazirabad and Multan. The districts were kept under a *Kardar* or district administrator, whose appointment was sanctioned by the Nazim (the local government head) with Ranjit Singh's approval. (The Mughal administrative system had been similar). There were 51 Kardars in Punjab; their duties were to collect revenues, customs, excise duties and taxes and remit them in time. They also administered justice and settled disputes, looked after agricultural activities and kept themselves in touch with the people. From 1826 to 1838, Charles Masson, the explorer and East India Company soldier, on his way to Harappa, travelled through Ranjit Singh's Punjab and reported that 'the State under Ranjit Singh's rule was better run and more prosperous than those parts of India under British administration'.

System of Revenue Collection

Ranjit Singh did not make any changes in the agricultural system or land revenue that had prevailed since the Mughal rule. Every village had a revenue collector (*muqaddam*) and a circle of villages (*tappah* or *taluqah*) was in the charge of a Chaudhri. In addition to these two officials, there was a keeper of fiscal records, the *quanungo*. Revenue was directly collected from the cultivator of the land. The amount and manner of payment varied but care was taken that all regular and irregular charges (e.g. supply of grass, timber, fruit, eggs, chicken etc) to touring officials which went under the title *mulba* (literally 'rubbish', or feudal dues in the forms of gifts on marriages or festivals to members of the royal family or the Rajas) never amounted to more than half of the gross produce calculated on the standing crop or after harvest: if the revenue was paid in cash, the sum was calculated on the value of half the produce. The rate was not considered exorbitant and allowed the agricultural community to flourish.

As important as the right over land, which was guaranteed to the actual cultivator, was the ownership of wells. As a matter of fact, the most reliable evidence of the ownership of land was the inscription on a well (sometimes placed on the inside to save it from mutilation). The right to dig a well was exclusively that of the cultivator. The proprietor who did not till the land himself or through hired servants had to be content with a nominal title. The same applied to a jaagirdar whose right to the revenue did not in any way invest him with a title to the land from which it was collected.[13]

At the end of Ranjit Singh's forty years of rule, the income in rupees of the State was as follows:

1.	Revenue (in rupee of the day) from the provinces of Lahore, Multan, Kashmir and Peshawar were...	17,557,741
2.	Nazranas	603,657
3.	Custom and Excise	1,531,634
4.	Jaagirs	9,196,000
		28,889,032

The figure of around three crore rupees sounds extremely modest today. It should, however, be borne in mind that at the time the price of staple food, wheat, was 14 annas (less than a then rupee which was equivalent of 16 annas) per maund (about 50 kgs of today). In 1961, it fluctuated between Rs 18 and 20 per maund, i.e. more than twenty times as much.[14]

Land revenue was the Lahore Durbar's main source of income. The assessment depended on various factors: the condition of the soil, irrigation and nearness to the marketplace. In case of famines, floods or any other natural disasters, the state gave up its share of crop. At such time, free seed, cattle and money were also distributed to the affected areas.

According to another estimate, the amount of revenue generated in the Punjab under Ranjit Singh vary between

Rs 25,000,000 and Rs 32,500,000 yearly. Captain William Murray, in 1832, gave the annual revenue figure as Rs 25,809,500, the break-up being: land revenue and tributes Rs 12,403,900; custom duties Rs 1,900,600; Jaagirs Rs 10,928,000; and stamp duties and the sealing of papers Rs 577,000.[15]

One report of the annual revenue generated from provinces under individual governors gave the following statistics: Multan under Diwan Sawan Mal, Rs 3,898,550; Kashmir under Colonel Mian Singh, Rs 3,675,000; Jalandhar under Misr Rup Lal, Rs 1,872,902; and Peshawar under Avitabile, Rs 1,834,738. There were eight salt mines in Punjab, which brought in an annual revenue of Rs 463,675.[16]

Law & Order and Justice

Maharaja Ranjit Singh's system of justice worked efficiently and swiftly. The panchayats or local village bodies, dealt with crimes, thefts, murders, disputes and, in fact, all civil or criminal cases. The victim or accused could appeal to the Kardar, if unsatisfied with the verdict, or even file a written appeal to the Maharaja himself. Ranjit Singh would sometimes ask for reports on certain judgements. There was no capital punishment in the land. The criminal was either fined, jailed or, in some serious cases, there was loss of limbs, nose or ears.

Ranjit Singh received weekly reports from every province of his kingdom. He often went on surprise visits to places where he thought things were not going as they should. Every day, he would be available either at the Lahore Fort or at his camp to listen to requests or complaints from the public. Throughout his long rule, he managed to give his people a sense of security, prosperity, growth, and, more than anything else, a sense of pride.

State Patronised Creative Talents

True to his name, Ranjit Singh grew to be a renowned warrior, but remained unlettered all his life. It is said that he could hardly sign his name on state documents. He never went to school as a child and when he grew up, he was left with little time to acquire learning. He was always busy pursuing one campaign or the other, chasing one enemy or another, celebrating one victory or another. However, Ranjit Singh consolidated the people of the Punjab and gave them a sovereign State of their own. This fostered in them a sense of confidence and pride in their ethos and tradition, which in turn gave a fillip to all-round creative activity.

Though illiterate himself, Ranjit Singh had men of letters like Fakir Aziz-ud-Din, the poet Hashim and others like them around him. Fighters and warriors were, no doubt, closer to him, but he did fraternise with those who wielded the pen, like Masson, the explorer historian. He founded institutions of learning and aided a number of those already functioning, irrespective of who ran them. These included schools – Muslim *Madarssa*s and Hindu *Pathshala*s. He instituted a calligraphy centre in Urdu and granted a jaagir consisting of several villages to one Mian Wada, who was devoted to the teaching of Persian. Similar bounties were bestowed upon several other individuals and institutions.

Syed Muhammad Hashim was a poet in Ranjit Singh's court. The Maharaja was immensely fond of his poetry. He was granted a village as jaagir. Besides Hashim, other renowned poets who wrote during Ranjit Singh's time, were Ahmad Yar and Qadir Yar. Ahmad Yar was commissioned by Maharaja Gulab Singh to write the *Shahnama* of the Sikhs in Persian. Accordingly, he wrote two volumes: *Fatuhate-e-Khalsa* and *Shahanchi Nama*. Qadir Yar wrote a ballad on Hari Singh Nalwa, besides a number of romances – *Puran Bhagat, Sohni*

Mahiwal and others. The creative talent of the time was generously patronised by the state during Ranjit Singh's reign. This gave birth to a considerable volume of *Bir Kavya* (heroic-Vir verses). Among the lesser-known poets of the age were: Ram Singh, Ram Dayal, Hakim Singh, Nihal Singh, Sahe Singh, Kahn Singh, Zafar Beg and Kavi Sobha.

Along with the heroic verses (*Bir Kavya*), popular folk romances such as *Hir Ranjha, Sassi Punnun, Sohni Mahiwal, Puran Bhagat* and *Raja Risalu* continued to be written and re-written. There appeared to be great demand for these in the newly-cultivated tastes of the society of the day. Maharaja Ranjit Singh was a man of fine sensibilities. He was fond of the company of artists like Attar Khan and poets and people too began to appreciate the esoteric.

It was not that only Punjabi was patronised during the period, a lot of literature was created in Persian and Hindi as well. Ahmad Yar's *Shahnama Ranjit Singh*, commissioned by Gulab Singh, was written in Persian. Similarly, Pandit Ganga Ram wrote in Hindi, praising Maharaja Ranjit Singh and the Khalsa rule. Ranjit Singh also arranged for Persian and Sanskrit classics to be translated into Punjabi.

It was during this period that the renowned Sikh theologian Bhai Santokh Singh wrote his well-known works *Nanak Prakash* and *Gur Pratap Surya*. Bhai Santokh Singh's works continue to be read and respected even today.

Though unlettered himself, the Maharaja had great reverence for the written word. A copy of the Holy *Granth* accompanied him, mounted on an exclusive elephant, even when he was in the field fighting his enemies.

Agriculture

During the forty-seven years of his reign, Maharaja Ranjit Singh took systematic care of the peasants who formed

66 per cent of the population, most of them living in some 31,000 villages (*mooza*). Ranjit Singh removed the *Zamindars* of the former Mughal administration and gave the land to the people who cultivated it. By 1839, about 40 per cent of the cultivators owned their land, and a systematic policy of resumption of wasted lands and rehabilitation of devastated areas was implemented by the Maharaja. He also promoted the restoration of old canals and the digging of new ones, and the surface of artificially irrigated areas increased from 400,000 acres in 1820 to 1,000,000 acres in 1839.

Ranjit Singh himself used to tour the countryside. Wherever he went, he inquired from the peasants about their problems and how efficient were the officers of the state and how they conducted themselves. The cultivated area in the kingdom in 1839 can be estimated at 13 million acres, which is the whole area which could be cultivated with technology of the time. In 1831, the Punjab was self-sufficient in food, had sufficient food in its main cities and could dispatch in an emergency 50,000 maunds of grain to Kashmir in 1833. The first British surveys in 1847 attested the very high level of agricultural production in the State, as good as in the best provinces of British India.[17]

Economy: Commercial Exchanges in 1832

The kingdom of Punjab maintained its economy very nicely during the reign of Maharaja Ranjit Singh. It exported its own productions and imported foreign goods according to the needs of the State and the population. It is interesting to draw up here a list of imports and exports, showing the state of the economy in 1832.

Exports from Kashmir: shawls, saffron and fruits. From Lahore: salt, arms (matchlocks, swords, bows and arrows), several kinds of cotton and silk cloth, mules and horses. From Multan: silk scarfs, indigo, carpets, rock salt.

Imports from British India: woolens, velvets, satins and silks, Muslin cloth, raw silk, wool, cotton, indigo, gold and silver, copper and iron as sheets, tin, lead, sulphur and arsenic, glasswares, pearls and precious stones, hardwares, shields, spices, drugs, sandalwood and ivory.

From Afghanistan: horses, green and dried fruits, some precious stones and opium.

From Persia: printed cloth and dyestuff, gold, copper in square flat pieces or made into vessels, needles, gold and silver from Bokhara which were acquired originally from the Russian market.

From Yarkend, Tibet and the Chinese frontier: rods of silver, shawl-wool, skins, musk, silk and tea of inferior quality. The wool from Tibet was in great demand.

An important part of the Indian trade since the 1770s was in the hands of the Marwari houses, based in Shekawat and Calcutta. Most of the caravans plying between North-West India and Central Asia were in the hands of the Lohni houses based at Shikarpur (Sindh).

The two networks were connected along a line crossing the Punjab. In 1832, the volume of import from British India to Amritsar was estimated at Rs 14 lakh. And the whole volume of exports beyond Sutlej (Punjab) and the Indus (Afghanistan, Central Asia) by the Marwaris was estimated at Rs 49 lakh. That is why in 1828, Ranjit Singh had 15 shops and a stable built in Lahore for Seth Mirza Mal of Choorchroo, head of the Marwari houses, to whom he accorded a discount of 25 per cent on the octrois of the city.[18]

Currency System in the Sikh Kingdom

The Sikhs rapidly evolved a complete monetary system of their own. Banda Bahadur struck the first Sikh coin in 1710 AD. During the misl period, coins were struck at Lahore in

1765 and 1772, and in Amritsar in 1775. The Amritsari issue had a Persian inscription in the name of Guru Nanak, hence the name *Nanakshahi* which was ultimately given to the Sikh coins. Maharaja Ranjit Singh extended this currency system all over his kingdom. Like the Sikh misls before him, he believed that he was but the servant of the Gurus and did not put his name on the coins, a significant difference from the coinage current in Punjab under the Muslim dynasties.

The currency system developed by the Maharaja comprised gold *mohur*s and silver coins in denominations of one, half, quarter rupees, inscribed in Persian script. The silver rupees had a high content of silver with a value of sixteen annas to the rupee and generally weighed 10.7g-11.1gramme. The main mints were at Lahore and Amritsar. As the Sikh domination increased, mints were established at Multan (1818 AD), Kashmir (1819), Derajat (1821) and Peshawar (1834). These coins exhibit a refinement in terms of calligraphy, style, artistry and workmanship. They are adorned with dots and flower, moons and stars, and encircled with beaded borders. A leaf is a common symbol of most of these coins, while a hand (*Panja*), royal umbrella, *Kartar* appear on some. At times, people became linked with a particular symbol on a coin or a certain legend connected with it. The *Nanakshahi* of Kashmir were called Hari Singhji after Hari Singh Nalwa, one of the governors of Kashmir. The *Morashahi* and *Arsiwallashahi* from the Amritsar mint were associated with Bibi Moran. Coins minted in Peshawar were known as *Peshawari Naunihal Singhji* rupees, after Kanwar Nau Nihal Singh, grandson of Maharaja Ranjit Singh and governor of Peshawar.

The political fragmentation of the Punjab and Northern India in the eighteenth century led to the development of local taxation – octrois and duties levied on goods by each and every petty zamindar, nawab and raja. In 1830, in the British protected territories between Ludhiana and Jagadhari, about 15 States levied duties on the goods transiting between the Sutlej and the Jamuna river.

The development of trade in Punjab and northern India in the 1820s, although impeded by the shortage of silver in 1829-1831, led to a reorganisation of financial and taxation structures of these areas with the introduction of the company rupee in British India in 1833-1836, and the unification of transit duties in the Punjabi kingdom in 1833. The consequence was the integration of Northern India and Punjab in an increasing world trade order, extending from Europe to China and the Americas.[19]

Development of Punjab's Towns

Two main cities dominated the heart of the Punjabi kingdom: Lahore, the former capital of the *Suba* (State), and Amritsar, the quickly-developing religious capital of the Sikhs. Both of them were flourishing markets in the 1800s with commercial networks extending from Russia to China.

Amritsar

Amritsar was a new city, organised around the Harmandir and protected by the Gobindgarh fort. As soon as Ranjit Singh captured it in 1802, he unified its administration and started constructing the walls of the city for which Fateh Singh Ahluwalia sent 1,000 masons and many other chiefs contributed in money and work force. To provide it water, Ranjit Singh extended a branch of the Hansi canal from Madhopur to Amritsar. New localities developed, and numerous gardens were built outside the ramparts. The most important was Ramgarh, built by Maharaja Ranjit Singh as his residence. Amritsar was perhaps a greater trading place than Lahore in the 1830s. Though there were already many shawl-makers there in 1831, but the famine of 1833 in Kashmir brought in many more Kashmiri families who started a good quality shawl industry on a large scale.

Maharaja Ranjit Singh not only beautified the Harmandir, but he developed the city as well. All the gardens of the kingdom, to whichever community they belonged, and the residences in the city were decorated and embellished with paintings. The *haveli* (residence) of Jamadar Khushal Singh, former deorhidar (keeper of the palace) of Ranjit Singh, had lovely paintings in the Durbar room, showing architectural landscapes and mirrors in the ceiling.

As described by the French Botanist, Victor Jacquemont on 8 March 1831: 'Amritsar is the largest city in the Punjab. It is said by the natives that its circumference is of nine kos. I put the population at 100,000 to 200,000. There is more movement and life in Amritsar than in any other town in British India, and it is the first city I have seen showing obvious signs of expansion. The bazars are very numerous. The rich bankers and merchants have houses three to four storeys high, the front being whitened and covered with coarse mythological figures. The rock salt of Lahore, which passes through Amritsar in enormous quantities to be exported to India, has its own quarter. Timber and firewood have another quarter. The wool spinners, the cotton weavers, and the Kashmiris usually occupy distinct quarters. There are a large number of Kashmiris and Afghans. The greater part of the Kashmiris is occupied in cleaning the shawls brought from Kashmir and destined to the Indian market.'[20]

Lahore

Right from the occupation in 1799, Ranjit Singh started a programme of renovation and embellishment of Lahore, with renewed building activity, which started with the complete renovation of the Lahore fort and its water works. The Sheesh

Mahal was repaired; a new *baradari* (corridor) was erected by Ranjit Singh, which was used as the setting for his grand painting, 'The Court of Lahore'. Some old residences of ministers were also renovated, and new buildings erected on the top of former Mughal structures. In 1818, Ranjit Singh built the Hazuri Bagh, in the midst of the former Aurangzebsarai. He also built the shrine of Guru Arjan with its pretty golden dome next to the Roshnai Darwaza. To keep on with former Mughal splendour, the Maharaja also entirely restored the Shalimar Gardens after cleaning and repairing the Hansi Canal.

The splendid structures erected during the Mughal period, which had not been managed properly, were restored by the Maharaja and others were also built anew. The havelis of Jamadar Khushal Singh, Raja Dhian Singh and Raja Dina Nath rivalled in splendour and beauty. All the paintings of the haveli of Nawab Imam-ud-Din, governor of Kashmir, were intact till the 1880s. None of these splendidly decorated residences exist today, except the haveli of Nau Nihal Singh, completed in 1837 for the marriage of the prince. This is a remarkable piece of architecture, with elegant balconies overlooking two squares and embossed with external decorations of elephants and birds which still have parts of their original painting.

The French officers were few, but their military and political influence was great, and they had their main residences in Lahore near the headquarters of their brigades. The residences of General Allard and Ventura still exist today, but without the magnificent paintings and embroidered mirrors which adorned them in the 1830s. The residence of General Court has disappeared, but a recently discovered miniature painting shows that it was a typical Punjabi farm house of the time. As far as Avitabile is concerned, nothing remains of his splendid house built at the top of the Budhoo-ka-Ava, and apparently no painting has survived. One has to rely on the following complimentary appreciation: 'The Maharaja happily proceeded to the Kiln-mound of Budhoo. He told the Raja Kalhan (Dhian Singh) that Avitabile had built a very good house. The Raja Kalhan replied that the glorious sahibs were fond of good buildings, Dar-us-Sultanat.'[21]

There had been frantic construction of Hindu temples and Sikh gurudwaras at Lahore under Ranjit Singh, and they dramatically changed the very sky-scape of the city, so long dotted with only the marble and glazed tiles of the domes of the mosques and tombs. This was one of the major irritants (not to be encouraged according to the Sharia) for the orthodox Muslims and ulema living for generations in the Dar-us-Sultanat. This was one of the major reasons for the biased description of Lahore under 'the Sikhs' by Muslim historians after annexation.

Lahore was the political capital of the kingdom. The government offices (*daftars*), the Crown Jewels (*toshakhana*) and the State archives were in the fort. There was also intense banking, trading and manufacturing activities in the city, and the military industries were also established there, like the gun foundries at Idgah. The cantonments were all around the city, with the new fashionable bazar of Anarkali and the 'Garden of the Soldier' on the bank of the river Ravi near Anarkali. European travellers of the time described the walled city of Lahore as 'an over-populated city with narrow lanes, and beautiful women with charming smiles, more attractive than anywhere else in India, appeared on the terraces and the balconies....'[22]

Other Towns

Descriptions of the smaller towns of Punjab are not available in detail because the historians and the European travellers did not say much about them. Gujranwala had been taken care of by Maharaja Ranjit Singh as it was his native place and the capital of his misl. It was also the residence of Hari Singh Nalwa, one of the most famous generals of the Punjabi army. In his haveli, he kept his collection of paintings. The town of Chiniot was extremely picturesque, with majestic houses that were beautifully painted and decorated. So were probably most of the medium-sized towns of Punjab.

There are a few precise descriptions of the city of Wazirabad, which commanded a strategic ford on the river Chenab, because of the modernising and beautifying drive decided and implemented by General Avitabile when he was governor of the city. It is said that Avitabile had pulled down a great part of the crumbling buildings of Wazirabad and had erected a big and specious bazar. General Avitabile built a new trading centre, a new sector named as Ram Katra inside the city, and erected a huge octagonal tower in the same bazar. Avitabile almost rebuilt the Wazirabad town in the European style, and pulled down the old bazar, making the streets wide enough to admit a carriage and four horses. Maharaja Ranjit Singh paid a visit to Avitabile at Wazirabad in June 1833. He was received there with an artillery salute. The Maharaja felt very happy to inspect a map of the town, which had been prepared very carefully and precisely.

There had been tremendous renewal of architectural and artistic activities under Maharaja Ranjit Singh. In Lahore and Amritsar, this happened right from the beginning of his reign, but in the second half of his reign it took place in almost each and every corner of the kingdom, in the hundreds of medium-size cities. These activities are a clear indication of the growing prosperity of the Punjab, and a staggering pool of artists available for decorating the temples and the Gurudwaras, the forts and the palaces, the private residences and sanctuary of the great and common men. All over Punjab, there were a great number of buildings with paintings during the Sikh period.

This was seen from Lahore and Amritsar, down to the smallest villages having a haveli, a Hindu temple or Gurudwara. Such a large distribution over the whole kingdom showed that prosperity was not confined to the capital or to the narrow political elite of the land.

THE BRITISH AND RANJIT SINGH

WHAT GREATLY HELPED Ranjit Singh strengthen the nation he had just founded was his statesmanship in dealing with the British during his lifetime. It is astonishing that someone so young and unversed in the ways of colonial powers should have risen to outsmart the British, who had boundless ambition, with an efficient army equipped with sophisticated weapons.

When in 1801, Ranjit Singh was crowned as the Maharaja of Punjab, the British were firmly settled in Delhi. Even though the Mughals still existed in name, they counted for very little by that time. It was Britain's writ via the East India Company, that prevailed over most of India, right up to Delhi. Beyond Delhi, Ranjit Singh was the man to reckon with. Even at that early stage, when he was barely 22, his designs for the future were on a grand scale. His intention was to exercise his exclusive writ over North India, the North-Western Provinces, the Hill States and the mountain ranges to the Khyber Pass. This vast territory was outside British control. Nor was it under the control of any single authority, although the Sikh nation was the most powerful in that part of the continent. But the Afghans possessed the most prosperous cities and towns and controlled major trade routes. They also had sizeable armies to enforce their writ. Besides Afghans, there were many other big and small Hindu and Muslim chiefs, aside of the tribes in the North-West of the subcontinent, who were a law unto themselves.

The only obstacle left between the British and their dominance of the whole of India was the land of the five rivers under Sikh rule. The British had very wisely observed the fighting qualities of the Sikhs, fueled by their religious beliefs, and sustained by their amazing self-confidence. So, it was clearly not in Britain's self-interest to get involved in any military showdown with them at this stage. Ranjit Singh too was intelligent enough to appreciate the importance of creating a well-defined boundary between the British possessions and the Sikh State. Both sides were perfectly aware of the advantages of this situation. But, as often happens, the twists and turns of fate play their part in influencing momentous events.

The British Governor General, Lord Richard Wellesley, had taken office at the age of 38. He was one of the important operatives of colonial expansionism. Aggressive and ambitious, he publicly proclaimed that British rule was undoubtedly in the best interests of the ruled. 'I can declare my conscientious conviction' he wrote, 'that no greater blessing can be conferred on the… inhabitants of India than the extension of the British authority, influence and power.'[1]

True to form, Wellesley set about adding Mysore (Karnataka), Tanjore (Tamil Nadu), Surat (Gujarat) and Oudh (Uttar Pradesh) to the British holdings in India. These territories lay in Southern, Western and Central India, but no attempt was made to show the flag in Northern India, or to the ruler of the new Sikh kingdom.

The haste shown by Wellesley was not taken kindly by the directors of the East India Company in London as they did not find it profitable, in terms of money, for the company. After watching their stocks falling steadily with no dividends coming in, the company decided to call Wellesley back. Accordingly, he was recalled in July 1805. His successor, Marquess Cornwallis, died within months of taking up his post. The next Governor General, Lord Gilbert Elliot-Murray-Kynynmound Minto assumed office in July 1807. By now Ranjit Singh had fully realised that though their initial aim was trade, the British were now moving on towards outright conquest.

The British, who were nibbling at the entire subcontinent of India, bit by bit, lost no time in establishing contact with Ranjit Singh, when he came to power. The East India Company sent their envoy, Yusuf Ali Khan, to Ranjit Singh with rich gifts and ample good wishes even before his formal coronation. Evidently, they wanted to make friends with him. Ranjit Singh's response to their overtures was most appropriate. The British, who had liquidated the Maratha power by vanquishing the Scindia's French General, Cuillier-Perron, had taken possession of Delhi and Agra by then and had made a virtual prisoner of the then emperor on the Mughal throne. Now they had their eyes on the Punjab.

When Holkar was chased across the subcontinent by the British Commander, Lord Lake, he came to Ranjit Singh, along with his Rohilla ally, Amir Khan to seek help. The Marathas held territories in the Punjab (known as the Malwa lands) and Holkar had run from central India, through Rajasthan, Haryana into Punjab. The Sikh fraternity who met at the Akal Takht passed a resolution offering to assist Holkar regain its territory, in accordance with the best tradition of the Sikh faith. Ranjit Singh was, however, aware of the fact he had yet to consolidate his power and that he could ill afford to make the Punjab a theatre of war at that hour. He, therefore, decided to mediate between the British and the Marathas and had Holker's territory restored to him.

A formal treaty called the Treaty of Lahore was signed on 1 January 1806 between Maharaja Ranjit Singh and Fateh

Singh Ahluwalia on the one hand, and the British on the other, according to which Holkar left the Punjab along with his army and the English were to remain where they were. During negotiations, Ranjit Singh pointed out tactfully that the Yamuna river (Jamuna) was the *de facto* boundary between the British and his own territory. It did not suit the British to take notice of this statement and they conveniently left it vague for the time being.

Maharaja Ranjit Singh wanted to ensure his suzerainty over the entire Sikh people and consolidate the whole of the Punjab under his influence. He was keen that the British remain on the other side of the Jamuna river. But the latter had their eyes on the Sikhs.

The British-Sikh Relations

The only weak point in Ranjit's claim to sovereignty over Malwa was that in 1805, when Lake had chased Holkar across the plains of Eastern Punjab, Ranjit, fearing that the English Commander would not only destroy the Marathas but might also invade his territory, had suggested the river Sutlej as the boundary between the two kingdoms. But neither Lake, nor the Governor-General, had taken any notice of this suggestion too. Their sole object was the annihilation of the Marathas. Once that was achieved, the Board of Directors of the East India Company, which had been brought to the verge of bankruptcy by the Maratha campaigns, gave strict instructions to their officers not to involve themselves in any more wars and to consider the river Jamuna as the western extremity of the English possessions in India.

In the three years between 1805 (when the Maratha campaign ended) and 1808, much water had flown down the Sutlej and the Jamuna. Ranjit Singh had resumed his claim to be the sovereign of the Sikhs and the Punjab and twice substantiated his title as far as the Malwa States were concerned, without a word of protest from the English. But in these three years, the East India Company had refilled its coffers and was ready for more adventures.

Ranjit Singh's action in taking over the territories of Tara Singh Gheba, who had died in 1807, had caused alarm amongst the Malwa chiefs. It was taken as concrete proof, if proof were needed, that he meant to reduce the chiefs to the position of pensioners. Soon after the confiscation of Gheba's estates, Mokham Chand crossed the Sutlej and, with more zeal than discretion, proceeded to take Anandpur-Makhowal and Whadni (near Ferozepur) along with fifteen neighbouring villages. Apprehension turned to panic and the Malwa Sardars turned to the only power that could preserve them and their families in their palaces and privileges – the English. The situation took a sudden and unexpected turn in their favour.

Napoleon, the English and the Russians

The events that brought this about occurred neither on the banks of the Sutlej nor the Jamuna, but on those of the Thames and the Seine. In the 1770s, Britain and France had been fighting with each other for dominance over the English Channel, the Mediterranean Seas and the Indian Ocean. France had also been siding with the American colonies across the Atlantic Ocean, supporting their bid to freedom from British rule. All in all, more than a billion French soldiers lost their lives in these conflicts with the British across the globe and the French revolution happened in 1789. By 1799, Napoleon Bonaparte had declared himself as monarch of France and he took on the Russian empire.

One after another, the European powers fell before him: Austria at Austerlitz, Prussia at Jena, Russia at Friedland. The Russians fought Napoleon's armies bravely for seven years, with the British siding with Tsar Alexander. However, unable to continue their fight longer, the Russians signed two treaties with the French in 1807, known as The Treaties of Tilsit.

The terms of the treaty obliged Russia to stop her maritime trade with Britain. This was a part of Napoleon's strategy to set up a common European economic zone under French domination. Britain was its competitor. Shutting down Britain's most important markets and force it to economically submit was what Napoleon wanted. So, the British were fighting the French again and took away French territory in India. And of course, they were fighting the Russians now. And Ranjit Singh stood in between British India and Afghanistan-Russia.

It was a not-too-secret fact that the treaty Tsar Alexander signed with Napoleon was an understanding that if England continued hostilities against France, Russia would join the French in combating her. Although the British Navy commanded the seas, the land route to India through Persia, Afghanistan, Sindh and the Punjab was open to the Franco-Russian armies. The British now decided to revise their policy of regarding the Jamuna as their western frontier. Lord Minto, who had taken over as Governor-General in June 1807, ordered troops to be moved up to Karnal to protect Delhi from the north. Then the grand strategy of erecting a series of dams against the tide of Franco-Russian invasion was taken in hand. The dams were to be in Persia, Afghanistan, Sindh and the Punjab. Four missions were consequently sent out: Malcolm to Persia, Elphinstone to Kabul, Portinger to Sindh, and Charles Metcalfe was chosen to negotiate with Ranjit Singh.

The idea of sending a British delegation to Lahore was mooted early in 1808. When intelligence was received that Ranjit Singh might come to Hardwar for pilgrimage, the British decided to exploit the situation by acts of kindness and attention to render the circumstances of Ranjit Singh's visit to the company's dominions subservient to the plan of pleasing and conciliating him, thereby rendering it the basis of future intercourse and friendly connection.

Metcalfe was ordered to proceed to the banks of the Jamuna and wait for the arrival of Ranjit Singh. On the return journey, he was to escort the Maharaja up to the British frontier, which was again the banks of the Jamuna. This kind of recognition was what the shrewd Maharaja had wanted. Having succeeded in his design, he quietly called off the pilgrimage.

The Malwa chiefs, however, were not dependable. While they accepted Ranjit Singh's supremacy, they also hobnobbed with the British. They sent a delegation consisting of the chiefs of Jind, Kaithal, Jagadhari, and the agents of Patiala and Nabha to meet the English Resident Archibald Seton, to seek his protection. Ranjit Singh got to know of the plans of the Malwais and sent his agent to accompany their delegation. The delegates met the English Resident three or four times but since Ranjit Singh's agent was also present, not a word was said about the frontiers. Then Ranjit Singh's agent, believing that his master's suspicions had been unfounded, left Delhi to proceed on pilgrimage towards Gaya.

The delegates at once went to Seton and presented a lengthy memorandum asking for protection from Ranjit Singh. Seton forwarded the memorandum to the Governor-General. The company's policy still being no-farther-than-the-Jamuna, the Governor-General decided that the delegation should officially be ignored. The delegates waited in Delhi for two months, then turned back to the Punjab without the guarantee they had sought. They awaited Ranjit Singh's reactions. Ranjit Singh invited the Malwa chiefs to Amritsar and gave them a solemn assurance that he would not annex their States and would treat them as equals. The chiefs agreed to come into Ranjit Singh's camp. 'Between the loin and the wolf, they had to come to terms with the deadlier of the beasts.'[2]

In this atmosphere of uncertainty, Charles Metcalfe was deputed by the British to acquaint Ranjit Singh with the developments in the West and the incursion that they feared from Napoleon. Metcalfe also wished to assess for himself how far the British could depend upon the loyalty of the Malwa chiefs.

The Treaty of Amritsar

It was indeed a fierce exercise in diplomacy. The Maharaja sent Fakir Imam-ud-Din, his home minister, to meet Metcalfe on his behalf at Patiala, thereby indicating to the British envoy that Lahore exerted sovereignty over the Malwa region. Simultaneously, the Maharaja invited the Malwa chiefs to meet him at Lahore so that Metcalfe did not associate with them unduly. However, some of them ignored the summons from Lahore and stayed back to tender their representations against Ranjit Singh to the British envoy.

Ranjit Singh gave audience to Metcalfe at Khem Karan rather than at Lahore where he was accompanied by his foreign minister. While he was well aware of what Metcalfe had to tell him, he avoided broaching the subject as long as he could. It was a virtual battle of wits. Eventually, when Metcalfe had his say and spelt out the threat of a French invasion, the Maharaja tried to dismiss the idea tactfully. This is how the dialogue proceeded:

> Ranjit Singh: 'Where exactly does the British army propose to meet the French invasion?'
>
> Metcalfe: 'Beyond Kabul if required.'
>
> R: 'Is the British army ready to march?'
>
> M: 'The British army is ever ready to march.'
>
> R: 'Any idea of the date of the French invasion?'
>
> M: 'The exact date cannot at present be ascertained.'
>
> R: 'In that case, we have enough time to think the matter over.'[3]

Metcalfe was on a defence alliance, whereas Ranjit Singh insisted on the British recognising him as the sole sovereign of the entire Sikh community. As Metcalfe evaded doing so, Fakir Aziz-ud-din reminded him again and again how an unequivocal declaration of the frontiers between the two powers was important as part of this defence alliance.

After a few days, Fakir Aziz-ud-Din again confronted Metcalfe, who happened to remark in arrogance, 'the boundaries of the government's territories are fixed. There is no desire whatsoever to exceed them'.

'Where has the government fixed its permanent boundary?' asked Fakir Aziz-ud-din.

'Karnal', Metcalfe replied.

'Karnal? It belongs to Gurdit Singh, an old friend of the Maharaja', intervened Prabhu Dayal. Prabhu Dayal was a trusted employee of Fateh Singh Ahluwalia, who was asked to assist Fakir Aziz-ud-Din in the negotiations on behalf of the Lahore Durbar.

Metcalfe then presented the draft of an agreement which had three main clauses:

a) A joint British-Sikh alliance in the event of an attack by Napoleon.
b) Safe passage of British troops through the Punjab up to the Northern Frontiers.
c) Establishment of an intelligence network beyond the Indus.

At this, the negotiators representing the Maharaja came forward with counter-proposals. These stipulated:

a) Most-favoured-nation treatment to the Lahore government.
b) Recognition of Ranjit Singh's suzerainty over the entire Sikh people.
c) No intervention from the British in the internal affairs of the Sikhs.

d) Alliance between the two powers in permanence.

Evidently, the two sets of proposal did not meet at any point and there was stalemate.

When Ranjit Singh realised that Metcalfe was being arrogant, he suddenly struck camp and set out towards the South, leaving Metcalfe to follow him if he so desired. Metcalfe was left bewildered. He, however, kept the matter alive, but without getting another opportunity to meet the Maharaja. The Maharaja went on to Malerkotla and received the Pathan ruler there. Metcalfe kept on watching the entire exercise. This was followed by similar visits to other chiefdoms in the Cis-Sutlej territory.

The British got panicky and decided to precipitate a crisis. They insisted that Sutlej and not the Jamuna was their line-of-control and that the Maharaja must restore to the British, all the Malwa States that had started paying tribute to Ranjit Singh. He must remain confined to the right bank of the Sutlej. The argument offered by the British was that, having defeated the Marathas, they had acquired suzerainty over this area and if they had not levied any tribute it was because they wished to treat these States liberally. Thus, while they substantiated their claim with what appeared to be a cogent argument, they also won the sympathies of the Malwa chiefs by claiming to be more considerate towards them than Ranjit Singh. In addition, the British sent a strong force under the command of Colonel David Ochterlony and instructed Metcalfe to prolong the negotiation until the British army reached the Sutlej and if need be, to force the decision.

Almost a War Before the Treaty

The Maharaja re-crossed the Sutlej into his territory and reached Lahore, where Metcalfe duly followed him. With the threat of a French attack having receded, the British were now determined to establish their foothold in the Punjab. They could do so only by asserting their suzerainty over the Cis-Sutlej Sikh States. As regards Ranjit Singh, in case the Malwa States were to be ceded to the British, he could not make claims over the entire Sikh people.

The Maharaja gave a call and the troops started closing in at Amritsar. The Gobindgarh fort was repaired and readied with provision for a prolonged siege. Troops and ammunition were collected from all quarters; the new fort of Gobindgarh was armed and General Mohkam Chand, the best of the Sikh generals and a bitter enemy of the English, was recalled from Kangra and marched to Phillaur on the Sutlej, opposite the town of Ludhiana, were he encamped. To this hostile movement, the British government sent force to Ludhiana under Colonel Ochterlony, who, passing Patiala and Nabha, was received with many demonstrations of satisfaction and regard.

While the Maharaja was determined to fight, Fakir Aziz-ud-Din, his minister for foreign affairs, counselled restraint. So did Sada Kaur (his mother-in-law) who had the reputation of being a warmonger. Fakir Aziz-ud-Din had his own reasons. He knew that the Malwa chiefs could not be relied upon. They only paid lip service to the Maharaja; at heart they were aligned with the British. The British had already become a mighty power in the subcontinent; a regular war with them might prove too costly and endanger the Maharaja's rule. Sada Kaur had other reasons. As her later conduct proved, she was playing a double game. She wanted Ranjit Singh to come to grief. There was not much love lost between them. She was aware that in the event of breaking apart from Ranjit Singh, the British would come to her rescue.

Meanwhile, the Maharaja moved to Amritsar to supervise the progress of military preparations there. Metcalfe also followed him, as he had been doing all the while. It was a dual game Metcalfe was playing. On the one hand, he appeared to be keen on proceeding with the negotiations. On the other, he sent word to the Governor-General that they should declare a full-scale war and take over the entire Punjab. On their part, the British had also entered into secret negotiations with the Afghan ruler to keep him on their side.

The cold war that had gone on during the preceding six months had produced such a state of tension that a small incident would have caused serious consequence. Muharram was observed on 25 February 1809 and the Shia Muslims in Metcalfe's escort took out a procession in the streets of Amritsar. It also happened to be the day of Holi, and a large number of Sikhs, mainly the Nihangs with their celebrated leader Akali Phula Singh, had already gathered in the city for the celebration. The Shia processionists insisted on passing through the streets which came to the opening in front of the Golden Temple where the Sikhs were at prayer. The Nihangs suggested, the processionists take another route. Arguments led to a scuffle and the Shia sepoys came to a head-on collision with Nihangs. It is not known who the first aggressor was. Even Metcalfe was doubtful and concede that the first shot had probably been fired by one of his escorts.[4] There were more casualties on the side of the Nihangs than that of the Shias. This fact, in view of Metcalfe's own admission that 'matchlocks of our assailants carried further and with surer aim than our own musquets', does not, however, lend support to the theory of Nihang aggression.[5]

Metcalfe could not utilise this incident as an excuse for war. His report blamed Akali Phula Singh, but not the Maharaja, who turned up at the scene immediately and personally helped to quell the riot. He also sent envoys to Metcalfe to apologise for the lack of courtesy shown to his guests and promised compensation. Resident Seton in Delhi received a distorted version of the incident and was sure that war was inevitable, being, as he confessed, 'in some measure influenced by the reflection that the Sikhs are a wild and ferocious people'.[6] Ochterlony also admitted that if any more incident had taken place (the Nihangs were threatening vengeance) he had made up his mind to cross the Sutlej.

Fortunately, before the news of the incident could reach Calcutta, the Governor-General had dispatched two drafts of treaties to be offered to the Durbar with orders to Ochterlony and Metcalfe regarding the details. The catastrophe of war was, thus, averted in the nick of time.

The two drafts consisted of three articles each and were almost identical. They provided for perpetual friendship and most-favoured-nation treatment for Lahore Durbar; recognition of the Maharaja's sovereignty over territories north of Sutlej; and permission to keep troops south of Sutlej to police his estates south of the river. One of the drafts had a clause appended to the second article to the effect that Ranjit Singh renounced all claim to sovereignty over Sikh chiefs to the south of the Sutlej and all rights of interference in their concerns. It was made clear that this was not to force Ranjit Singh to cede his 'ancient conquests' and if he did not like it, it was not to be pressed.

The wrangling over Faridkot went on for some weeks more. Metcalfe again lost his patience and advised Major St Leger, who was asked to be prepared to join at short notice, to take the town by assault, assuring him that by the time the Sikhs assembled their forces, the monsoons would make the Sutlej expensive. So, on 3 April, Faridkot was evacuated.

On 25 April 1809 a treaty with the British was signed at Amritsar, without the additional clause of the second draft. There was a week of farewell parties. Metcalfe left the Punjab on 2 May, well pleased with himself.

THE TREATY OF 1809 WITH LAHORE

Treaty between the British Government and the Raja of Lahore (dated 25 April 1809)

Whereas certain differences which had arisen between the British Government and the Raja of Lahore, have been happily and amicably adjusted; and both parties being anxious to maintain relations of perfect amity and concord, the following articles of treaty, which shall be binding on the heirs and successors of the two parties, have been concluded by the Raja Ranjit Singh in person, and by the agency of C.T. Metcalfe, Esquire, On the part of the British Government.

Article 1. – Perpetual friendship shall subsist between the British Government and the State of Lahore, the latter shall be considered, with respect to the former, to be on the footing of the most favoured powers, and the British Government will have no concern with the territories and subjects of the Raja to the northward of the river Sutlej.

Article 2. – The Raja will never maintain on the territory which he occupies on the left bank of the river Sutlej more troops than are necessary for internal duties of that territory, nor commit or suffer any encroachments on the possessions or right of the Chiefs in its vicinity.

Article 3. – In the event of violation of any of the preceding articles, or of departure from the rules of friendship, this treaty shall be considered null and void.

Article 4. – This treaty, consisting of four articles, having been settled and concluded at Amritsar, on the 25th day of April 1809, Mr. C.T. Metcalfe has delivered to the Raja of Lahore, a copy of the same in English and Persian, under his seal and signature; and the Raja has delivered another copy of the same under his seal and signature, and C.T. Metcalfe engages to procure within the space

> of two months a copy of the same, duly ratified by the Right Honourable the Governor-General in Council on the receipt of which by the Raja, the present treaty shall be deemed complete and binding on both parties, and the copy of it now delivered to the Raja shall be returned.
>
> (Ratified by the Governor-General, Lord Minto, on 21 May 1809)[7]

Treaty is Advantage Ranjit Singh

Despite the treaty and the festivities that followed, ill-will continued on both sides for quite some time. On the Durbar's side, there were people like Diwan Mohkam Chand and Akali Phula Singh of the do-or-die school who felt that the Maharaja should tear up the treaty and fight. They felt that the Treaty of Amritsar was a grievous blow to Ranjit Singh's dream of unified Punjab. Contacts were made with the Marathas, and the air in northern India was thick with rumours of a Sikh-Maratha alliance to expel the British from India. The British were perturbed by these rumours and moved detachment of troops to Hansi to prevent Scindia or Holkar from joining up with the Punjabis.

The Maharaja kept a cool head. He listened to Mohkam Chand, for whom he had great respect and admiration, but refused to take his assurance of Maratha collaboration seriously. 'Let the Marathas make the first move, and I will join them', he said.[8] As months went by, these rumours died down, the clouds of suspicion cleared and relations between him and the English became cordial. By the end of that year, the Governor-General was able to write to the Maharaja expressing satisfaction at the relations existing between them. Replied Ranjit Singh with enthusiasm: 'Judge by the state of your own heart, what is the state of mine'.[9]

The British fully honoured the Sutlej Treaty despite

being irked by the rapid expansion of the Sikh State. They turned down appeals for help against Ranjit Singh from both Sansar Chand of Kangra and the Gurkhas. During the first unsuccessful siege of Multan in 1810 by the Lahore Durbar, the beleaguered city's governor was similarly told that, in view of the treaty, there was little the British could do to help him.

The British were to adhere to the treaty, to Ranjit Singh's advantage, on other occasions as well. In 1819, Kashmir's Afghan governor, Azim Khan, pleaded with the British to place Kashmir under their protection but was refused. Shah Zaman and Shah Shuja, the grandsons of Ahmed Shah Abdali, who also asked for British intervention, were turned down. When an overzealous British envoy to Afghanistan, Alexander Burnes, tried to persuade East India Company officials to help the Afghans take back Peshawar from Ranjit Singh, the British Governor-General, Lord George Eden Auckland, after some thought, turned down the suggestion.

Did the Sutlej Treaty benefit Ranjit Singh more than it did the British? A consideration of the different mindsets of the two signatories will help to begin answering this question. The British, of course, were past masters in the art of diplomacy; they were able to judge precisely where their self-interest lay, and had centuries of experience in wars, battles, victories, defeats, annexations, treaties and much else. Ranjit Singh, by contrast, a school dropout in his twenties had no experience of negotiating treaties or dealing with Europeans. Yet, relying entirely on his own unaided perception and evaluation, he arrived at a clear and intelligent assessment of his adversary's strengths. After the eight-month negotiations, he got what he wanted from the treaty.

Having witnessed how the British had dealt with the Marathas in 1803 after Jaswant Rao Holkar had seized Delhi and ravaged the East India Company's territories between the Jamuna and the Sutlej, Ranjit Singh had a prime example to go by. Holkar had got no help from the Punjab Sardars of that region, and subsequently he had been defeated and forced to come to terms with the British. The conclusion Ranjit Singh drew from this episode was that he could never build up his Sikh State without accurately assessing his own limitations against his adversary's advantages.

Some of his critics suggest that the treaty snowed him in a poor light since he abandoned all the Sikhs living between the Jamuna and Sutlej, but accepting this view is to discount his evolving strategy and his vision for the future. He wanted the Sikh State to extend far beyond the boundaries of the Punjab. He had his eyes on prized Afghan possessions all the way up to Kabul, as also other vast territories in North India. So, the first article of the treaty assured him that the British would not concern themselves with his territorial acquisitions north of the river Sutlej. It was because of his decisive victories against the Afghans, that he was able to seal the routes through which invaders had entered India for centuries. Had he not signed the treaty and secured his southern boundary effectively, he could not have achieved what he did spectacularly.

Ranjit Singh's success as a statesman with regard to the Sutlej Treaty can only be judged with this consideration in mind. Even Metcalfe, who was often at odds with him, and robustly represented British interests in the period preceding the finalisation of the treaty, acknowledged Ranjit Singh's gain. His courteous remark to the Maharaja on signing the treaty, 'your Excellency will reap the fruits of the alliance with the British in a period of 20 years'[10] was to be proved right – in fact, in less than 20 years.

CONQUESTS AND THE KOHINOOR

HAVING ATTENDED TO important state affairs, essentially organisational and civil in character, for the next few months after signing the treaty with the British, Maharaja Ranjit Singh launched a number of military expeditions one after another. It is significant that all these initial campaigns, big or small, were carried out under his own command. Each one of these was marked by daring, foresight and strategy.

The danger of external aggression had, for the time being, receded. Zaman Khan had sent the Maharaja presents on the occasion of his coronation. Ranjit Singh, in return, had restored to him 15 pieces of cannon that Ahmad Shah Durrani had lost while returning from Punjab. The British had also sought his good will by deputing an envoy, Yusuf Ali, to greet the new monarch and make known to him their appreciation of the political situation. They were particularly keen that the Maharaja should befriend Zaman Khan. They looked upon Ranjit Singh as the most prominent leader of the Sikhs.

Kasur

The Maharaja was, however, determined to overcome the hostile elements close by. The Nawab of Kasur was the first to receive

Ranjit Singh's attention. Kasur was barely forty miles from Lahore. Nizamuddin, the Pathan Nawab of Kasur, was not reconciled to Ranjit Singh's occupation of Lahore. He had earlier joined hands with the Sikh misldars when they were vanquished by Ranjit Singh. He now conspired with Sahib Singh Bhangi of Gujrat again, and they started challenging Ranjit Singh's authority. The Maharaja himself led an attack on Gujrat and sent force under Fateh Singh Kalianwala to simultaneously invade Kasur. Both Sahib Singh and the Pathan ruler were defeated. They accepted the Maharaja's overlordship, paid war compensation and surrendered hostages as guarantee of future good conduct.

The Nawab of Kasur, however, did not sit still for long. The Maharaja sent another force to hammer him, followed by attack under his own command. Kasur came under fire. The town was mercilessly sacked. The Nawab sought peace by surrendering the fort. He re-confirmed allegiance to the Maharaja.

Kasur continued to cause concern to the Maharaja. Nawab Nizamuddin was, however, assassinated and he was succeeded by his brother Qutb-ud-Din. The new Nawab also assumed a defiant posture. As a result, another force had to be sent to Kasur. The Nawab shut himself in the fort and he kept himself there for months. Eventually, his resistance collapsed. This time the Nawab was overthrown, and his territory annexed. The Maharaja, however, allowed him a jaagir for maintenance. This put an end to the tiny Pathan enclave, irritating in the heart of Punjab.

Kangra

After the loss of face which followed the debacle in Malwa, Ranjit Singh had to achieve something spectacular to restore his prestige amongst his people. As soon as the Treaty of Amritsar was signed, troops were withdrawn from the Sutlej and ordered towards Kangra.

The Gurkhas under Amar Singh Thapa had advanced westward along the Himalyan ranges, sweeping the forces of the hill chieftains before them and were trying hard to capture the fort of Kangra. Sansar Chand appealed both to the English and Ranjit Singh for help. To counteract Sansar Chand's move, the Gurkhas also asked the British to help them conquer Kangra and offered tribute to Ranjit Singh, if he would stay away. The British turned down the Gurkha request and the Rajput plea on the grounds that by the Treaty of Amritsar, they could not interfere in the affairs of people living to the west of the Sutlej.

The Lahore Durbar rejected the overtures of the Gurkhas because it considered Kangra to be a part of the Punjab and would feel obliged to defend it against all outsiders. Sansar Chand's request was favourably received but it was considered necessary that Kangra should first declare itself a part of Punjab and surrender the fort to the Durbar's troops. Sansar Chand, who was fighting a losing battle against the Gurkhas, agreed to the Durbar's terms.

The Durbar ordered the hill chiefs of the Kangra region to stop selling provisions to the Gurkhas, and its troops cut the Gurkhas' supply lines with Nepal. Ranjit Singh arrived in Kangra and demanded admission to the fort. Sansar Chand began to vacillate. The fort, he promised, would be handed over as soon as the Gurkhas withdrew. Ranjit Singh was not the one to be taken in by this deceit, particularly by Sansar Chand, who was known not to be a man of his words. Since there was no time to argue, Ranjit Singh promptly put Sansar Chand's son, Anirudha Chand, whom he held as hostage, under arrest. Sansar Chand yielded and on 14 August 1809, a detachment of the Durbar's troops took possession of the Kangra fort.

The Gurkhas held on stubbornly despite their limited rations. Ranjit Singh let them run out of provisions and when they started to retreat, attacked them in full force a couple of miles beyond the fort. Amar Singh Thapa turned back to face the Punjabis and placed his troops in battle position along a hillside known as Ganesh Ghati. The hill Rajputs, who had suffered at the hands of the Gurkhas, opened the attack. The Gurkhas disposed of the Rajputs without much difficulty. Punjabi artillery also made little impression on the Gurkhas, who had entrenched themselves behind a rock.

Knowing that Thapa's men had been short of food for many days and would be unable to stand the strain of hand-to-hand combat, Ranjit Singh ordered the infantry to charge. The Sikhs with their long curving Kripans, closed in on the Gurkhas with their short Kukris. Ranjit Singh, who was watching the action from a mound, mounted his horse and plunged into the fray! The battle was won and the Gurkhas retreated from Ganesh Ghati in disorder.

The stubborn fight put up by the Gurkhas impressed Ranjit Singh. When the action was over, he not only allowed Amar Singh Thapa time to retire without further injury, but also ordered his Sardars to help the Gurkhas in collecting their equipment. Some of the hill Rajas, who utilised the opportunity to plunder their vanquished foe, were severely reprimanded and made to restore the loot. The Gurkha menace to the Punjab was thus ended forever.

On 4 December 1809, the Maharaja entered the fort of Kangra. Amongst the chiefs who paid him homage was the rulers of Kangra, Chamba, Noorpur, Kulu and Datarpur.

Ranjit Singh could face his people once more. The towns and villages through which he passed on his way homewards were decorated to welcome him. When he reached Amritsar early in January 1810, the guns of Gobindgarh fort barked their greetings and at night all the houses in the city and the Golden Temple were illuminated in his honour. The Maharaja rode through the brightly lit streets on the back of his biggest elephant and showered silver coins on the populace. The scenes of jubilation were repeated at Lahore, Patiala, and Jind. The short eclipse of the sun on his fortunes was over.

The victory of Kangra was an important milestone in Ranjit Singh's life. Ten years earlier, when he had become Maharaja of the Punjab, there was a cordon of hostile powers bordering his kingdom. Now he had only one powerful neighbour (the English) and they were friendly.

Jhang

Maharaja Ranjit Singh's love for horses led him to attack Jhang. He came to know that Ahmad Shah Sial, the Nawab of Jhang, had a number of well-bred horses in his stable. He first sent word to the Nawab, asking for some choice horses. The latter's reply was rude and provocative. The Maharaja dispatched a force against him under the command of Fateh Singh Ahluwalia. Ahmad Shah had collected a large force of tribals and the fighting lasted for three days. The resistance collapsed on the fourth day, when the Maharaja's forces ransacked the town and plundered it to their full satisfaction. Ahmad Shah became a tributary of the Maharaja. He paid 1,200,000 rupees to Ranjit's Durbar as a token his allegiance.

Uch, Sahiwal and Garh

After the subjugation of Jhang, the Maharaja's forces vanquished the Bokhari Syeds of Uch, the Baluchis of Sahiwal and the Maharaja of Garh before they returned to headquarters.

Jammu

The State of Jammu was in turmoil owing to the death of its ruler. Ranjit Singh had sent a force in 1806 to take possession of the town. It seems, at that time, the commander of the Sikh force was satisfied with the Nazrana (presents, a placatory tax) and had returned to Lahore. The Maharaja sent another force under Misr Diwan Chand the next year. He too was bought off by the affluent residents of the town. Two years later, the Maharaja sent yet another force under Diwan Bhawani Das. This time the family of the Raja fled. The town was captured and Diwan Khushal Chand was appointed governor. He was later replaced by Gulab Singh, who was made Raja of Jammu. He paid an annual tribute of 400,000 rupees to Ranjit Singh's treasury.

Attock

Ranjit Singh had to teach a lesson to Fateh Khan of Attock for his deceitful moves during the joint expedition to Shergarh. Ranjit Singh did not take the duplicity kindly. He asked his general Mohkam Chand to annex Attock. After the battle that took place at Haidru on 9 July 1813, the Sikh forces walked in without any resistance. Four months later, Fateh Khan, now constrained by the loss of a major invasion route that the Afghans had traditionally taken into India, resorted to letter writing in lieu of armed retaliation. On 25 December 1813, he wrote to Mohkam Chand: 'Still nothing is lost. Give the fort of Attock to me so that the relations of friendship between the two parties may become strong.' Mohkam Chand replied: 'The fort of Attock will never be handed over to you and the country of Kashmir will soon be conquered by us.'[1] Unable to reconcile to the loss of Attock, Fateh Khan died in 1818, still obsessed with getting it back.

It is scarcely possible to list comprehensively all the territories Ranjit Singh annexed to the Sikh state, because in addition to outright annexations, many were left under the political and administrative control of chieftains or rulers while being under his suzerainty and subject to a tribute they paid annually to him till they were eventually taken over. Other such interim arrangements, with many variations, were also entered into.

Some idea of how the Sikh empire grew out of this bewildering chequerboard of territorial acquisitions can be had from a glimpse provided over a nine-year period by the Sikh historian J S Grewal. These were the years between signing the Sutlej Treaty in 1809 and the conquest of Multan in 1818. It was during this period, and the conquest of Kashmir and the North-West in 1820s and 1830s, that Ranjit Singh's realm emerged as an empire.

Grewal lists a number of towns, which are familiar names: 'The Sikh territories annexed by Ranjit Singh included Jalalpur, Manawar, Islamgarh, Bajwat, Gujrat, Chunian, Dipalpur, Satghara, Jethpur, Haveli, Muhiyuddinpur, Jalandhar, Patti, Fatehgarh, Sujanpur, Hajipur, Mukerian, Rawalpindi, Sri Hargobindpur and Miani....The Hindu territories annexed by Ranjit included Kangra, Sayyidgarh, Kotla, Jandiala, Samba, Kathua, Guler, Nurpur and Jaswan.

'With the exception of Jandiala, all these territories were in the hills close to the plains. In the process, about half a dozen chiefs were subverted, and the most powerful hill principalities of Kangra and Jammu suffered curtailment.... The Muslim territories annexed by Ranjit Singh included Khushab, Kachh, Sahiwal, Kusk, Attock, Makhad, Jhang, Julamba, and Kot Nall. In the process, some Baloch and Sial chiefs were subverted, and the rulers of Bahawalpur, Multan and Kabul lost some of their territories. Thus, before the conquest of Multan, the lower hills and upper and middle portions of all the five *doab*s fell under the effective control of Maharaja Ranjit Singh.'[2]

Kashmir

Ranjit Singh was attracted by the idea of Kashmir because it was the prized possession of the Afghans, who had in turn, taken it from Mughals in 1752. Ranjit Singh was drawn to Kashmir for many reasons. He was lured as much by its wondrous lakes, valleys, snow-covered peaks, saffron fields, flora and fauna and flowering trees as by its exquisite crafts – carpets, shawls, walnut woodwork, jewellery, beautiful women and much else. In 1812, the excuse he needed for a dramatic entry into Kashmir was, ironically enough, again provided by the Afghans, just as in the case of Attock and Multan.[3]

When the sitting Emir of Afghanistan, Zaman Shah was blinded by a half-brother from the Barakzai clan, Mahmud, Shah Shuja had become the Emir in 1803 as a blind man could not rule, according to Afghan laws. Shuja, from the Sadozai clan, married into the Barakzai clan to bring peace and remained Emir till 1809. The Elphinstone mission reports extensively on this ruler's possessions. When Mahmud attacked Kabul again in 1809, Shah Suja fled to India with the Kohinoor.

The Kohinoor

A belief in India connects diamonds with high spirituality and power, be it the Syamantaka of the *Vishnu Purana*, Ashvatthama's jewel in the *Mahabharata*, the Triratna of the Jaina tradition, or the Seven Jewels – the last one a real one – worn by a 'Chakrawartin' king in the Buddhist tradition.

The anonymous Punjabi artist who painted the 'Durbar of Maharaja Ranjit Singh' and August Schoefft in his 'Court of Lahore' have both represented Maharaja Ranjit Singh wearing the Kohinoor on his right arm. In his painting Schoefft has shown the brilliant jewellery and strings of pearls worn by the Maharaja, and those decorating his horses or carried in trays by young servants of the household.[4]

Kohinoor is a diamond the like of which the world has not known. It belonged to India, and the belief is, it existed in the times of the *Mahabharata* and even earlier. It came from the Kollur mines in Golkonda that yielded other famous diamonds of the world – Great Mughal, the Orlov, the Pigot, the Regent,

Sancy and Hope. The oval shaped, colourless Kohinoor measured 31.9mm by 36mm and was owned by the Kakatiya dynasty in the 12th century. It has been cut and shaped several times.

It was seized around 1306 AD from Rai Mahlak Deo, ruler of Malwa in the Deccan, by Alauddin Khilji, then Delhi's ruling Sultan. Emperor Ibrahim Lodhi of the Lodhi dynasty then acquired it for a time, before it was taken by the Mughals. Babur records in his memoirs, the *Baburnama,* that 'every appraiser has estimated its value at two-and-a-half days' food' for the whole world. Apparently, it weighs eight misquals (approximately 188 Carats). Humayun (his son) offered to me when I arrived at Agra; I just gave it back to him.'[5]

The Kohinoor disappeared for about a hundred years, during Akbar-Jehangir's time, and then surfaced again in 1656 at the court of the emperor Shah Jehan, who set it in his peacock throne. Nadir Shah, during his sack and plunder of Delhi, had carried it away to Afghanistan. Nadir Shah is credited with naming the diamond Kohinoor. When Nadir Shah was hacked to death in a family coup in 1747, Ahmad Shah Abdali removed the Kohinoor from his body.

In the late eighteenth century, it ended up with Ahmad Shah's grandson Shah Shuja Durrani. Shah Shuja was hopeful of regaining the Afghan throne. Intrigues of Afghanistan's power game threw Shah Shuja into the hands of Ata Mohammad, the governor of Kashmir. Shah Shuja was cut off from his wife Wafa Begum and his blinded brother Zaman Shah.

Desperate over her husband's fate, Shah Shuja's wife, Wafa Begum, begged Ranjit Singh to rescue him from Ata Mohammad's hold in Kashmir before the latter dispatched him in the style of her fellow Afghans. She offered Ranjit Singh the Kohinoor (Light of the Mountains) diamond in return for sending in a military expedition to Kashmir.[6] As luck would have it, at last Maharaja Ranjit Singh got his dream opportunity to recover the diamond, and he left no stone unturned to do so.

Fateh Khan of the Barakzai tribe in Afghanistan, who had caused Zaman Shah to be blinded, wanted to lay hands on Shah Shuja, the possessor of the famed Kohinoor and currently a captive of Kashmir's governor. But there was no way he could get to Kashmir with his forces since Ranjit Singh's Sikh army stood on his way at Attock. So, he had to ask Ranjit Singh for his help in the invasion of Kashmir. With the modalities carefully worked out to the advantage of the Lahore Durbar, the combined Sikh and Afghan forces headed for Shergarh, were Shuja was imprisoned.

The man Ranjit Singh handpicked to command the Sikh army in this joint expedition was Diwan Mohkam Chand, an outstanding commander. It didn't take him long to see through the game the Afghans were planning to play – to outspace Diwan Mohkam Chand, reach Shergarh before him, and take custody not only of Shuja but of the treasury as well. The Diwan informed Ranjit Singh of this plan. The Maharaja advised his Diwan to outwit Fateh Khan and, if the Khan persisted in his double-crossing, to deal with him accordingly. He also assigned Desa Singh Majithia, the governor of Jammu, Nihal Singh Attariwala and Jodh Singh Kalsia to assist the Diwan. On his part, Ranjit Singh crossed the Jhelum and camped at Rohtas to provide any support needed by his generals.

Mohkam Chand rose to the occasion by taking a more steep but shorter route to the Shergarh fort and mounting an assault on it before the Afghans were anywhere in sight. Completely taken aback by being so easily outwitted, Fateh Khan hastened to join in the assault, and when Shergarh fell he and his men put their energies into looting the treasury, while the Sikhs mounted a massive search for Shuja. On finding him in fetters in a dungeon, they swiftly transferred him to the Sikh camp and from there to Lahore. Thus, the first incursion of

Ranjit Singh into Kashmir in 1812 had been a spin-off of the seductive lure of the Kohinoor.

With Shah Shuja and Wafa Begum reunited in Lahore, the Kohinoor became the bone of contention, this time between Shuja and Wafa on one side, and Ranjit Singh on the other. Having promised the Kohinoor to Ranjit Singh when she was fearful for her husband's life, Wafa and her husband, Shuja, were now reluctant to hand it over to their rescuer.

Shuja's contention was that the subject of the Kohinoor was never mentioned until Ranjit Singh had him safely in Lahore in the house assigned to him for his residence, when he started demanding the Kohinoor. Shah Shuja denied having the stone with him even when Ranjit Singh offered a large estate in exchange. Shah Shuja again asserted that the stone had been placed for security in the hands of a *shraf* or moneylender, but that it would become available only when the friendship between the Maharaja and himself had taken a definite shape and was secured by sufficient guarantees.

Ranjit Singh lost his temper, placed a guard of soldiers round the Afghan house, and searched anyone who entered it or came out of it, allowing no food to be sent in. Forged letters were produced, which, it was stated, had been intercepted from Shah Shuja to his friends in Afghanistan, calling upon them to invade the Punjab and liberate him.[7]

The Shah was threatened with imprisonment in the fortress of Gobindgarh, and at length after two months of resistance with perpetual harassment, seeing his family and servants half-starving and feeling that longer refusal would only end in his death, he promised to give up the diamond if the Maharaja, on his part would promise his protection and friendship in the most solemn manner. 'This the Maharaja did, having a document drawn up in which he promised on the *Adi Granth* and the *Granth* of the 10th ascendancy, to be ever the friend of Shah Shuja and to endeavour to restore him to the throne of Kabul.'[8]

Shah Shuja then invited Ranjit Singh to come and receive the diamond in person. He arrived with a few attendants and was received in silence which was unbroken for an hour, when the Maharaja reminded his new friend and prisoner, of the object of his visit. The Shah ordered one of his servants to bring the diamond. A packet was brought in and unwrapped, and when the Maharaja saw that it was really the coveted stone, he seized it and left the house without even bidding farewell to the prince.

Sometime later, hearing that his visitors were still the possessors of some magnificent jewels, Ranjit Singh sent Bhai Ram Singh with one of his wives to search the house and even the room of the wife of Shah Shuja and bring all the valuables that were found. This was done, and it is said the lady even searched the persons of the wives and female attendants of the Shah, and everything worth carrying away was kept by the Maharaja.

The manner in which the Maharaja possessed the Kohinoor, and the mare Leili belonging to the Afghan governor of Peshawar, an animal as famous in her time as the Kohinoor itself, are excellent examples of the character of the Maharaja and his ruthless determination. The Maharaja felt very proud regaining the Kohinoor and vindicating the honour of his country.

The Kohinoor remained with the Sikh dynasty for over 36 years. The diamond at the time was set in an enameled coating at the base, with strings, to be worn as an armlet. The Maharaja wore the diamond and admired it. He then put it back in a topaz box and sent it to his *toshakhana* (treasury). He wore it on ceremonial occasions, and it was carried wherever he went, under strong guard. Just before his death on 27 June 1839, the Maharaja sent for the Kohinoor and desired that it be presented to the temple of Jagannath at Puri. He was, however, dissuaded from doing so.

After the annexation of the Punjab in 1849, the Kohinoor was usurped by the British. It now adorns their sovereign crown. It is said that in order to ease her conscience, Queen Victoria had handed over the diamond to Prince Dalip Singh, Ranjit Singh's minor son who the British dethroned and then kept under the protection of the British, asking him, the next moment, to present it to her out of gratitude for all that the British had done for him. This is the only justification for the Kohinoor remaining with the British, after India has won her independence.

The new Governors of Kashmir

There was little doubt in anyone's mind that with the Sikhs' conquest of Multan – the richest addition yet to their State – the next in line would be Kashmir, the second richest. And indeed, the very next year, the Sikh forces defeated the Afghan army led by its governor, Azim Khan, at a hard-fought battle at Supaiya (now Shopian) on 3 July 1819. Once again it was the Nihangs who decided the day, with their do-or-die charge against the Afghan horsemen and infantry. The remnants of the shattered Afghan force fled into the hills, and the Sikh forces entered Kashmir's principal city, Srinagar on 5 July 1819.

With the Afghans on the run from most of Punjab, Ranjit Singh's thoughts now turned increasingly to the North-West Frontier, the gateway to Afghanistan and Central Asia, Peshawar being the pivotal town of this wild and unruly region. But before he launched any major moves in this direction, the administration of Kashmir had to be placed on a sound footing.

Srinagar was made the capital of the Kashmir valley, and from here, the governors, appointed by the Lahore court, would administer this vast region. That a great deal had to be done in Kashmir after the years of Afghan misrule, was evident.

The first of the governors appointed to improve conditions

in the woefully-run and neglected valley, Moti Ram, was the son of Diwan Mohkam Chand, who had outmaneuvered Fateh Khan during the rescue of Shah Shuja ten years ago. He gave priority to the restoration of law-and-order and the administration of even-handed justice; he was considered an outstanding governor, compassionate, popular and by all accounts incorruptible. Kirpa Ram, son of Moti Ram, also had a reputation for honesty and good governance and did much to add to Srinagar's appeal by laying out beautiful gardens like the Rambagh Garden on the eastern side, and another, Bud Dal, on the western side of the Dal lake and the Diwan Kirpa Ram Ka Bagh.

Another outstanding governor of Kashmir under Ranjit Singh was Hari Singh Nalwa. Like Ranjit Singh, he too was born in Gujranwala and lost his father at the age of seven. His father and grandfather had fought alongside the Maharaja's, the Sukerchakia chiefs Mahan Singh and Charhat Singh. Hari Singh Nalwa had distinguished himself as a soldier time and again, at the siege of Kasur in 1807, Multan in 1810 and 1818 and Kashmir in 1819. He was a non-nonsense man, a strict disciplinarian, and considered, at times, to be too harsh. Yet, he was a spiritualist, a reformer, and a man with strong social concerns who constructed gurdwaras at Kathi, Darwaza, Srinagar, Matan and Baramula – places that had been visited by Guru Hargobind.

He did away with all restrictions that the Afghans had imposed on Kashmiri Pandits regarding worship, dress and various customs, freed Hindus who had been made to convert to Islam and conscripted to forced labour and let them return to their original religion. He encouraged the cultivation of saffron by reducing the government share in its production and enforced correct weights and measures. He accorded priority to the government's humanitarian responsibilities, especially during the famine of 1820-22, when at a time of complete economic, social and political chaos, he geared up the entire government machinery to mount a rescue operation.

Ladakh

Ranjit Singh's agenda after Kashmir included the trans-Himalayan region of Ladakh, with its borders touching Kashmir, Baltistan and Tibet. It was a 30,000 square-mile tableland in Ranjit Singh's time, at a height of 14,000 feet, surrounded by mountain ranges of 26,000 to 28,000 feet high. Its Buddhist population was of Mongolian descent, while its neighbour Baltistan, with its capital at Iskardu, was ruled by a Muslim prince, Ahmed Shah. Ranjit Singh's governor of Jammu, the Dogra Gulab Singh, also had his eyes on Ladakh. A highly ambitious man, Gulab Singh annexed Ladakh in 1834 with Ranjit Singh's consent. Since Ranjit Singh was the ruler, Gulab Singh stayed subservient to Ranjit Singh during his lifetime, but after his death the shrewd Dogra was to show his true colours.

Conquest of the Derajat Territories

Peshawar, the last major symbol of Afghan rule in northern India, was also very much on Ranjit Singh's agenda; but before that, a number of lesser foreign territories throughout the Derajat belt had to be brought under Sikh rule. These included Dera Ghazi Khan, Dera Ismail Khan, Leiah, Mankera and Bannu. While the first two and the last lie west of the river Indus, the remaining two are located east of it. This entire region north-west of the Indus, whether part of the Peshawar province or outside it, was of great importance to anyone with designs on the strategically important city of the Peshawar, which dominates the Khyber Pass through which all invaders have always entered India.

So, a year after annexing Kashmir, in 1820, Ranjit Singh personally led an expedition on Dera Ghazi Khan and got it in his bag successfully. It was a valuable acquisition since it brought Sikh forces near the route that Central Asians and Afghans had customarily taken into India on their way to its other rich regions, and nearer realisation of the Sikhs' aim of cutting it off altogether from the invaders further west.

The following year, the busy trade centre Dera Ismail Khan was annexed, and then when the key fort of Mankera fell, its Afghan governor was made a feudatory of the Sikhs. After the capture of Leiah towards the end of the same year, Ranjit Singh had the 1,650 square miles of Bannu district in his sight. Its annexation accomplished in 1825, consolidated the hold of the Sikhs on this area west of the Indus, inhabited by some of the most turbulent people who harboured a fierce hatred of Hindus and Sikhs.

Bannu was first made a tributary of the Dera Ismail Khan region before being brought under direct control of Lahore in 1836. The warrior tribes of this volatile region – Pathans, Baluchs, Sials, Awans, Saiyads, Quereshis and others – have lived by their own laws and codes of conduct for centuries, right up to the present time. In establishing his control over these formidable people, Ranjit Singh succeeded where many other colonial powers in this part of the world had often faced grave problems.

Before the prized city of Peshawar was brought under Sikh control, many more possessions of the Afghans and other regional chieftains were taken over: Kohat, Manzai, Rawalpindi, Bhera, Jhang, Kangra, Kasur, Waziristan, the land of Waziri Pathans, and a number of other lands. Finally it was the turn of Peshawar.

LEILI AND THE CAPTURE OF PESHAWAR

LOCATED ALMOST NEXT to the Khyber Pass, Peshawar was perhaps the most strategically vital city in India at that time. It had been used as the gateway into the Indian subcontinent over centuries by the Lodhis, Mughals, Durranis, Nadir Shah of Persia and many others. Its name has many variants. The Chinese pilgrim Hiuen Tsang referred to it in the seventh century of the Common Era as Po-lu-Sha-pu-lo, while the eleventh century Muslim historian Alberuni called it Peshawar and sometimes Purshur. The Mughal Emperor Babur referred to it as Parashawar, which was preferred by Akbar too, although Akbar's court historian Abu Fazl used the name Peshawar (frontier town) as well.

The original name of the city appears to have been Poshapura. It became the seat of Gandharan art and culture around the middle of the first millennium before Christ and an important fountainhead of the Buddhist faith, despite the alien environment in which it found itself. Several historians hold the view that Peshawar was a part of the Kushan Empire (first to third century CE).

Since Anang Pal's defeat at the hands of Mahmud of Ghazni in the early eleventh century, India had suffered a ceaseless incursion of invaders from the North-west. They came in unhindered hordes, indulged in pillage and arson, destroyed temples and shrines, mercilessly ransacked villages and towns, slaughtered young men and took young women as slaves. This was repeated time and again. The subcontinent had suffered a thousand year of such plunder and pillage by the time Ranjit Singh's rule began. And Afghan raiders still tried to hold hostage bits of the land of the five rivers.

It remained for Ranjit Singh to stem this tide. It was under Maharaja Ranjit Singh that a united and powerful Punjab carried the battle to the very home of the plunderers and this round occupied *their* lands. He made repeated assaults and completely demorlised the Afghan principalities. Punjabi soldiers came to be dreaded by the Afghan masses. Remembering the fearsome onslaught of Hari Singh Nalwa, Pathan mothers frightened their erring children by telling them 'Haria Rawada'. This was, perhaps, the greatest achievement of Maharaja Ranjit Singh. The Sikh soldier is respected by the valiant Pathan even today.

Ranjit Singh was, no doubt, a man of destiny but the times were also in his favour. Opportunities offered themselves and he availed himself of these unerringly. An ambitious soldier, he wanted to consolidate his power, carrying those he had already vanquished with him. As far as possible, he never made an enemy of his foe after the opponent had been defeated. He generously provided for those who lost to him in battle. More often, he allowed those he defeated to continue where they were as long as they accepted his sovereignty and agreed to pay tribute. Whenever he annexed a territory, he granted a suitable jaagir for maintenance of the deposed ruler. He never made any distinction between the Hindu and the Muslim. He was, in fact, more liberal in his dealing with the non-Sikhs. It is this that made him universally respected by the Hindu and the Muslims, the Punjabis and the non-Punjabis.

The Maharaja's conquest of Peshawar and the hill territory of Hazara – which was a difficult and lengthy operation costing him much in money, officers and troops – must be taken note of, together with the submission of the Muslim tribes of the Punjab, who were quite fond of fighting and as gallant soldiers as the Sikhs themselves. What they did not possess was the power of organisation and combination, for which the Maharaja was so conspicuous, and which enabled him to subdue separately, tribes, which united might have successfully resisted him. There was no genius leader to gather all the Muslim tribes of the region under the green flag of the Prophet and rival the Sikh monarchy of Lahore.

A few fanatics like Saiyad Ahmad Shah, at the head of heterogeneous assemblies of mountain warriors, at times gave the Maharaja's forces a lot of trouble but at the end victory rested with the strong and stubborn Sikhs, directed by the persistence of their great Maharaja, slow, and sure, and irresistible as the rising sun.

For example, the fact that Fateh Khan had not shared the spoils of Kashmir with Mohkam Chand's forces, had annoyed the Maharaja and he was looking for an opportunity to teach him a lesson. Finding Fateh Khan pre-occupied in Kashmir, he sent out a force which occupied Attock. Its governor, Jahandad Khan, was granted a jaagir and retired. Fateh Khan hastened towards Attock. The Maharaja sent troops under Fakir Aziz-ud-Din and Diwan Devi Das, followed by more troops under Diwan Mohkam Chand. The Afghans were defeated in a fierce battle fought at Haidru on 13 July 1813. Vanquished, Fateh Khan returned to Kabul, entrusting Peshawar to his brother, Yar Muhammad Khan. Attock opened the gates for Peshawar to Ranjit Singh.

Akali Phula Singh

An opportunity came his way when in August 1813, governor Fateh Khan was murdered by Prince Kamran, whose father

Mahmud had been raised and kept on the throne of Kabul for many years by Fateh Khan. Fateh Khan's numerous brothers who were spread out in different parts of Afghanistan, Peshawar and Kashmir called for vengeance and Afghanistan was plunged into civil war.

The Maharaja sent for Akali Phula Singh, who knew the North-West Frontier well, and questioned him about Attock and its environments. Phula Singh told him that Attock was like a small island in the midst of a sea of turbulent tribesmen. If the north-western bastion was to be made secure against the Afghans and Pathans, the frontier would have to be pushed farther north to Peshawar, or better, right up to the entrance of the Khyber Pass. The close alliance between the Afghans and Pathan tribesmen would then be broken, and the most important gateway into India be locked in the face of the invaders.

There was no time to lose. The strife between the Barakzai brothers (Fateh Khan's brothers) and the Mahmud branch of the Sadozais (from Kandahar-Multan areas) had begun. In their anxiety to wrest Kabul, the rival factions had left their south-eastern frontier with the Punjab practically undefended.

The Maharaja lost no time. He led out an army under his own command. On 15 October 1818, Ranjit Singh marched out of Lahore at the head of his troops. He was accompanied by two of his most able generals, who knew these lands and the people, and whose names were becoming a terror amongst the hill tribes – Hari Singh Nalwa and Akali Phula Singh.

The Durbar army passed through Rohtas, Rawalpindi, Hassan Abdal and arrived in the plains of the Hazarajat hills. A surveillance party was sent across the river Attock by boat; the rest of the army halted on the eastern bank till scouts could locate a suitable place.

This surveillance party was ambushed by Khattak tribesmen and completely destroyed. The place where the ambush took place was within the Durbar's territories and the Khattaks paid tribute to the Maharaja. Their attack was, therefore, one of treacherous rebellion. The news of the disaster infuriated Ranjit Singh. He ordered the troops to be lined up along the riverbank and after hurling a tray full of gold coins into the stream as an offering, he rode his elephant into the turbulent waters. The melodramatic gesture had the desired effect. His troops plunged their horses into the river or swam across.

The Khattaks did not put up much resistance. Their stronghold at Khairabad and Jahangirpura were occupied and the defeated chief of the Khattaks, Feroz Khan, proceeded towards Peshawar without encountering any opposition. Ranjit Singh pressed on to Naushera (the Peshawar valley).
The defeat of the Khattaks disheartened Yar Mohammad Khan, the Afghan governor of Peshawar, who fled to Kabul through the Khyber Pass, leaving fourteen big guns and other war equipment intact.

On 19 November 1818, Ranjit Singh entered the famous citadel of the Pathans. Contrary to the traditions of most of the Afghan and Pathan conquerors who had always plundered the towns and cities of North India, Ranjit Singh forbade his soldiers to lay their hands on any person or property. A proclamation was made by beat of drum assuring the citizens that they would not be molested and advising them to carry on their occupations as usual. The next morning, the Maharaja rode on his elephant through the markets of Peshawar. It was the first time in 700 years that the city saw an Indian conqueror ride through its streets.

The occupation of the city of Peshawar was a slippery win and Ranjit Singh was well aware of it. He needed a strong garrison to be maintained in the region if he wished to retain his hold over the province. The Maharaja could not afford this, for he had other priorities too. He, therefore, entrusted Jahandad

Khan of Attock with the additional charge, and receiving a nazrana of a paltry sum of 25,000 rupees from the citizens of Peshawar, Ranjit Singh returned to Lahore after four days. Yet, once again, he was welcomed home by jubilant crowds and the cannons of the fort barked out his victory.

No sooner had Ranjit Singh left Peshawar, Yar Muhammad Khan retook Peshawar, driving away Jahandad Khan. For the time being, Ranjit Singh chose to let Peshawar be, he knew he could retake it any time. Ranjit Singh now concentrated on the trans-Indus territory and subdued Mankera, Dera Ghazi Khan, Dera Ismail Khan, Bannu and Tonk that belonged to the Afghan rulers.

Meanwhile, an interesting development took place. Dost Muhammad Khan, one of the Barakzai brothers who had left Afghanistan after Fateh Khan's assassination, sent his emissaries to the Lahore Durbar, offering an annual tribute of 100,000 rupees if he was allowed to occupy Peshawar. The Maharaja accepted the offer and sent a force under Prince Kharak Singh and Misr Diwan Chand to finalise the deal.

In 1822, when the tribute form Peshawar was not received, the Maharaja deputed Fakir Aziz-ud-Din to collect it personally. Yar Muhammad Khan, who had succeeded Dost Muhammad Khan in Peshawar, was not willing to honour the commitment. In fact, Afghan people had not reconciled to the truth that Peshawar had become a permanent tributary of the Sikhs and therefore, the Afghans had raised the war cry. The Afridis, the Yusufzais, the Khalbaks and the tribals from Swat and Bannu got together along with the *ghazis* and *mujahids* and launched what they called a holy war against infidels, virtually a *jihad.*

A fierce fight took place in which around 2,000 soldiers of Ranjit Singh's army, including Akali Phula Singh, the renowned warrior, perished. But Naushera (the valley) was in his hands. This marked the complete annihilation of the Afghan power.

The Maharaja's forces marched into Peshawar. With a view to teaching the people a lesson, the city this time was given to plunder and sacked. However, the Maharaja had still not made up his mind to annex Peshawar. He would be content to have it as his tributary. He appointed Yar Muhammad Khan as its governor again. The province was divided into five districts to secure better administration.

As a mark of respect to the memory of Akali Phula Singh, Maharaja Ranjit Singh had a *Samadhi* built at Naushera on the banks of the Kabul river, which continues to be a place of pilgrimage for devout Sikhs in the subcontinent.

The permanent Sikh occupation of Peshawar, however, was still years away. It wasn't until 1834 that the Sikhs brought it directly under the control of the Lahore Durbar. In the intervening years, the Afghan rulers made repeated attempts to re-establish Kabul's suzerainty over Peshawar, but Ranjit Singh always foiled them.

Hari Singh Nalwa

In 1834, feeling it was time to take direct charge of Peshawar, the Maharaja chose an able and trusted man to annex it. The chosen man was Hari Singh Nalwa, who has been called 'The Murat of the Khalsa' after Nepoleon's brother-in-law, Joachim Murat – an outstanding marshal of the French army. With a force of 9,000 men, Hari Singh crossed the Indus and took up an unexpected position to the west of Peshawar. His moves unnerved the Barakzai Sardars, who fled and left the city to the Sikhs. In 1835, the Afghans under Dost Muhammad made an unsuccessful attempt to retake Peshawar, but it remained a part of the Sikh kingdom, with Hari Singh Nalwa in charge of it, with a force of 10,000 men.

Nalwa, like Murat, was known as a general's general, and lived up to his reputation. He soon initiated a project to build a fort at Jamrud, which dominates the entrance to the Khyber Pass. Within a year of its construction in 1836, the resentful Kabul regime, furious at the audacity of the Sikhs building a fort in their territory, overlooking the traditional route they had taken into India for centuries, mounted an attack against it with a large force. They opened up with their guns to the walls of the fort and were about to begin an assault when Hari Singh, who had held back until the enemy advanced, suddenly fell upon them with his customary vigour, broke their rank without much loss and put them to flight.[1]

Soon, however, with the arrival of Afghan reinforcements, the ebb and flow of the battle resumed with intensity. The outcome was, however, in favour of the Sikhs, but at a terrible cost – the death of Hari Singh Nalwa. Badly wounded, this great warrior died the same night. His contribution to upholding the valour of the Khalsa is reflected to this day in the inscription still to be seen on the inner gateway of the Bala Hisar or the High Fort of Peshawar: 'Victory of Purakh (the Supreme Being). Through the Grace of Sri Akal.'

Love for Horses and the horse Leili

Ranjit Singh's passion for horses was immeasurable, almost to insanity. He is said to have had 12,000 horses in the royal stables of which 1,000 horses were exclusively for his use. He could ride for hours without feeling fatigued. Even when he was stricken with paralysis, he would, somehow, heave himself up on horseback. Once in the saddle, he was his usual self. He felt fit and completely at peace with himself. When something upset or annoyed him, he would go out riding and thereby regain his composure. Two horses were always kept ready for him, so that he could ride out any moment he fancied. His thinking was most active when he was on horseback. He enjoyed talking about his horses with his guests and visitors, and took them out riding.

He gave his horses poetic names such as Naseem, Ruhe, Gauharbar and Sufaid Pari. Out for a ride or on hunting expedition, he would sometimes feed the horse in his service with his own hands. He was never fond of wearing jewellery on his person but he would attire his favourite horses with belts of diamonds.

Once Ranjit Singh learnt about a rare horse, he left no stone unturned to possess it. It is said that no horse in the royal stables had been purchased for less than 20,000 rupees. The Maharaja's friends and admirers were aware of his weakness for horses of good breed. The English presented him with Scottish horses. The Nizam of Hyderabad sent him a large number of Arab horses. The hill tribes sent him pedigree ponies with a view to securing Ranjit Singh's goodwill and favour. If Ranjit Singh heard of a horse of particular beauty or grace, he had to have it, no matter what the cost. He would willingly spend the equivalent of £30, 000 or more for one that caught his fancy.

The Maharaja's love of horses led him to undertake military expeditions as well. The earliest victim of this passion was the Nawab of Jhang who was said to have celebrated horses in his stable. Ranjit Singh sent him word, asking for the gift of some of these. The Nawab refused. Ranjit Singh attacked the Nawab who fled with the prized horses, which he subsequently returned and presented them to the Maharaja.

When negotiating with Shuja-ul-Mula (Shah Shuja), one of the terms Ranjit Singh had stipulated was that in the event of regaining Afghanistan, he would present the Lahore Durbar with 101 horses every year.

Ranjit Singh's most favourite hobby even as a youth was horse-riding and hunting. His stamina as a rider was amazing. At times, he would be on horseback for 24 hours at a stretch, and still not be tired. When he heard about Sardar Hari Singh Nalwa's death, he mounted a horse and left for Peshawar, covering the entire distance from Lahore to the Jhelum in one day. It is, therefore, not difficult to imagine how keen the Maharaja was to take possession of Leili. It was in the 1820s that Ranjit Singh had been captivated by stories of a horse called Leili (or Leila, as in the ballad). Leili's reputation had spread throughout Persia and Afghanistan.

War for Leili

The owner of Leili was Yar Muhammad Khan Barakzai, the governor of Peshawar, who in spite of the Maharaja's persistent request was not willing to part with Leili. Therefore, the infuriated Maharaja in 1826, sent Sardar Budh Singh Sidhanwalia, one of the best Sikh generals, to Peshawar to take possession of the mare Leili. Budh Singh was also tasked to attack Khalifa Saiyad Ahmad, who was preaching a jihad against the Sikhs in the Peshawar hills.

Budh Singh defeated the enemy, with great loss on both sides, but when he reached Peshawar, he was informed that Leili had died. On his return to Lahore it was ascertained that this story was false.

Another force, under the command of Prince Kharak Singh, was despatched to Peshawar with orders to either buy the horse or seize it, and if Yar Muhammad would not part with it, then to depose him from governorship. The prince marched to Peshawar and Yar Muhammad, who considered that his honour was involved in not surrendering the horse, fled to the hills. Prince Kharak Singh, after holding Peshawar for eight months, retired, leaving Sardar Sultan Muhammad Khan as governor. But the Sikh army had not proceeded further than Attock when Yar Muhammad returned and drove out the new governor.

General Ventura, who had been left in command of the Sikh army at Attock, was now directed by the Maharaja to try his hand at the business of acquiring this horse, for which he was to offer any price which would be accepted, but if refused, was to renew hostilities. While Yar Muhammad was still hesitating to part with the horse, Saiyad Ahmad again descended from the hills, ravaged the villages north of Peshawar and Yar Muhammad who attempted to drive Saiyad Ahmad back, was killed.

Leili, however, had not been surrendered, and General Ventura, after having defeated Saiyad Ahmad, camped at Peshawar and demanded the animal from Sultan Muhammad Khan, who he promised to confirm as the governor if he gave up the horse. But Sultan Muhammad was also evasive like Yar Muhammad Khan, till Ventura had him arrested and confined to his own palace and threatened to hold him a prisoner until Leili was handed over to him. Finally Sultan Muhammad succumbed to the pressure and thus, General Ventura became the owner of the coveted horse, which he took to Lahore where it was received with much rejoicing by the Maharaja.

Baron Hügel claims to have been told by the Maharaja himself that it (Leili) cost him 60,00,000 rupees and 12,000 soldiers – such was the Maharaja's desire for this horse.[2]

Leili was, indeed, a rare beauty. It is said that when Leili arrived at Lahore, the Maharaja's happiness knew no bounds. There was jubilation throughout the capital. The Maharaja would, at times, decorate Leili with the Kohinoor. Qadir Yar, an eminent contemporary poet, wrote a poem on Leili. He was richly rewarded by the Maharaja. It is not known whether it was a horse or mare. While the name Leili indicates that it belonged to the fair sex, the rest of the description proves otherwise. 'The more I see Leili, the more remarkable and intelligent he seems to me', the Maharaja told W G Osborne.[3] Leili, the legendary sweetheart of the ballad's Majnu, was black in colour but Maharaja Ranjit Singh's Leili was dark grey.

The Maharaja's long-cherished ambition had been fulfilled

and it is said that the jewels and ornaments brought out to decorate Leili were worth several lakh of rupees. Its bridle and saddle were laid with diamonds and rubies. There were rings around its neck which were studded with precious stones.

Leili had its finest hour when at Ropar, during his meeting with William Bentinck in 1838, Ranjit Singh performed great feats of skill on the horse. He picked up with the point of a spear a brass pot five times, riding at breakneck speed. As the spectators marvelled, the Maharaja walked up to Leili and kissed it on the mouth.

When Leili died the Maharaja shed bitter tears. A 21-gun salute was fired at the time of its burial.

CONQUEST OF MULTAN

ONE OF THE MOST important achievements of Maharaja Ranjit Singh was the taming of the plundering and cruel tribes in the North and border districts of the subcontinent and the acquisition of Multan. The province of Multan was a rich and fertile land with a network of irrigation canals. It produced wheat and cotton as its major crops. The town of Multan was situated on the trade route to Sind, Afghanistan and Central India. It had a flourishing market.

The ancient city and district of Multan were ruled by an Afghan family, who were appointed Nawabs by the Mughals in 1738, at the time of Nadir Shah's invasion, when the Mughals were anxious to strengthen their outlying provinces by a system of decentralisation, as they were too weak to control these. Between 1771 and 1779, the city was held, with some intervals, by the Bhangi Sardars. But they were finally ousted by king Timur (Ahmad Shah Abdali's son) and Muzaffar Khan was appointed its governor. He was a brave and energetic man and held his own against both – the Sikhs and the neighbouring tribes, Sials and others, who attacked him.

In 1802, Muzaffar Khan first saw the young Sikh chief, Ranjit Singh, who had marched from Lahore to spy out the land. The Nawab came out to meet him, thirty miles from the city and interchanged valuable presents. Again, in 1806, after having reduced Jhang, Ranjit Singh marched towards Multan and reached there, twenty miles north of the city, when the Nawab, who had no wish to fight, gave him Rs 70,000 to retire. The next year, his appetite stimulated by what he had so easily won, the Maharaja returned and attacked Multan with full force. The town was captured in part, but the fort held out against all the Sikh efforts. However, an agreement was concluded through Sardar Fateh Singh Kalianwala, by which the Maharaja retired on receiving a large sum of money.

Nawab Muzaffar Khan, now old and weary of war, made a pilgrimage to Mecca, and on his return vainly tried to induce the English to take him under their protection. But the British declined as Multan was remote and beyond the sphere of their then desire to influence global imperialisms.

Nawab Muzaffar Khan of Multan had, in 1803, repulsed an attack from the Afghan, Shah Shuja's, troops and in the hope of conciliating him, had more than once offered him an asylum at Multan, but Shah Shuja had wished to obtain the city and province as his own by conquest. Ranjit Singh treated the weak-minded Shuja with great respect, but failing to obtain any money from him, determined to take Multan on his own account. When Ranjit Singh met the Afghan Shah Shuja at Khushab, the exiled monarch wished the Sikhs to 'capture Multan and make the city over to him'. On 24 February 1810, Ranjit Singh arrived before the walls of Multan.

For some time, the fort was bombarded without effect; mining was then resorted to; but the Afghans repulsed the Sikh attack with success, and blew up the battery of Attar Singh Dhare, killing him and twelve of his men. On the 21st of March, a general assault was ordered, but the Sikhs were repulsed with great loss, and they now grew disheartened, for provisions had become very dear in the camp. Diwan Mohkam

Chand, their general, was seriously ill, and several leaders had been slain. However, on the 25 March again, another assault was made with the same result. It was necessary to lift the siege, and Ranjit Singh had to accept from Muzaffar Khan the terms which he had many times rejected, namely, two and a half lakh of rupees, twenty war horses, and a contingent in time of war. Having received Rs 30,000 in earnest of the ransom, the Maharaja retired from Multan on the 14 April 1810.

According to David Ochterlony, who visited Lahore when Prince Kharak Singh got married, the Maharaja took his failure at Multan very much to heart. He was determined to overpower the Nawab. It is claimed that the Maharaja even sought British assistance to defeat Multan but the East India Company declined to oblige. They would much rather keep out of the trouble. The time was yet not ripe for Fort William to meddle in Ranjit Singh's affairs.[1]

Muzaffar Khan

In February 1816, the Sikhs launched an irregular attack on Multan. A strong force had been sent to Bahawalpur and Multan to collect tributes, and there being some delay in Muzaffar Khan's payment, Akali Phula Singh, mad and bhang (cannabis) induced, led a storming party of fanatics like himself against the town. With such intensity did they attack that they gained possession of some of the outworks of the citadel. Fakir Aziz-ud-Din duely apologised and the Nawab paid his tribute quicker than he would otherwise have done. The Sikh army then proceeded towards Mankera.[2]

The year 1817 witnessed one more attempt by Lahore to capture Multan. This also remained infructuous. The Maharaja realised that if he wished to subdue Nawab Muzaffar Khan, he would need to make military preparations of a better order. In 1817, again, a Sikh army under Diwan Mohkam

Chand marched against Multan and attacked the fort but was repulsed, and retired on payment of ten thousand rupees. These attempts, however, were not made in a determined fashion. The Maharaja was collecting his strength for a greater effort and had sworn that Multan, which had so often defied him, should yet be his.

Thus, Ranjit Singh had made four attempts to take this city, but had only succeeded in capturing the town outside the fort. The enormous mud and brick Multan fort which rose in the middle like a mountain had defeated him every time. Without the fort, possession of the city did not amount to very much.

Early in 1818, the Durbar resolved to put whatever it had into capturing Multan. The chain of small Muslim States around the city had already been broken. All that remained was Multan itself. The decision was obviously influenced by the pre-occupation of the Afghans with the Persians on their western front. An indecisive engagement was reported to have been fought at Khorasan; Wazir Fateh Khan was reported to have been injured and likely to remain out of action for some time.

A force of 20,000 men under Misr Diwan Chand was dispatched to Multan. To avoid bickering between the Sardars who looked upon Diwan Chand as an upstart, Prince Kharak Singh was made nominal commander of the army. Artillery, which had to play a major role in reducing the fort, was under the command of Ilahi Baksh.

Preparations were made on an elaborate scale. All the boats on the Sutlej and the Ravi were commandeered to ensure a regular supply of provisions. Depots were opened along the route. The overall charge of maintaining a free flow of war material and food grains was given to Kharak Singh's mother, Mai Nakkain, who set up her headquarters at Kamalia. The big Bhangi gun Zamzama was ordered down to Multan. So also, were platoons of Nihangs.

The Maharaja stayed on at Lahore. A dispatch rider was posted at every third mile between the capital and the army camp at Multan so that the Maharaja could obtain the latest information and be able to transmit orders.

Nawab Muzaffar Khan was aware of these large-scale preparations and realised that this time, he would not be able to bribe or buy off the Durbar. He roused the sentiments of the populace of the countryside to fight a 'holy war' and prepared the city and the fort for a long siege.

Nawab Muzffar Khan had planned to defend himself in three stages: in the countryside, in the city and in the fort. The first engagement was in the open where he let his Ghazis do most of the fighting. This battle lasted for only one day and the Ghazis gained the martyrdom they sought: they were equipped with swords and spears and had to contend with a disciplined army equipped with muskets and field batteries. Muzaffar Khan, by now a veteran of many battles, withdrew his regulars behind the city walls, as he had planned. The second round began with the Lahore troops surrounding the city and bombarding the walls. The defenders held them at bay for a couple of weeks till the city was blown up at several points. The defenders retreated into the fort to fight the third and last round.

Multan fort was surrounded by a large, deep moat. Although at that time of the year (March) there was no water in the canal, it prevented cannons from being brought close enough to do any serious damage to the walls and it seriously impeded the laying of mines under the battlements. For a whole month, Ilahi Baksh's batteries pounded the mud-and-brick structure without making any impression. March turned to April and the heat became unbearable. Ranjit Singh's messages became angrier. He told Diwan Chand how much money the state had put into the venture and what a disgrace it would be if they did not succeed. Diwan Chand also knew that if he did not capture the fort before the monsoons, he would never do it, for then the canal would be filled with water.

Ilahi Baksh redoubled his efforts and subjected the fort to intensive bombardment. The 80-pounder Bhangi cannon, the Zamzama, arrived in April which fired solid metal balls, hurtling them into the wall and tore huge holes in it. A spy sent out by Muzaffar Khan witnessed the enthusiasm with which the Sikh gunners under Ilahi Baksh fought. When a cannon lost one of its wheels and could not be properly fired without support, soldiers wrangled amongst each other for the privilege of having it rest on their shoulders. Many were killed with the jerk of the gun. The defenders' energies were concentrated on blocking the damage done by the cannon when a party of Nihangs stole down the canal under cover of darkness and laid a mine under another portion of the wall. Next morning, a huge segment of the battlement was blown sky high.

Muzaffar Khan had had enough of fighting and sent his envoy to Ranjit Singh to discuss terms of his surrender. He was offered Shujabad, Khangarh and a big jaagir if he gave up the fort. Muzaffar Khan accepted the terms and asked for a treaty to be drawn up. The news of Muzaffar Khan's acceptance of the terms offered made Ranjit Singh delirious with joy. Cannons were fired to celebrate the victory and Lahore was illuminated at night. But, when the draft treaty was presented to Muzaffar Khan in Multan, he was dissuaded from signing it. 'It is better to die in honour than to live in shame', said his soldiers. 'We will fight the Sikhs to the finish', they avered.[3]

Angry at this turn of events, the Maharaja ordered resumption of the fierce bombardment of the artillery and his cannons blew up the bags of earth which had been hurriedly placed to repair the breaches. The Nihangs came to the fore again. On 2 June, an Akali by name Sadhu Singh, determined to surpass what Phula Singh had done in 1816, rushed to an outwork of the fort with a few desperate followers, and captured this battlement. The Sikh forces, seeing this success, began an assault at the Khizri Gate. Here the Nawab Muzaffar Khan, with his eight sons and all that remained of his garrison, stood, sword in hand, resolved to fight to the death.

The grey-bearded Nawab and five of his sons fell fighting. The sixth son was gravely injured and the remaining two surrendered and were given protection. Few in the garrison escaped with their lives. The whole city was given up to plunder. The fort of Shujabad was also reduced and five guns taken from it. After this the walls of Multan were repaired, a garrison of six hundred men was placed in the fort and the Sikh army returned to Lahore.

The news of Muzaffar Khan's death reached Lahore three days later. This time, nothing could contain the Maharaja's joy. He gave the messenger who brought the news of the victory a pair of gold bracelets and rode out on the back of his elephant to shower his people with gold and silver. Misr Diwan Chand was honoured with the title of *Zafar Jang Bahadur* – Brave Victor of Battles.

It is said that after the surrender of the fort, the town of Multan, which the Sikh soldiers had seized after years of continuous fighting, was plundered mercilessly. However, when the Maharaja came to know of this, he stopped it immediately. He gave stern orders to his men to surrender whatever they had plundered and desist from any further pillage. A few days later, one of Muzaffar Khan's sons was brought into court. The Maharaja heard of the valour of the old Nawab and since he admired bravery above all manly virtues, he got up from his seat and took the young Nawab in his arms. Five days later, Misr Diwan Chand arrived in Lahore with the second of Nawab Muzaffar's captive sons. The Maharaja embraced the boy and made him sit beside him.[4]

The surrender of Multan in 1818 was an important landmark in Maharaja Ranjit Singh's career as a conqueror. Multan brought to his kingdom a territory with an annual revenue of 700,000 rupees and a town strategically situated on a flourishing trade route. The most important feature of this victory was that it established Ranjit Singh's superiority over the Afghans who had overawed and overrun the land of the five rivers for centuries.

The Maharaja appointed Diwan Swan Mal as the governor of Multan. He proved an efficient and a benevolent administrator. His tenure lasted for 25 years.

Three weeks after the victory at Multan came the Muslim festival of *Idul Fitr*. The Maharaja thought it the best occasion to pay homage to the memory of his faithful servant Mian Ghausa, who was also father of the Durbar artillery to which Ranjit Singh owed many of his victories, including that of Multan. He also went to the mausoleum of Shah Abdul Maali and spent some time in silent prayer amongst his Muslim subjects.

Multan's population in 1827 was about 40,000 with 8,000 houses. In 1831, its population rose to 60,000, 30 per cent Hindus and the rest Muslims. It had 500 soldiers in the Sikh garrison. According to the court artist, Godfrey Vigne: 'The Hindu was to be distinguished by his caste mark on his forehead, his rose colour turban and red flowing trousers. The Multan Mussalman usually wore white dress of the same kind of pattern. The Sikh, generally was recognised by his sword, matchlocks and accessories, his scanty turban and his earrings.'[5]

With the conquest of Multan, finally, Ranjit Singh was in a position to stop the Afghan invasions of the subcontinent year after year.

AFGHAN INVASIONS AND THE PUNJAB

THE BIGGEST MENACE to a free and powerful Punjab were the Afghans who, ever since Abdali's conquest, had looked upon most of northern India as a part of their empire. Abdali's attempts to treat it as such had been frustrated largely by the Sikhs. Although his son and successor, Timur, kept up pretensions to northern India, the best he could do was to retain his hold on Kashmir and eject the Bhangis from Multan. Timur's son, Shah Zaman, was the most ambitious and as soon as he took his father's place, he announced his intention of re-establishing the Afghan empire in India. Fortunately for the Punjab, all that Abdali's progeny had inherited from him were dreams.

Ranjit Singh's first brush with Zaman Shah's army occurred when he invaded India for the second time in 1795; the first had been in 1793. In December 1795, Zaman Shah headed for Hasan Abdal, which as *Panja Sahib*, holds sacred memories for the Sikhs since Guru Nanak had visited the place in the late fifteenth century. While Zaman Shah remained entrenched at Hasan Abdal, his general, Ahmad Khan Shahanchibashi, marched from Attock on the Indus river, some 200 miles to the town of Rohtas, which belonged to Ranjit Singh.

To confuse Zaman and draw his force away from its base in Hasan Abdal, Ranjit Singh withdrew his men from Rohtas to

Pind Dadan Khan, in the salt ranges. When the Afghans attacked Ranjit Singh, he crossed the Jhelum river, reassembled on its southern bank, and sent his messengers to the regional Maratha chief, Daulat Rao Scindia, at Aligarh in Uttar Pradesh, inviting him to join the Sikhs and expel the Afghan invader. There was, however, no response from the Maratha chief. But, as fate would have it, Zaman Shah had to return home to prevent an invasion of his own country from the Persians. As soon as his back was turned, Ranjit Singh expelled the Afghans from Rohtas. But Zaman's ambition continued to overrun the Sikh lands.

Zaman counted on the Rajput prince, Sansar Chand of Kangra. Whether Sansar Chand would favour the Afghan's plans was doubtful, as he too had visions of extending his kingdom from the mountainous regions to the plains. He had already taken areas adjacent to his domains from the Sikh chiefs and discovered that their disunity made them an easy target. At about the time when Ranjit Singh came into his own, Sansar Chand was busy planning a conquest of the Punjab.

Meanwhile, a people hitherto only known as a warrior race had become a formidable power in the eastern Himalayas. These were the Gurkhas under a very formidable leader, Amar Singh Thapa. They had begun to move westward, along the mountain ranges until they came face-to-face with Sansar Chand. The choice for the Gurkhas and Rajputs lay between fighting each other, or joining hands to take the Punjab and share the spoils. Disunity amongst the Punjabis made the latter alternative more feasible.

At that time, there were just two great eastern powers in India – that is the Marathas and the English. The Marathas had extended their arms across the sub-continent. They had suffered a severe defeat at the hands of the Afghans on the field of Panipat in 1761, but it did not take them long to recover from the blow. Within a few years, they again took Agra, reduced the Mughal emperor at Delhi to subservience and re-entered southern Punjab. Their soldiers were better disciplined than the Sikhs and they were led by more experienced commanders. In the north, they had French generals De Boigne, Cuillier-Perron and Bourquin to direct their conquests. Meerut had become the centre of the French generals and they were full of enthusiasm to defeat the British and extend the Maratha empire to all corners of India, right across the Punjab to the Khyber Pass. However, with the Maratha Princes quarrelling amongst each other, it was too much to hope that the whole country would fall in their lap.

The English were less conspicuous but potentially more formidable than the Marathas. Ostensibly, their only interest in the region was to protect the Nawab Wazir Ali Khan of Awadh, whose territories extended up to the river Ganges. The English were the most far-sighted of all the external forces threatening the Punjab. They had agents in the big cities of India, Sindh, Persia and Afghanistan, and were fully informed of what was going on.

Many years earlier they had sensed the danger to themselves of a Sikh-Maratha alliance. Even then, they, more than anyone else, had realised that Zaman Shah's aggressive designs spelt danger to the whole of India and had shrewdly guessed that the people who could be counted on to put up an effective resistance to the Afghans were not the Marathas or the Rajputs, or the Gurkhas but the Sikhs. They also figured out that the one man who could organise the Sikhs was the unknown lad in his teens, Ranjit Singh. The English strategy displayed the political genius of their race. Through their agents they urged the Sardars to unite under Ranjit Singh – the English were willing, even eager, to fight the Afghans as much as the last Sikh.

Zaman Shah was back again by October 1796, for the third time, camping in Peshawar for a month. Ranjit Singh's rapid manoeuvres once again had the Afghans baffled. He established himself with a force of 10,000 men across the Jhelum, not far from Peshawar, then moved to Pind Dadan Khan, then on to Miani, then suddenly crossed the Jhelum for a surprise attack on Zaman Shah at Pind Dadan Khan before re-crossing the river once again. At this point Zaman Shah addressed a letter to Ranjit Singh, asking him to desist from opposing him. Ranjit Singh's powerful reply was: 'Through the grace of the Guru, every Sikh is bound to be victorious.'[1] He was just 16 years old.

Still on his third invasion, Zaman Shah entered Lahore in January 1797 with a formidable force. Lahore had been officially made an Afghan province in 1752, after the Abdalis had wrested it from the Mughals. Zaman Shah didn't want to waste time in Lahore, because he was keen to reach Amritsar and settle the Sikh problem once for all. Ranjit Singh could barely wait to take him on. When a detachment of the Afghan army first went on the offensive and attacked Amritsar on 11 January 1797, it suffered a humiliating defeat with much loss of blood. A furious Zaman Shah, beside himself with rage, now took personal command and arrived in Amritsar the next day. He too was not only vanquished but was chased all the way to the gates of Lahore by the Sikh army.

To make certain that the Afghan forces would never again set foot in India, Ranjit Singh invited Sahib Singh to join him in expelling the invader. Sahib Singh was the chief of the Phulkian misl, whose great grandfather, Ala Singh, had been made Raja of Patiala by Ahmed Shah Abdali during a previous invasion of India in 1763. This was the same Abdali, who, a year before, had blown the Harmandir Sahib apart, filled the sacred pool with human bodies and carcasses of cows, killed thousands of pilgrims and made a pyramid of Sikh heads on the site. Not surprisingly, Ranjit Singh received no reply from Sahib Singh. Most of what the Patiala family owned had been acquired through Abdali's generosity.

Punjab Plundered by Afghans

Going back to the history of the plunder of Punjab by the Afghans at a time when the Sikhs accounted for only 7 per cent of the population of Punjab, as against 50 per cent Muslims and 42 per cent Hindus (these figures are extrapolated from the census figures for 1881).[2] Before attaining their golden period, they had to face huge and continuing adversity. To start with, Zakariya Khan, a jaagirdar near Amritsar, had taken the scholar Bhai Mani Singh, a close companion of Guru Gobind Singh, into his custody and cut to pieces without purpose or provocation. He then laid siege to Amritsar, plundered the Harmandir Sahib, filled the pool with slaughtered flesh, animal and human and threw revered Sikh relics into the pool.

When Zakariya Khan had died in 1745, his son Shah Nawaz Khan succeeded him as governor of Lahore. This man was a greater sadist and Nawaz Khan's favourite past-time had been to watch the bellies of captive Sikhs being ripped open and iron pegs stuck into their heads. On 10 March 1746, the first of the two *ghalughara* (disasters) took place: a large body of Mughal troops under Yahiya Khan massacred 7,000 Sikhs, while an additional force was captured and taken to Lahore for public execution. This came to be known as the *Chhota* (small) *ghalughara.* The *Wada ghalughara* or great disaster took place in February 1762, this time at the hands of the Afghan invader Ahmad Shah Abdali.

The sixteen years between the two ghalugharas saw extensive bloodshed in Punjab, with the forces of the Khalsa continually set upon by one or another of their three principal enemies. While Nadir Shah of Persia, in repeated incursions into the subcontinent in the 1730s, played havoc with the seat of the Mughal empire at Delhi, he dealt more sagaciously with the Sikhs. Despite the fact that they plundered the loot he was returning with, he was perceptive enough to avoid armed conflict with people whose homes were their saddles.

Ahmad Shah Abdali of Afghanistan invaded India eight times between 1748 and 1768. He declared Punjab to be a new territory of a new Afghanistan, after defeating the Mughal governor of Lahore. Thus, the Sikhs became the sole target of both the Mughals and Abdali. However, the Khalsa was determined to take on both adversaries.

The Sikh stand was anathema to Abdali. The last straw came when, in 1757, the Sikhs waylaid Abdali's baggage train full of the wealth he had plundered from Delhi, Mathura and Vrindavan. The Sikhs also rescued hundreds of captive Hindu girls and returned them to their homes. This was especially more humiliating for the Afghans. An outraged Abdali now told his son, Timur Shah, the governor of Lahore to eliminated the accursed infidels and their Golden Temple, once and for all.

Attacks and counter attacks between Sikhs and their prosecutors formed a continuing dance of death on the landscape of the Punjab, culminating in the Wada ghalughara on 5 February 1762. In a surprise attack on a large assembly of Sikhs, at Kup near Srihind, Abdali's army, having covered 110 miles in two days, massacred 10,000 to 30,000 Sikhs. In the ferocious fighting, the odds were heavily stacked against the Sikhs.

Abdali now headed for the Golden Temple and struck on 10 April 1762, at a time when thousands had gathered there for the Baisakhi celebrations, which included the most sacred ritual of all – a dip in the holy pool. The blood bath was horrific. The Harmandir was blown apart with gun powder. The pool was filled with the debris of destroyed buildings, mutilated human bodies, carcasses of cows and much else. Topping it all, a pyramid of Sikh heads was created. However, within a few months, early in 1763, Charhat Singh, the head of Sukerchakia misl – whose grandson Ranjit Singh was to be born one and half decades later – managed to wrest back control of the Golden Temple.

The very next year, however, Abdali was back in India – and once more attacked the Sikh shrine. Defending the shrine, 30 Sikhs died, and the shrine was once again demolished. No wonder, the Sikhs were determined to stop the Afghans and Mughals from setting foot in the Punjab. To drive home this point to their adversaries, the Sikhs in a swift military action, not only annexed Lahore on 16 April 1765, but also declared their sovereignty over the whole of Punjab. To make absolutely clear that political power in the region now rested with them, they struck coins and declared Lahore the mint city, *Dar-ul-Sultanate* (Seat of Sikh Power).

Thus, Ranjit Singh's kingdom was already in the making, even before he was born. To rule from Lahore was his destiny.

Unfulfilled Afghan Ambitions

Coming back to Abdali's grandson Zaman Shah's misadventure, his defeat at the gates of Amritsar in 1797 had put a stamp of humiliation on the Afghan's mind. After this defeat, Zaman Shah left Lahore for Peshawar, en route Afghanistan. With India still very much on his mind, Zaman launched his last invasion in September 1798, eager to drive out the Sikhs from Punjab and put a decisive end to Ranjit Singh's rising power.

The various battles and skirmishes that took place during this visit took him no further towards ending Sikh power, and when he received news from Afghanistan of serious threat to his throne in Kabul, he hastened back to his capital. Taking advantage of his absence, the Persians had invaded Khorasan in Afghanistan and were making their way to Kabul.

In this hasty departure, Zaman lost 12 of his prized cannons in the Jhelum river, which was in spate. The loss of these crucial guns, in fact, proved a turning point in his relationship with Ranjit Singh who, on receiving an urgent appeal for his help in recovering the guns, magnanimously complied. Zaman Shah then assured Ranjit Singh that he would not oppose Ranjit's taking over of Lahore. Days went by and there seemed no possibility of the Afghans breaking through the Sikh barricade and proceeding towards Delhi. Zaman Shah exhorted his Afghans, but so great was their terror of Ranjit Singh and his Sikhs that they would not come out of their barracks after night fall. Zaman Shah gave up talk of holy war and exterminating the Sikhs. He sent his agent to Amritsar assuring the Sikh chiefs that their possession would not be disturbed and asking them what they wanted. The first reply was unanimous; they wanted nothing but that the Afghans should return to their own country and leave them in peace in their own land.

Time was against Zaman Shah. His brother Mahmud was again stirring up trouble in Afghanistan. His soldiers had not been paid for many months and were clamoring for permission to loot the Punjabi cities. When Zaman Shah refused, they told him bluntly that they would not fight any more. The Shah was compelled to give up his plans of conquest and ordered his troops back to Kabul. Before leaving, he proclaimed that as soon as he had settled matters with his brother Mahmud, he would return to conquer India.

Zaman Shah indeed came back to the Punjab twelve years later, but not as conqueror. His brother Mahmud had captured and blinded him, and he turned his sightless eyes towards the Punjab, tapping his way with his cane, to beg asylum from Ranjit Singh.

A SENSUALIST

NO MATTER WHAT others thought of him, Ranjit Singh lived his life in just the way he wanted to. He compromised neither in his drinking nor in his sexual appetite. He indulged in them to the fullest – but never at the cost of his commitment to the nation that he had founded. He did not permit his driving passion and goal – to create a strong Sikh state – to be compromised by anything in his personal life, and any judgement of him needs to take this aspect into account.

On the subject of Ranjit Singh's personal life, Fakir Syed Waheeduddin has this to say: '… he was susceptible to feminine influence, but as a man and not as a ruler… there was little of debauchery in the way he used to spend his time in the company of his singing and dancing girls. He loved singing and dancing for their own sake and took a connoisseur's interest in them. The performances, therefore, used to be displays of art and not the *orgies of dissipation* which some people have imagined them to be.… Being fond of *repartee* and *badinage*, he would now and again engage in a wordy duel with some particularly vivacious girl; and usually such a one served as his cupbearer. There was, however, never any coarseness or vulgarity in the process. The singing and dancing *soirees*, thus, used be quite sober and dignified affairs.'[1]

The Maharaja was a hard drinker, and it was his indulgence in ambrosia which killed him, as it has killed a large number of Indian princes. The Maharaja's favourite was a fierce potion distilled from corn – a brandy mixed with the juice of meat, opium, musk and various herbs. Of this he drank large quantities in the evening and at night. Most of his courtiers, with exception of the Fakirs, were ready to please him by joining in his drinking bouts and indeed were habitually as drunken as himself. But with all this hard drinking, which was the custom in his time and should not be regarded as anything unusual, the Maharaja was always fit for business at the proper and assigned time.[2]

Every foreign visitor to his court was struck by his intelligence, eager curiosity, and general information, and there was nothing of which he was fonder than to discuss the manners and constitutions of other countries and to hear about the armies and campaigns of Europe. His manners to strangers were particularly pleasing and courteous, and many accounts by travellers to his kingdom survive, from those who visited Lahore during the latter years of his reign, which attest to the fascination he exercised over those in immediate contact with him.

Ranjit Singh's drinking parties were much talked about events, and one day he invited W G Osborne, Military Secretary to the Earl of Auckland, then Governor-General of India, to one of them. Osborne quotes him as saying: 'You have never been to one of my drinking parties, it is bad work drinking, now the weather is so hot; but as soon as we have a good rainy day, we will have one.'

Osborne in turn recorded his views: 'I sincerely trust it will not rain at all during our stay, for, from all accounts, nothing can be such a nuisance as one of these parties. His wine is extracted from dried fruit, with a quantity of pearls ground to powder, and mixed with it, for no other reason (that I can hear) than to add to the expense of it. It is made for himself alone, and though he sometimes gives a few bottles to some of his favourite chiefs, it is very difficult to be procured, even at the enormous price of one gold mohur for a small bottle. It is as strong as *aquaforties* (nitric acid) and as such, at his parties he always helps you himself, it is no easy matter to avoid excess.'

Talking about the snacks at these parties, Osborne writes: '.... The only food allowed you at these drinking bouts are fat quails stuffed with all sorts of spices, and the only thing to allay your thirst, naturally consequent upon eating such heating food, is this abominable liquid fire.' Mentioning Ranjit Singh's opinion about other wines, Osborne states: 'Ranjit himself laughs at our wines, and says he drinks for excitement, and that the sooner that object is attained the better.'

'During these parties, he generally orders the attendance of all his dancing girls, whom he forces to drink his wine, and when he thinks them sufficiently excited, uses all his power to set them by the ears, the result of which is a general action, in the course of which they tear one another almost to pieces. They pull one another's nose and earrings by main force, and sometimes even more serious accident occurs; Ranjit sitting by encouraging them with the greatest delight and exclaiming to his guests, *Burra tomacha, burra tomacha* (great fun, tamasha).'[3]

A Benevolent Lover

Like most men who have been distinguished in history for administrative vigour and military genius, Ranjit Singh was very susceptible to feminine influence. His experiences were not, however, such as to give a favourable impression of the manners and morals of the ladies of the Punjab. His grandmother, Mai Dessan, was killed by his father for an intrigue with a Brahmin; and Ranjit Singh is said to have killed his own mother Raj Kaur, popularly known as Mai Malwai, for a similar offence. Of his own wives and mistresses, the chronicle is too scandalous for more than passing mention in this place.[4]

When he had secured a legitimate succession in the person of his son, Kharak Singh, he cared little for the intrigues of his harem. Many children were said to be fathered by Ranjit according to his women, for political objects or in the hope of obtaining his special favour; and although the astute Maharaja was never deceived, he generally accepted the children as his own, with a certain grim amusement, and would ask why fortune had favoured him in so extraordinary a manner. To his son Kharak Singh, and to his grandson, Nau Nihal Singh, he sent several ladies of more than doubtful reputation from his own harem; One of these being the beautiful Isar Kaur, who was forced to become a *Sati* on the death of Maharaja Kharak Singh.[5]

However, Ranjit Singh was not one to force anyone to grant him favours, and went out of the way to be nice to those who made him happy; his generosity and civilised conduct towards them were well known. There is a particularly appealing case of a courtesan named Moran he was so deeply in love with that he not only married her and had a mosque named after her in Lahore and also a village in Amritsar district, but also had a coin struck in her name – the only woman so honoured.

Moran, a Kashmiri dancing girl from Amritsar, completely captivated Ranjit Singh when he first set his eyes on her. He was 22 then and Moran 12 or 13. Her glowing face, large eyes, beautiful black hair, seductive voice and quickness of mind, completely won him over. She danced with grace and dignity. Lean and wiry himself, Ranjit Singh, despite his short stature, one eye and smallpox scars, was still a very striking-looking man with a mesmerising face, penetrating right eye, a long slightly upward nose, firm mouth, great teeth, broad shoulders and a beard which cascaded down to his chest. He had an exceptional presence and personality.

Even though Moran was a courtesan and, Ranjit Singh the ruler of Punjab, he was gracious enough, in 1802, to ask her father's permission. The man was terrified at the idea of marrying his daughter outside his class and tried to frighten the royal suitor away by making a condition, one that was, in fact, a tradition – that the bridegroom-to-be should build and 'blow ablaze with his own breath a fire' in his father-in-law's house.[6] Ranjit Singh unhesitantly accepted the condition.

Ranjit Singh's behaviour speaks of the firm and unusual character of a man who could have the dancing girl even without the consent of her father, but he not only sought consent of her father but also agreed to the condition laid down by her father. Although his bride was a Muslim, he never, even once, asked her to convert, respecting her right to abide by her own faith. Ranjit Singh acknowledged the supremacy of his own faith no less, as is revealed by his response to Sikhism's highest authority, the temple in Amritsar, concerning this affair.

Orthodox Sikhs protested at the idea of their Maharaja marrying a Muslim courtesan. They met at the Akal Takht and by common counsel, imposed punishment of a hundred lashes on his back in public. The Maharaja readily agreed to abide by the writ of the Akal Takht. Learning of this, the Five Elect at the Akal Takht took a lenient view. They reduced the sentence to a fine of 125,000 rupees.

According to the author of *The Real Ranjit Singh*: 'The wedding was celebrated with great *éclat* or show. The bridegroom's party, which formed a procession of elephants, horses, *palki*s and people on foot, stretching from Lahore fort to Shalimar Garden, a distance of some miles, went all the way to Amritsar. The bride was given away by Mian Samdu with a dowry of several lakh of rupees worth of jewellery, clothes and household effects, as if she had been a princess.'[7]

There is yet another interesting story about Ranjit Singh's

love for Moran. After his meeting with Lord and Lady Bentinck at Ropar in 1831, an observer of the scene wrote of the deep impression one particular moment made on him: 'As soon as the Begum Sahiba crossed the river by a boat, the Nawab Sahib personally went forward to receive her and, taking her by hand, made her sit in a chair in such a way that it indicated his heartfelt affection and deep love between the two. The Maharaja said at that moment that he was put in mind of his connection with Biwi Moran, for he said that he had exactly the same kind of love and unity with her and could not prepare his mind to accept separation from her even for a moment and every moment they remained fully aware of each other's doings.'[8]

Moran, it is said, was most queenly in her looks and Ranjit Singh was extremely fond of her. She would not observe *purdah* and appeared with the Maharaja publicly. She sat with him on elephant and came out in state processions. While Ranjit Singh would not permit his own name to be carried on coins struck by him in his regime, he had a series issued in Moran's name. They were called Moranshahi currency.

Given Ranjit Singh's limitless capacity for love, it wasn't long before Moran's sister Mamola also caught his fancy, and he married her as well. She was also a dancer. Later in life, Ranjit Singh became infatuated with yet another Kashmiri girl 'of Amritsar', Gul Badam, and he married her with pomp and splendour in 1833.[9] The newly-wed ruler, wanting to show off his new bride Gul (later called Gul Begum) to his subjects, would often put her before him on his favourite horse and ride through the streets of Lahore. Badami Bagh, the park near Lahore Fort, was named after her, and she was buried there in 1863.

Wives and Concubines

It should be mentioned that Ranjit Singh kept all his wives happy by giving them handsome jaagirs and maintenance allowances so that they wouldn't feel either rejected or overlooked.

Ranjit Singh's regiment of women literally numbered hundreds if the count includes all his wives, concubines and the horde of house-women he had created with an eye on both their physical fitness and striking looks. And then there were the ladies, mostly widows, who came under the category of *Chadar dalna* (under his protection).

It was far from Ranjit Singh's nature and temperament to confine himself to just one of his loves; another Amazon he was irresistibly drawn to was Bashiran. Because she had gorgeous cat-like eyes, he would call her *Billo*, which in Punjabi is slang for cat; with a beautiful voice and exceptional singing talent, she would keep the Maharaja entranced. Ranjit Singh made her rich with his gifts of land and jewels.

One woman of colourful character and exquisite beauty was called Lotus. She was sent as tribute from Kashmir to Ranjit Singh in the mid 1830s. He was totally captivated by her and assumed she was madly in love with him. Lotus was gifted seven prosperous villages by Ranjit Singh as token of affection. She was devoted to him till the end and committed Sati when he died.

In addition to the magnificent girls, there were others of equal versatility to entertain and enchant the Maharaja with their collection of dances. Osborne, invited to dinner by the Maharaja, describes a memorable dance by four recently-arrived Kashmiri girls, whose large, luminous eyes and expressive countenances might have entitled them to be considered 'beautiful anywhere in the world'. Writes Osborne: 'They were richly and gracefully dressed in scarlet and gold embroidered shawl dresses, with large and enormously loose petticoats of handsomely worked silk. Their head ornaments were singular and very becoming; their glossy black hair hanging down the back in a number of long plaits, with gold coins and small bunches of pearls suspended to the ends....'[10]

The number of Ranjit Singh's wives is generally placed at around 20, which includes those in the 'chadar dalna' category. While the latter did not fully qualify as wives of the first order, but they had religious and social acceptance because they too had to go through a religious ceremony. Hindu, Muslim and British historians vary slightly in their calculations of the number of Ranjit Singh's wives. While Hari Ram Gupta settles for 20,[11] Waheeduddin's figure is at 18, with nine in each of the two classifications.[12] However, according to Lepel Griffin: 'Ranjit Singh married eighteen wives: nine by the orthodox ceremonial and nine by simpler rite of throwing the sheet (*chadar dalna*).'[13] As to the number of concubines, it is anybody's guess. Only a few among these wives require any special notice.

Mehtab Kaur

Mehtab Kaur was the first in order, married in 1786, a match which gave Ranjit Singh his commanding position, she being the granddaughter of and heiress of the powerful Kanhaya baron Jai Singh. Her mother, the widow Sada Kaur, a truly remarkable woman, who realised that if her daughter was to retain her influence she must present her husband with an heir, procured a boy during one of the Maharaja's expeditions. The child named Ishar Singh, only lived a year and half. Sada Kaur was now determined to try the effect of twins.

When Ranjit Singh had started on his Cis-Sutlej expedition of 1807, it was given out that Mehtab Kaur was pregnant, and on his return twin sons were presented to him, one purchased from a cloth-weaver, and the other the offspring of a slave-girl in Mai Sada Kaur's house. Ranjit Singh at first refused to have anything to say to the children, but the following year, when he was almost at war with the English over the Cis-Sutlej question, he thought it necessary to conciliate his terrible mother-in-law who had the Kamgarhia barons at her back, and acknowledged the boys, treating them as his own and allowing them the title of Prince.

One of them, Tara Singh, was an idiot; the other Sher Singh, grew up an exceedingly handsome, brave and stupid man, and succeeded to the throne after the death of Nau Nihal Singh, but was assassinated in 1843 by the Sindhanwalia chiefs.[14]

Sada Kaur, Ranjit Singh's mother-in-law, helped her son-in-law realise not only some of his goals but some of her own as well in the process. Although his marriage with her daughter did not last long, Sada Kaur, while no doubt disappointed, was a pragmatic and clear-headed woman. She was determined as ever to exploit the opportunities the alliance with the Sukerchakias had opened up for her. Her eventual goal was to dominate the whole of Punjab.

The friendliness between Ranjit Singh and Sada Kaur was not destined to last long, because as the energetic lady began to expand her role in the affairs of his kingdom, Ranjit Singh's resentment at her arrogance grew. While the two boys were growing up, the ever-ambitious Sada Kaur's strategy was to get Ranjit Singh to settle handsome jaagirs on them. She wished to induce her son-in-law to settle an estate on Sher Singh, independent of her own,[15] her aim being to establish a solid claim on Ranjit Singh's territories through Sher Singh in the years to come. But the Maharaja, no novice in this game, insisted that Sada Kaur present the Prince with a jaagir appropriate to his status out of the extensive Kanhaya territories, which were now hers. With the steady souring of their relationship over the years, Ranjit Singh had his own eyes on the Kanhaya possessions and Sher Singh, ironically enough, was now pivotal to the game plan of each.

By October 1820, matters came to a head. Ranjit Singh ordered Sada Kaur to set aside half of her own estates for the maintenance of the two princes, Sher Singh and Tara Singh. Sada Kaur was unwilling to obey the order, threatening to cross the Sutlej and place her estate of Wadhni under British protection.[16] With this ill-advised threat she overreached herself and sealed her fate. It was now clear to Ranjit Singh that if his mother-in-law was prepared to resort to the ultimate treachery of turning for help to the British, an enemy-in-waiting, she had to be debarred from any future role not only in his affairs but even in those of her own misl.

After a few more moves and counter moves, including an unsuccessful attempt by Sada Kaur to cross over to the British, she was confined to the Lahore Fort, from which she managed to escape, but a force was sent to apprehend her, returning with a good deal of Kanhaya wealth from their stronghold of Batala. The Kanhaya misl now became Ranjit Singh's property, and Sada Kaur remained confined in a fort for the rest of her life, first in Lahore and then in Amritsar, where she died in 1832 at the age of 70.

Ravi Raj Kaur

The second wife of the Maharaja was Raj Kaur, the daughter of Ram Singh, a Nakkai chief. She was married in 1798, and four years later gave birth to Kharak Singh, who was possibly the only child ever born to Ranjit Singh. Kharak Singh succeeded his father without opposition, but was a man of weak intellect and was no more than a puppet in the hands of his ambitious son, Nau Nihal Singh, and the intriguing Rajas of Jammu, who poisoned him when they had enough of him. Nau Nihal Singh, in his turn, was assassinated as he was returning from his father's cremation.

Gul Begum and Moran

The other wives were of less importance. One of whom the Maharaja married in 1833, in orthodox fashion and with great splendour, was a courtesan named Gul Begum of Amritsar city. When still a young man, in 1806, a yet more famous courtesan named Moran, obtained great influence over him, and Ranjit Singh was not ashamed to parade, very drunk, on an elephant, during the Holi festival with Moran by his side. She obtained a grant of Firozpur and coins were struck in her name.

Jindan

Another woman who rose to fame, or rather to notoriety, after the death of the great Maharaja was Jindan, reputedly, the mother of Maharaja Dalip Singh. She was the daughter of Mann Singh, a trooper in the service of the palace, and was a clever mimick and dancer. She attracted the notice of Maharaja Ranjit Singh and was taken into the harem where her open intrigues caused astonishment even in the court of Lahore.

A menial servant, a watercarrier, by the name of Gulu, was accepted as the father of Dalip Singh. At any rate, the father was not Maharaja Ranjit Singh, who was paralysed several years before the birth of the child. Nor did he ever marry Jindan by formal or informal marriage, contrary to his practice of sealing a relationship.

Many believed that Dilip Singh was not born of Jindan at all; but was brought into the palace by the Jammu Rajas Gulab Singh and Dhian Singh, who required a child to put forward when all the other possible heirs, real or reputed, of the Maharaja should have perished. It is certain that Jindan and the child were for some time sheltered at Jammu and only produced at a convenient time.[17]

Jindan, with her last professed lover, Raja Lal Singh, played a conspicuous and infamous part, and her debaucheries were in large part the cause of the Sutlej war and the ruin of the Sikh kingdom. 'Dilip Singh, a child of nine years, was the titular Maharaja when the British army reached Lahore after the campaign; and as it was convenient to accept the *status quo*, and as a nominal ruler was required for a country which the English government had then no desire to annex or permanently occupy, the reputed child of the servant-maid and the water-carrier was confirmed on the throne of the Lion of the Punjab. Fortune, with her ever-turning wheel, must have laughed at the transformation.'[18]

Guddan and Raj Banso

Guddan and Ravi Raj Banso, the two Rajput hill princesses, were the most charming women in Maharaja Ranjit Singh's harem. It is said that people came from far and near to have a glimpse of the new brides as they arrived at Lahore. Their father, Raja Sansar Chand, was a great patron of Kangra art. Guddan too seemed to have acquired a love for the arts from her father. She had a rich collection of miniatures. She was deeply devoted to her husband. When the Maharaja died, she committed Sati in the true spirit of a Rajput queen of her time. No amount of dissuasion could make her change her decision. Before the funeral fire was lit, Guddan sent for Prince Kharak Singh and Prime Minister Dhian Singh, to pledge devotion to the memory of the Maharaja and remain loyal to each other.

Her sister, Raj Banso, had earlier committed suicide when equated by Ranjit Singh with Moran who, according to her, was only an ex-courtesan and no more. Her self-respect as a Rajput princess could not tolerate this.

The Maharaja had a number of Muslim wives in his harem. They had complete freedom to practice their faith. In fact, the monarch encouraged his wives to participate in one another's ceremonials and festivals like Id, Dussehra, Diwali and Baisakhi.

It is said that the example set in the palace was followed in the country at large. It became practice in the time of the Maharaja for Hindus and Sikhs to participate in Muslim festivals and for Muslims to take part in Hindu and Sikh festivals.

Thus, the personal life of Ranjit Singh was as colourful as his political career. Although an ugly man himself, he loved to surround himself with handsome men and beautiful women. He was small of stature and slight of build, but he was bold and daring. In many campaigns, he led his troops himself and fought sword in hand. He lived the life of a soldier and worked like a monarch.

FOREIGNERS AT THE LAHORE DURBAR

Secret Visit to the English Camp

GENERAL GERARD LAKE, in 1803, had defeated the Marathas at Delhi, who had opposed him under the Holkars, pursued them across the trans-Sutlej States and reached the banks of the Beas river.

Young Ranjit Singh had not been idle either. Through his intelligence network, which he had set up early in his rule, and the information he had, which he combined with his common sense, he assessed far more accurately than most the threat the British would eventually pose to the Sikh Kingdom. Taking advantage of the presence of General Lake's troops on the Beas, Ranjit Singh paid a secret visit to the English camp, and noted the machine-like drill of the sepoy battalions, the mobility of the company's artillery and the solidarity of the British regiments, horse and foot.[1]

In all likelihood, it was this secret visit to the British army camp that convinced Ranjit Singh of the need to introduce into his own military formations, those weapons, battle tactics, training methods and innovative ideas that had given the Europeans a lead over the armies of Asia. This, perhaps, is what, in due course, convinced Ranjit Singh to recruit European officers to help smarten up his army. Hence forth, he made it a point of assembling material and systematically updating his intelligence about the British in India, which helped him to develop his own insights into their moves, motives and methodology. This way, as long as he lived, he kept his kingdom safe.

Ranjit Singh's army at that time consisted essentially of irregular cavalry – the *Ghorchurra*s, made up mostly of soldiers from the misls, called *Misldar Sowar*s. Distinct from these two, was a cavalry regiment called the *Ghorchurras Khas.* This was the first standing unit that Ranjit Singh formed as Maharaja, composed of leading Sardars and their kinsmen, eventually numbering up to 2,000 men. Together with a similar regiment formed later, this force became known to admiring foreign visitors as 'the Maharaja's bodyguard', and was considered the elite of the Sikh army.

Maharaja Ranjit Singh consolidated his empire by the age of twentyone. His quest for knowledge, both to better his empire and army, continued unabated. A contemporary of Napoleon, he was greatly interested in the happenings in Europe, the wars, military organisations, tactics and weaponry. His inquisitiveness, touching on impatience, was geared towards improving his military arsenal and capability, and thereby his military strength and efficiency. He had the hostile Afghans on the western border, and a potential threat, the British in the east. No matter how friendly and conciliatory the British attitude was at that time, their conquest of the rest of the Indian subcontinent indicated their ultimate objective – the subjugation of his kingdom at an appropriate time. He never lost sight of this fact.

This period coincided with the end of the Napoleonic wars and a number European soldiers of repute, formerly of the French Army or those of their allies, looked east in order to soldier on. Persia became the destination of many as Ranjit

Singh's reputation had not yet reached Europe at the time. Once in Persia, however, tales of Ranjit Singh and stories of his kingdom and his military prowess drew many to Lahore to offer their services to him. By the end of his reign in 1839, thirty-nine European officers, including generals, were in his service. In addition, there were three doctors.[2]

The first reorganisation on modern lines and consolidation of the Lahore Army took place in 1822. The entire emphasis then was on cavalry and artillery. The infantry component was geared towards garrison duty. Sikhs in those days were great horsemen and as a consequence, the emphasis was on the cavalry.

It was only after the arrival of the European officers and Ranjit Singh being convinced of the role the infantry played in the major battles fought between Wellington and Napoleon, both during the Peninsular wars and in Northern Europe, that the infantry was reorganised along the lines of the European armies. As a result, its role in battle was recognised by the Sikh army, many of whom then opted to join it.

The military genius of Maharaja Ranjit Singh was not so much shown in his generalship, for in this he was surpassed by many of his officers and Sardars. It was in the Maharaja's skill as an able steward of the unruly Sikhs of the region from whom he was able to draw respect and loyalty, obedience and valour. He was able to form a powerful, disciplined and well-equipped army out of the raw Sikh talents, turbulent and independent, who had been accustomed to carry their swords from one leader to another as they saw the best chance of plunder, and who changed their masters as often as it suited their inclination or convenience.

When his grandfather Charhat Singh, and his father Mahan Singh, had commanded the Sukerchakia confederacy, the Sikhs were a thoroughly republication body – chiefs and leaders arose with more or less authority, as was inevitable in those anarchic days, when every man owned what he could take by force and hold against all comers, but this leadership gave no man a more intrinsically honourable position in the eyes of the people. The Sikh theocracy had equality and fraternity for its foundation far more literally than has been the case with modern republics of Europe and America.

Then, in the organisation and system of then armies, the fighting Sikhs were essentially horsemen, not footmen. The infantry soldier was considered altogether inferior to the cavalry, and was, in time of war, left behind to protect garrison forts, to look after the women or to follow, as best he could, the fighting force, until he, in his turn, could afford to change his status and buy or steal a horse for his own use.

Maharaja Ranjit Singh, very early in his career, recognised, with his usual wisdom, that the Sikh system was unsuited for any nineteenth century, modern war, and that until it was modernised, he could not hope to win solid victories over regular troops like that of the English, whose drill and tactics he studied with infinite patience, or even over the Afghans, who in the time of Ahmad Shah Abdali, were fairly disciplined, and formidable opponents even in the open country, while in the hills they were almost invincible.

Upgrading the Infantry

When he had thoroughly mastered the secret of the superiority of the British army's organisation, against which all the military races of India had tried their strength in vain, he resolved to create an army on similar lines, while he determined, no less resolutely, to keep peace with the only power which he had learned to respect. With these objectives, the Maharaja changed the entire organisation of the Khalsa army. The cavalry ceased to be the most important arm, and the infantry became the favourite service. The change was facilitated by the employment of European officers, French and Italian, whom the Maharaja engaged when he failed to obtain the services on loan, of officers of the East India Company.

These foreign generals introduced the system which had become the general practice in the armies of Europe, where the value of infantry as against cavalry was universally acknowledged. Some of them were men of considerable ability and quite competent to perform all they promised in increasing the efficiency of the Lahore army. The Khalsa infantry, under their mentorships, became the most formidable body of troops, well-disciplined and steady, though slow in manipulating. Their endurance was very great, and a whole regiment would march 30 miles a day for many days together.

Enlistment in the Maharaja's Army

Enlistment in the Maharaja's regular army was entirely voluntary, but there was no difficulty in obtaining recruits, for the service was exceedingly popular. The cavalry was constituted much in the same manner as in the early days of the Khalsa, when clouds of horsemen hung on the skirts of the Afghan armies, afraid to venture an attack upon regular troops, but cutting off convoys and endangering the communications of the enemy. This is, no doubt, one of the principal duties of any light horse brigade; but the Sikh cavalry were, as a rule, miserably mounted and armed, and became more celebrated for taking to flight when attacked than for any display of valour.

'On foot, the Sikh is the bravest and steadiest of soldiers; but on horseback, although there are some crack cavalry regiments of Sikhs in the English service that can hold their own with any horsemen in the world, they are surpassed by Afghans and Hindustanis who are inferior to them as infantry.'[3]

In the Maharaja's army, the infantry were the pick of the youth; only the handsomest and strongest men were selected.

The cavalry were the irregular troops, the contingents of his different Sardars, and not appointed for any considerations of bravery or strength. As Lepel Griffin observed: 'The horses were small, weak, and ill-bred, in the armies of the Sikh States at the present day, all of which I have often reviewed and inspected, and one of which it was my duty to reorganise, the same practice prevails. The infantry are in size and physique equal to the Sikhs in the British army; while the cavalry regiments have been turned into a hospital for old and aged pensioners, who can sit on a horse, although they cannot fight or perform any service requiring bodily exertion.'[4]

The Fanatic Akalis

In the old Khalsa days, Akalis as infantry soldiers enjoyed consideration. The Maharaja was afraid to interfere too closely with these men; for though little better than drunken brutes, they were supposed by the Sikhs to be those who possessed a semi-sacred status and were, moreover, useful when desperate deeds were to be done which the rank-and-file of the regular army might have hesitated to do. They nearly involved the Maharaja in a fight with the English by their fanatical attack upon Metcalfe's Muslim escort in 1809; however, their reckless valour turned many a wavering fight into a victory.

According to Lepel Griffin, 'They (Akalis) were identical in character and in the manner of their onslaught with the Ghazis of Afghanistan and Sudan, whose fierce and terrific attack shakes the nerves of all but the steadiest and most seasoned troops.But the Sikh soldiers of God drew their courage more from drink and maddening drugs, than from the depths of religious enthusiasm which inspires the wild children of Islam. They were deadly nuisance and danger during the Maharaja's reign, and more than once they made attempts on his life.'[5]

While describing his experiences and impression about the

Akalis, Osborne says: 'During my evening's ride (at Lahore, 18 June 1838) I unfortunately got amongst a band of Akalees, and had to endure the usual quantity of abuse and blackguardism they make a point of so lavishly distributing to everyone they meet. They are, without any exception, the most insolent and worthless race of people in all India. They are religious fanatics and acknowledge no ruler and no laws but their own; think nothing of robbery, or even murder, should they happen to be in the humour of it. They move about constantly, armed to the teeth, and it is not a uncommon thing to see them riding about with a drawn sword in each hand, two more in their belt, a matchlock at their back, and three or four pairs of iron chakras (or rings with sharp cutting edges, used as weapons) fastened around their turbans.... He (Ranjit Singh) has raised some irregular regiments composed entirely of Akalees, which he always employs on any dangerous or desperate service; and as they fight like devils, he continues to make them useful, as well as to expend a great number of them in this way.'[6]

Their (Akalis') rude behaviour and hatred for Europeans made them so nasty during the early years of the British occupation and annexation that visits to the temple of the Darbar Sahib at Amritsar, where the Akalis had their headquarters, were always fraught with risks. The Maharaja was tolerant but desired his Muslim subjects in Amritsar to perform their ceremonies with restrain, prohibiting the Muezzin's call to prayer, as this roused the Akalis to fury.

The Maharaja tried to bring some order among these fanatics, by forming them into a corps of irregular cavalry, 3,000 strong, but this had little effect, and they always dismounted for a charge, in which, the two-handed sword was their favourite weapon. The steel disc which they invariably wore on their turbans, six to eight inches in diameter, thin and with a sharp cutting edge, was dangerous to friends and foes.

Foreigners in Maharaja's Services

Maharaja Ranjit Singh employed a number of foreign experts and professional soldiers to modernise the way of life in his kingdom, his army and public administration. There were more than sixty such officers in his service. They included three Englishmen, twelve Frenchmen, four Italians, four Germans, two Spaniards, one Russian, one Scot, seven Anglo-Indians and three Americans.[7]

The Maharaja took exceptional care before deciding to employ a foreigner. The applicant had to undergo all sorts of tests and screening. But, once he made up his mind, he trusted those he took into his service. The foreigners were employed on well-defined terms, paid liberally, several times more than their local counterparts, and looked after with utmost care. At the same time, no foreign employee could be careless or casual in his duties. The Maharaja was a hard task-master, more particularly in the case of his foreign officers.

Ventura and Allard

The first two foreigners to join the Maharaja's service were an Italian and a Frenchman. The Italian was Jean-Baptiste Ventura and the French soldier was called Jean-Francis Allard. They had served in Napoleon's army and having lost their jobs (when Napoleon was defeated at Waterloo) they came out in search of suitable employment.

These men first tried their fortune in Egypt and Persia, but finding no opening under Shah Abbas, the ruling monarch, they travelled to India, via Herat and Kandhar, and attracted by the tales about the grandeur of Ranjit Singh's court, they reached Lahore in 1822. On their arrival, they at first stayed in a caravanserai. When the Maharaja heard about them, he asked them to make proper applications for jobs in his army. After checking the applicants' antecedents, he offered them ranks in the army. They were given generous emoluments with fairly lavish houses to live in. From time to time, they received from the Maharaja gifts and bounties. Both served Ranjit Singh long and faithfully.

While in the service of Napoleon's army, Ventura had served in Spain and Italy. He later became a soldier of fortune ready for adventure in any part of the world. He was asked by Ranjit Singh to train his infantry. He raised four battalions of Fauz-i-Khas. Soon Ventura was placed in command of this elite special brigade, the first in rank, discipline, and equipment in the Sikh army. Its normal strength was four infantry battalions and two regiments of cavalry, and although the Maharaja at one time raised it to five battalions of infantry and three cavalry regiments, it was afterwards reduced, at Ventura's request, to its former numbers.

In command of this force, the General served in many campaigns with distinction, chiefly in the hills and around Peshawar. Ventura served in the campaigns of Multan, Derajat and Peshawar. He was appointed governor of Dejarat. The Maharaja always treated him with confidence and respect and later appointed him Qazi and governor of Lahore, which gave him the third position in the Durbar.

A wedding gift of 40,000 rupees was made to Ventura at the time of his marriage. Ventura was also given land and advanced a large sum to enable him to build his own house in the neighbourhood of Anarkali, at Lahore.

Of similar character and standing was General Allard, another of Napoleon's officers, who had won distinction by his ability and gallantry in many campaigns. Allard was allowed to raise a corps of cavalrymen. Allard had married an Indian woman. The Maharaja encouraged his foreign employees to marry local women. Allard's daughter, Marie Charlotte, unfortunately died an untimely death. Allard had her buried in the palatial house that he had built for himself. The building came to be known as Kudi Bagh, in the memory of the deceased.

Allard was put in charge of training the Maharaja's cavalry. He also raised four regiments. During his tenure of service with the Maharaja, Allard went back home on leave. When he returned, he brought a warm message from the king, Louis Phillipe of France, together with a number of gifts for Ranjit Singh. Louis Phillipe had appointed Allard as his ambassador to the Maharaja's court. The text of King Phillipe's letter to Maharaja Ranjit Singh indicates the high esteem in which the Lahore ruler was held by the French monarch: '… As the sun confers light on the distant parts of the world, the true love unites hearts, physically separated, in a common rhythm of friendship and harmony.'[8]

Claude Auguste Court

Colonel Claude Auguste Court, a Frenchman, educated at the Ecole Polytechnique of Paris, commanded two battalions of Gurkhas. Court was the most respected of all foreign officers in the Maharaja's service. He was a man of literary pursuits and had a quiet nature. His most distinguished contribution was as the Maharaja's ordnance chief. He turned the Maharaja's soldiers into excellent gunners. The ordnance factory at Lahore produced high quality guns under his charge. His foundry manufactured all types of guns, heavy, medium and light. Whatever armaments were sent to the Maharaja as gift from foreign powers were copied in Court's foundry, almost to perfection. Court drew a salary of 2,500 rupees per month and was promoted to the rank of General. He served the Lahore Durbar until 1843, when Maharaja Sher Singh was assassinated.

Court is the author of several works in French, *Memoir of a Journey from Persia to Kabul via Herat and Kandhar* and *A Brief Narrative of the Anarchy in Punjab 1839-1845.*

Colonel Alexander Gardner

Colonel Alexander Gardner was an Irishman of little education but of considerable ability, employed in the artillery. He is best known for his *Memoirs of Alexander Gardner*. His account of the times is very graphic, though not very authoritative.

Colonel Henry Charles Van Cortlandt

Colonel Van Cortlandt was another officer of mixed parentage, who on the downfall of the Sikh monarchy, entered the service of the British in a civil capacity, and also performed excellent military service during the 1857 Mutiny.

General Avitabile

General Paolo di Avitabile was a native of Naples who came to Lahore some years later than Ventura, after he had served in Persia. He was generally employed in administrative work, first in charge of the Rechna Doab, the country between the rivers Ravi and Chenab. Thereafter, he was appointed as governor of Peshawar, after Hari Singh Nalwa's death. He was another soldier of fortune who came to Lahore after the defeat of Napoleon's army. He secured service at the Sikh Durbar through the good offices of General Ventura.

Joining service on a salary of 200 rupees per month, he had phenomenal rise and was appointed as governor of Wazirabad along with the Command of his military brigade. He proved to be a ruthless administrator. Wazirabad made remarkable progress during his tenure in office. He spoke Italian, French, Persian and Hindustani fluently. As governor of Peshawar, he curbed the querulous Pathans with an iron hand. His stern and ferocious methods reduced that wild tract to something like order for the first time in its history. His name is still remembered with awe by the turbulent tribes in the neighbourhood of the Khyber, a numbers of whom, thieves and murderers, he hung them around the walls of the city.

His code of punishment was Draconian, and although the later English rule was mild in comparison with that of this ferocious Italian, it is generally accepted that those who have to administer law and maintain order on the North-West Frontier of India must have a quick and heavy hand; and the slow and cumbersome procedure of High Courts and barrister Judges is mere folly when compared with the gallows after a criminal is caught, caught red-handed before he has reached his asylum in the hills.

Here is, in his own words, the way Avitabile went about it: 'When I marched to Peshawar, I sent in advance a number of wooden posts, which my men erected around walls of the city. The Pathans scoffed at them and laughed at the madness of the *firangi* and louder still when my men came and left coils of rope at the foot of the posts. Gun and swords, said they, were the arms to rule the city and not sticks and ropes. However, when my preparations were completed, they found one morning dangling from these posts fifty of the worst characters in Peshawar, and I repeated the exhibition every day till I made scarcity of brigands and murderers. Then I had to deal with liars and tale bearers. My method with them was to cut out their tongues. And then a surgeon appeared and professed to be able to restore their speech. I sent for him and cut out his tongue also. After that there was peace, and in six months there was no crime.'[9]

He had a rough and ready manner of administering justice. He had two Qazis, two Hindus, and two Sikhs to assist him in disposing of disputes referred to him. When he retired, he was drawing a salary of 60,000 rupees per annum. He is said to have amassed a lot of money, maintained a regular harem and lived in a palatial building of his own in Lahore. He was a man of numerous vices and many virtues. Avitabile was also a scholar and an engineer, who worked very closely with the most brilliant Sikh engineer of the time, Lehna Singh Majithia.

Avitabile's control of Peshawar brought him in contact with the British army during the First Anglo-Afghan War (1839–42). As governor of Peshawar, Avitabile controlled the southern entrance to the Khyber Pass. Although the Maharaja did not allow for the British to move through the Sikh empire to reach the Khyber pass, he ordered Avitabile to assist the British through the pass itself, into Afghanistan.

During Elphinstone's advance in 1839 (Elphinstone was the first British envoy to the court of Kabul), the British were well received in Peshawar and their officers received a princely treatment. Captain Henry Havelock spent a month in Peshawar and describes the splendour of Avitabile's court in his memoirs. He also paints a favourable picture of the governor: 'He is, moreover, a frank, gay and good-humoured person, as well as an excellent and skillful officer.' When the British returned in 1842, to avenge the defeat of Elphinstone, they were given every possible assistance by Avitabile's government, while he was still in the employ of the Sikh empire, as the Afghans had been a longtime enemy of the Sikhs.

Dr Honigberger

Dr Johann Martin Honigberger was another foreigner in the service of the Maharaja. He was a Hungarian. A Homeopath by profession, he became the personal physician to Ranjit Singh. Like Ventura and Allard, he too came to the Punjab drawn by Ranjit Singh's reputation. On arrival at Lahore, he was employed on a salary of 800 rupees which was subsequently enhanced to 3,000 rupees. It is said that the Maharaja came to have so much trust in Honigberger that he offered him a governorship. On his declining it, he was offered the command of the department of artillery. But Honigberger's love of his own profession would not allow him to accept this also.

The Maharaja eventually made him accept the management of the gunpowder and gunstock factory. Honigberger also married an Indian and had two daughters who were sent to Mussoorie for schooling. Honigberger went back to his hometown, Kronstadt, during his service with the Maharaja and returned to take up his job again, as General Allard had done earlier.

Dr Josiah Harlan

Josiah Harlan was an American adventurer, serving the British army as Assistant Surgeon. He wanted to become a king, travelled to Afghanistan and was known as the Prince of Ghor. He fought with the Afghans and was arrested in the North-West Frontier by Ranjit Singh's forces. Listening to his story, the Maharaja told him, 'I will make you governor of Gujrat, and give you 3,000 rupees a month. If you behave well, I will increase your salary; if not I will cut off your nose'.

Harlan is a typical example of a turncoat. The Maharaja appointed him governor of Jasrota and Nurpur. But, after having served Lahore for about seven years, he played false and walked over to Afghanistan again and sought service with Dost Muhammad Khan. He described Ranjit Singh as a monarch 'absolute and luxurious'. Harlan claims to have fought the Maharaja's forces at Jamrud and defeated them. 'The Sikhs were defeated and Ranjit Singh's Commander-in-Chief with 2,000 of his men was killed. The Afghan lost 1,000 men. The King of Lahore exclaimed: This is all Harlan's work. He has avenged himself.'[10]

Rev John C Lowrie

Among the foreigners who visited the Maharaja in Lahore was an American missionary, Rev John C Lowrie. He wished to establish a Christian Mission on behalf of the Western

Missionary Society. Ranjit Singh was keen to have a school in Lahore for his own children and for the children of the nobility. Before the Maharaja received Rev Lowrie, he sent Fakir Nur-ud-Din and then Fakir Aziz-ud-Din to see him. They asked him searching questions about his methods of teaching and curriculum to be introduced. The negotiations fell through on the question of teaching the Bible in the school, on which Lowrie insisted. The Maharaja could not accede to this. He was, nevertheless, highly impressed with his personal character and pious manner and loaded him with gifts and honours as he left Lahore to return to Ludhiana. At Ludhiana, Lowrie set up a Punjabi printing press – the first of its kind in northern India. From this press he issued the first dictionary and the first grammar of the Punjabi language.

Among other more important foreigners who sought service with the Lahore Durbar were:

1. Dotten Weiss, a German, who served as engineer.
2. Hommns, a Spaniard, who was an officer in the artillery.
3. Moevius, a Russian, who held a rank in the infantry.
4. Fitzroy, Gillimore, Leslie, Harvey and Campbell, all Englishmen, who held various civil and military positions.

'It is difficult to get an appointment here, but still more to get one's dismissal', General Allard once told Dr Honigberger. The remark characterises Ranjit Singh's treatment of his foreign employees.[11]

Distinguished Sikh Commanders

The foreign officers entertained by the Maharaja, especially General Ventura in command of the Fauj-i-Khas, and General Court in charge of what was known as the French brigade, very much improved the discipline and tactical power of Ranjit Singh's army. They were not, however, entrusted with the supreme command in expeditions which was nominally given to one of the princes, Kharak Singh or Sher Singh, or one of the principal Sardars. Of all the Generals of the Maharaja, the best was probably Diwan Mokham Chand, a Khatri by birth, who from 1806 to 1814, when he died, was the virtual Commander-in-Chief of the Sikh army, and was associated with all his conquests.

His grandson, Ram Dayal, killed in Hazra in 1820, was also a skilful commander, who would have risen to distinction, had he lived. Misr Diwan Chand, another Hindu of the trading class, and as such disliked by the Sikh Sardars, was the Conqueror of Multan in 1818, and the leader of the successful expedition against Kashmir in the following year. Among the Sikh chiefs who were most distinguished were Sardar Fateh Singh Kalianwala; Sardar Nihal Singh Attariwala, who took a distinguished part in almost all the Maharaja's campaigns from the year 1801 to 1817; Sardar Fateh Singh Ahluwalia, the ancestor of the Kapurthala Rajas; Sardar Budh Singh Sandhanwalia, and his brother, Attar Singh, who after the death of Sardar Hari Singh Nalwa at Jamrud in 1836, were considered the champion of the Khalsa. Hari Singh was a leader of infinite dash and gallantry, and was adored by the army; ever ready to fight and win, without counting the odds against him.

Hari Singh Nalwa's son, Jawahir Singh, inherited all his father's valour, and it was he who led the splendid charge of the irregular cavalry against the English at Chillianwala, which so nearly turned the victory into a catastrophe. Besides the names mentioned herewith there were many other famous captains of the Maharaja whose names were household words in Punjab.

Organisation and Training

The organisation and the training of the army was on the lines of the French army, so would be the drill, words of command and tactics employed in the battle. The principal formation was a brigade; there was no higher command till much later. Though the French commanders used French tactics and the English Commanders used tactics learnt in the British army, there was no confusion. Both nationalities had recently finished fighting eachother in the European wars, and had undoubtedly, learnt enough from eachother during the process to enable them to evolve standard procedures.

To begin with, in 1799, Ranjit Singh's army was, as elsewhere in India, based on the feudal concept. It comprised 2,500 Ghorchurras (irregular cavalry) and existing *derah*s including a sprinkling of retainers and soldiers of fortune.[12] The second phase of reorganisation was undertaken by Ranjit Singh in 1808, where some semblance of a modern military structure began to evolve. What must be remembered, however, is that in 1808 he was young, uneducated without any professional military training.

The reorganisation of the army gave a clearer picture of the forces available and fixed the responsibility for putting them into the field. Once the responsibility had been fixed, Ranjit Singh set most exacting standards of efficiency in march, manoeuvre and marksmanship. If the troops were careless in dress or ill-trained, he did not hesitate to punish the officer responsible by reducing his rank and levying heavy fines. But his usual method was to encourage men by reward rather than to threaten them with penalties. He made it a point to spend three to four hours of his day watching his troops at parade and never did a day go by when he did not reward a gunner or a cavalier for good performance. And since he invariably accompanied his armies to battle, he was always on the lookout for acts of bravery which he rewarded with handsome grants of land and pensions.

One authoritative answer to those who insist that Ranjit

Singh's military victories were only made possible by European officers is given by Joseph Davy Cunningham, himself a British army officer and assistant to the British political agent at the Sikh frontier in 1837: 'It has been usual to attribute the superiority of the Sikh army to the labours of these two officers (Generals Allard and Ventura) and of their subsequent colleagues, the Generals Court and Avitabile; but, in truth, the Sikh owes his excellence as a soldier to his own hardihood of character, to that spirit of adaptation which has distinguished every new people, and to that feeling of a common interest and destiny implanted in him by his great teachers.'[13]

Before Ranjit Singh, the Punjab had enjoyed international reputation in the seventh century during the reign of Harshavardhan, because of the visit of the celebrated Chinese pilgrim Huen Tsang who wrote about the land. In the eighteenth century, it once again came into limelight under Ranjit Singh, mainly on account of the Sikh Army which was equal to any armed force in the world at that time.

Ranjit Singh created his kingdom with the help of this army. He maintained peace and order in the country and checked foreign invasions by it, but the army was not given a position superior to civil authority. The army was not allowed to interfere in administration, nor was it permitted to indulge in political brinkmanship. It did not challenge his authority at any time, nor did it attempt to tyrannise people.

Every Jat village in Majha, Doab and Riarki supplied a number of soldiers to the Maharaja's army. The village paid State revenues from the salaries of its sons. Having lived in big cities like Lahore and Amritsar, the Sikh soldiers did not lose interest in village life. Possession of some cultivable land was an emblem of respect and prestige. Every Jat father, while selecting a bridegroom for his daughter, attached supreme consideration to his possession of arable land.

On account of the army's requirements, trade, commerce and industry flourished in the country. The standard of living in the villages were considerably raised.[14]

From an entirely hostile environment west of the river Sutlej, Ranjit Singh, with this army, carved out his Punjab which remained as it is till 1947. He was a man full of insight and intelligence. A man who used his cunning, treachery and ruthlessness, along with military diplomacy to create an empire to achieve his ambitious. All mortals have to die but a few like Ranjit Singh leave a legacy, creating, consolidating and ruling a vast kingdom for thirty-nine years with extraordinary qualities and an iron first.

THE LAST BATTLE

RANJIT SINGH HAD suffered several afflictions in his lifetime. At the age of six, he contracted smallpox, which left him scarred and blind in one eye, but had not affected his dynamism. He was once more stricken in 1806 by an undiagnosed illness, and again in 1826 with a far more serious one, which included a paralytic stroke. But in less than five years, he had made himself fighting fit to participate in the ceremonial occasion with Lord Bentinck at Ropar in 1831, which was a strenuous event where he had to pass through horsemanship and tent pegging.

The undeterred Ranjit Singh again fought with the same spirit, when in 1834, at the age of 54, he had another stroke of even more sever a nature. But it could not discourage him, because the most momentous years of his life seemed to lie ahead of him. Of these, 1837 was one of the more significant because that year had its good and bad. The first high point of that year was the wedding of his favourite grandson, Nau Nihal Singh, the son of heir Kanwar Kharak Singh, in March at Amritsar, which was celebrated at a grand scale.

Shortly after this event came a second high point, the repulse of a determined Afghan efforts to take back Jamrud Fort, near Peshawar, from the Sikhs, even though the Sikh forces were outnumbered. The result was a magnificent triumph for the Sikhs but with a cruel blow for Ranjit Singh because of the loss of his dear childhood friend, Hari Singh Nalwa, in the battle field. Not only had the two known each other all their lives, but they had together fought against great odds, side by side, in countless battles. The Maharaja ranked Nalwa as one of his most dependable generals, and when the news of his death reached him, he first sent a contingent led by Prince Kharak Singh and thereafter rode out himself – a grueling ride of several hundred miles – to be present at the site of his friend's death.

Six months after Hari Singh Nalwa's death in April 1837, Ranjit Singh's other great friend Fateh Singh, the Ahluwalia Sardar, died of high fever at Kapurthala. He and Ranjit had formed a formal alliance in 1802, to underscore their friendship and mutual regards for each other. They had exchanged turbans, a practice confined to very special relationships among Sikhs. Fateh Singh had been with Ranjit Singh on his Cis-Sutlej expeditions in 1806 and 1807, and had also taken part in the Bhimber, Bahawalpur, Multan and Mankera campaigns. Fateh Singh's death hit Ranjit Singh as hard as his other friend's had done a few months earlier.

Ranjit Singh experienced a third stroke in December 1838 during Governor-General Lord Auckland's visit to Amritsar. After feasting for three days at Ferozepur, he invited the Governor-General to Amritsar where he was accorded a royal reception. He was taken to the holy Harmandir, which was illuminated at night. A display of fireworks was also held in honour of the visiting dignitary. It is said that after the dinner hosted by the Governor-General, the Maharaja was escorted to a *shamiana* (marquee) to inspect a number of guns to be presented to him. The Maharaja, according to the British records, stumbled and fell head long during the inspection. The general perception was his overdrinking was responsible, especially what his own concoctions did to his system.

After the third stroke at Ferozepur (December 1838), the Maharaja was a broken man. This stroke completely deprived the Maharaja of his power of speech, and he had to communicate by signs. The only courtiers who could interpret the sign language were Bhaiya Ram Singh and Fakir Aziz-ud-Din – particularly the latter whose devotion to his sick master is said to have been greater than that shown by a son to his father.

Even the most unintelligible stammer meant something to him. To catch the words, Aziz-ud-Din would put his ear close to Ranjit's mouth. According to Lord Lawrence: 'A curious and interesting sight it was now to behold the fast-decaying monarch, his mind still alive, by signs giving orders; still receiving reports, and assisted by the faithful Aziz-ud-Din, almost as usual, attending to affairs of the state. By a slight turn of his hand to the south, he would enquire the news of the British frontier and most anxious was the intelligence from Afghanistan….'[1]

The winter rain and biting cold of January did not do the Maharaja much good. He kept indoors in an overheated room, taking medicines that the native doctors gave him and getting massages of almond oil. His cold became heavier, and he developed a husking cough. His spirits were further dampened by the news of the death of his friend, Monsieur Allard, on the North-West Frontier. The weather became milder in February and the Maharaja was able to be in the sun. His health improved.

The Maharaja went to Amritsar to pray for his health. He gave away large sums to charity: Cows with gold plated horns, elephants with gold or silver howdahs, images of gold and silver. The chief recipient were Brahmins, but shrines of all religious denominations, Hindu, Muslim and Sikh received their share. Although by March 1839, the Maharaja was reported by the local newspapers to be enjoying better health, there was no real improvement and once more the Agent at Ludhiana was asked to send an English doctor. Doctors Murray and Steel came to Lahore.

Dr Steele made a thorough examination of the Maharaja for a week and dispatched a confidential report to be transmitted to the Governor-General. The report stated: 'He is in that state that the least unfavourable accidental occurrence in the form of disease may be decisive and likely to be so. He may live for a short time, perhaps for a few months or even a year, but a latter period I think, improbable, although I consider that he has still some remaining energy and the natural powers of his constitution to be great and his rallying powers, from what I have heard, to be extraordinary.'[2]

The summer's heat made Ranjit Singh more restless than ever; by the end of May, he had no doubt in his mind that his days were numbered. Fifty Brahmins were employed to pray for his recovery; Fakir Nur-ud-Din was ordered to distribute ten maunds of bread to the poor every day and large numbers of cows, horses and elephants and quantities of gold and silver were given away to holy men and shrines. By June 1839, the Maharaja had six European doctors – three sent by the Governor-General and three of his own beside a large number of *hakeem*s and *vaid*s attending on him. He preferred to take the medicine given by the homeopath, Dr Martin Honigberger – drops of nightshade mixed with sugar and his favourite brandy – to the bitter mixtures prescribed by the English physicians.

Around 20 June 1839, there were all indications that the end was not far off. Being convinced about the end, the Maharaja confided his concern to his foreign minister, Fakir Aziz-ud-Din, to whom he also conveyed his wish that Kharak Singh succeed him, with Dogra Dhian Chand as his Prime Minister. On 21 June, he ordered all his senior officers, European and Indian, to be assembled in his presence and take oath of allegiance to their heir-apparent, his son Kanwar Kharak Singh; this supposedly to ensure that he succeeds without opposition to his father's throne.[3]

The investiture was carried out in time. The next day the Maharaja had a relapse while in court. He lay down on his bed and no one was allowed to speak. The ministers were greatly distressed; Kharak Singh and Raja Dhian Singh sent their guards to the doors of the palace and the fort gates.

On the afternoon of the 24th he had another setback and at the idea of departing from all his worldly wealth, the Maharaja ordered his treasures and jewels to be brought forth. Cows with gilded horns, one hundred decorated horses and five of the best breeds, all equipped in gold and bejeweled saddles, four elephants with gold and silver howdhas, a golden chair and cots, plates, string of pearls, swords, shields, gems and innumerable other valuables were given in alms to be distributed in all parts of India at all sacred Hindu shrines and temples. Reporters attributed the value given away that day as to be about two crore of rupees.

The same day the Maharaja sent for the Kohinoor and desired that it be presented to the temple of lord Jagannath at Puri. He was dissuaded from doing so by his courtiers. Dhian Singh was among those prominent courtiers who opposed the Maharaja's wish to donate the Kohinoor to a temple. Dhian Singh's view was supported by the Sardars, to whom possession of the diamond signified the independence of the Sikh Kingdom; it was, after all, a favourite saying of the Maharaja that whoever owned it would be the ruler of Punjab.[4] If this last wish of Ranjit Singh had been carried out, the Kohinoor would still have been in India and not a possession of the British crown.

The Maharaja's last act was that of a dying soldier. He summoned his courtiers to his bedside and gave away his weapons: swords, shields, spears, pistols and matchlocks with his own hands. The courtiers wept loudly as they took the gifts; the Maharaja tried to console them but broke down many times himself. At the end of the ceremony, he washed himself with the water of the Ganges.

On 26 June, the Maharaja lost his consciousness. Kharak Singh summoned a special durbar at which he confirmed his father's grants to the estate holders, and the ministers and senior officials made overtures of mutual concurrence. The ministers said that they should observe strict unanimity, similar to that of British Councils, for the safety of the state and the preservation of Kunwar Kharak Singh and Kunwar Nau Nihal Singh's right to the throne.

The end came on the evening of 27 June 1839. By a curious coincidence, it was exactly forty years to the day that he had entered Lahore as a victor. The *Lahore Akhbar* described the touching scene: 'The death of the Maharaja being known, the Ranees, Koonwar Kharak Singh, Raja Dhian Singh, Jumadar Khooshal Singh and others raised voices in lamentation, tearing their hair, casting earth on their heads, throwing themselves on the ground and striking their heads against bricks and stone. This continued during the night by the side of the corpse. Every now and then, looking towards the corpse their shrieks were shriller.'[5]

Precautions were taken against civil disturbances and incursion from abroad. A large quantity of ammunition was distributed to the troops and specific orders issued to the officers posted along the Sutlej ferries, to keep the boats on the western bank, leaving only one for the use of passengers crossing the river.

During the night the body of the Maharaja lay in state on the floor of the Durbar hall, with oil lamps burning on all sides; and all night the wailing and the lamentation went on. Dhian

Singh, who appeared more emotional than the rest, announced his intention to immolate himself on the Maharaja's funeral pyre. Kharak Singh and the principal sardars placed their turbans at his feet to make him change his mind.

But nothing could dissuade four Ranis and their seven maid servants from their resolve to immolate themselves as Satis. Rani Guddan, daughter of Raja Sansar Chand of Katotch, thought it the most appropriate occasion to obtain an oath of loyalty to the state, she took Raja Dhian Singh's hand, placed it on the chest of the corpse and made him swear never to betray Kharak Sing or his son Nau Nihal Singh, and always to be attentive to the welfare of the state. In the same way, she made Kharak Singh swear that he would not be led away by misrepresentations of interested parties against Raja Dhian Singh. 'The torments of hell due for the slaughter of a thousand cows were to be visited on him who should violate this oath.'[6] The Dogras did betray the Maharaja, though.

The next morning, the Maharaja's body was bathed with the water of the Ganges once again and placed on a sandalwood coffin, designed like a ship; its sails were made of silk and brocade. Ministers and courtiers paid their last homage by placing shawls on the coffin. The funeral procession left the fort with the ranis and their maidservants, who were to immolate themselves, walking immediately behind the procession. They were dressed in their bridal costumes and jewels. Every now and then they took off a bangle, a necklace or an earring and flung it into the midst of the crowd of beggars or gave it to someone in the parties of hymn-singers or the Brahmins chanting mantras. The procession passed through the narrow streets of the city, jam-packed with mourners and came to a garden at the foot of the massive wall of the fort – not far from the Gurdwara, marking the site of the martyrdom of Guru Arjan Dev. A news report describes the scene in these words:

'Having arrived at the funeral pyre, made of sandalwood, the corpse was placed upon it. Rani Guddan sat down by its side and placed the head of the deceased on her lap; while the other Ranis with seven slave girls seated themselves around – with every mark of satisfaction on their countenances.'[7]

The last prayers were said by members of all communities, Hindus, Muslims and Sikhs. Brahmins performed their prayers from the shastras; Sikh priests recited passages from the *Granth Sahib* and Muslims chanted, 'Ya Allah, Ya Allah'.[8] At the time fixed by the Brahmins, Kharak Singh lit the pyre and the ruler of Punjab, with four queens and seven slave maids, was reduced to ashes. Raja Dhian Singh attempted four times to jump into the burning pyre but was held back by the assemblage.

'The consuming of his pyre occupied two days', writes Honigberger: 'On the third, some bones and ashes of each of the bodies were collected in the presence of the court only, and separately placed in urns.' The citizens of Lahore paid their final farewell to the ashes of their monarch and his consorts, 'upon the procession leaving the fortress, traversed the streets and bazars, the ministers and some of the principal Sardars on foot, with numerous others mounted on their elephants and horses. Thousands of persons were assembled in the streets, bazars, and on the top of houses, by whom flowers were thrown upon the palanquin.... Upon the arrival of the procession outside Delhi Gate, a final and profuse royal salute was given by the thundering of cannon from the fort and ramparts of the city'.[9]

His final resting place is very near to the Samadhi of Guru Arjan Dev, which Ranjit Singh had built with deep reverence for the fifth Guru. As was customary, the architectural form of his own Samadhi was influenced by the Hindu and Islamic forms prevalent in those times. The material used was red stone in the main structure, with very little marble. Under the central vault and beneath a carved canopy of marble is the symbolic urn, also in marble, beneath which Ranjit Singh's ashes lie. There are several stone and marble forms beneath this vault to commemorate his wives and maids who immolated themselves on his pyre. In the increasing chaos that overtook the realm, the Durbar's functionaries found little time to assemble the most sensitive designers and craftsmen to design a truly memorable memorial for one of the most exceptional men of the age.

Ten years later, Sir Alexander Cunnigham's brother, Joseph Davey Cunningham was to sum up what Ranjit Singh stood for, from the age of ten onwards: 'Ranjit Singh found the Punjab a waning confederacy, a prey to the factions of its chiefs, passed by the Afghans and the Marathas, and ready to submit to English supremacy. He consolidated the numerous petty states into a kingdom, he wrested from Kabul the fairest of its provinces, and he gave the potent English no cause for interference. He found the military array of his country a mass of horsemen, brave indeed, but ignorant of war as an art, and he left it mustering fifty thousand disciplined soldiers, fifty thousand well-armed yeomanry and militia, and more than three hundred pieces of cannon for the field.'[10]

What followed is a tale of unbelievable chaos, treachery, greed and betrayals greater than Napoleon's.

THE WORM WITHIN

BRITISH PLANS TO dismember the Sikh State were initiated with enormous zeal and attention soon after the death of Maharaja Ranjit Singh. British historians themselves and recordkeepers with military service themselves provide the best accounts of those times and the British chicanery against the Sikhs despite the British claims of being proud to be doing the right thing. Their detailed accounts prove, there was nothing called the British national traits of honour and truth for a greedy, expansionist colonial power headed by Queen Victoria; that the Queen was as much just a titular head as her ward Dalip Singh; and she could little control the deceit and lies of her cunning men who annexed and plundered India in the nineteenth century.

The first and foremost step taken was not only to identify and win over by whatever means possible, those in the Lahore Durbar who were susceptible to treasonous offers, but also to create further rivalries and rifts, which were already simmering to weaken Ranjit Singh's famous court, the once-formidable centre of Sikh power. After the death of Ranjit Singh, the British saw no reason to stand by the Sikhs, especially as all the difficult peoples of the northern regions – the Afghans, Pathans, tribal chiefs and others – had been subdued and brought under control by Ranjit Singh and his Khalsa Army, who had done their job of crafting one concrete kingdom, which was now up for grabs. From the British point of view, within the first seven years of Ranjit Singh's death, it was obviously time to take over what clearly belonged to the Sikhs, because they were no longer united enough to defend it.

To start with, in a General Proclamation of 20 August 1847, the East India Company's Governor-General Lord Henry Hardinge, ostensibly speaking for the British crown, announced that he felt 'the interest of a father in the education and guardianship of the young prince (Dalip Singh)' and that 'he had at heart the peace and security of this country (the Punjab), the firm establishment of the state, and the honour of the Maharaja and his ministers'. In order 'to maintain the administration of the Lahore State during the minority of the Maharajah', the Governor-General was armed with supreme and plenary power, and was 'at liberty to occupy with British soldiers such possessions as he may think fit, for the security of the Capital, for the protection of the Maharajah, and the preservation of the peace of the country'.

The British Resident was placed at the head of the administration with 'full authority to direct and control all matters of the administration with full authority to direct and control all matters in every department of the state'.[1] These excerpts from the secret papers maintained by the British place in perspective the many devious means by which they created their Indian empire. The possession of Punjab was justified because of the Governor-General's *fatherly interest* in the *education and guardianship of the young prince,* to ensure which, it would be necessary to bring peace and security to the state and country.

This 'peace and security', of course, would require the presence of British soldiers, who would after all be for *'the protection of the Maharajah*'. To quote Barbara Tuchman, a contemporary American historian, on this particular English talent: 'No nation has ever produced a military history of such verbal nobility as the British. Retreat or advance, win or lose, blunder or bravery, murderous folly or unyielding resolution, all emerge alike clothed in dignity and touched in glory.... Other nations attempt, but never quite achieve the same self-esteem. It was not by might but by the power of her self-image that Britain in her century dominated the world.'[2]

In planning moves towards the annexation of the Punjab after Ranjit Singh's death, no limits were set to encouraging betrayals in the Sikh ranks, nor entering into dirty deals of any kind. Several British writers, though very few, have shown concern at their fellow countrymen's use of traitors amongst their adversaries in the pursuit of military and political ends. 'The Sikh army fought valiantly and stubbornly', writes British military historian, Donald Featherstone: 'In spite of poor generalship from commanders who, for political reasons, did not want to win the war and were constantly in touch with the British commanders to ensure them of the fact.'[3]

The two wars between the British and the Sikhs were a matter of touch-and-go for the British, and had they not resorted to every dubious tactic in the book, the outcome would have been entirely different for them. Yet when the history of those times is read in the accounts of British historians, the verbal nobility so beloved of their nation comes through at every turn, referring to actions of men of influence in the British administration that were questionable to say the least. While some British writers had the integrity to point to the misdeeds of their countrymen when battle was finally joined between the two armies, few – if any – wrote of how betrayals in the enemy's forces were encouraged to turn the tide of war in Britain's favour. The one outstanding example in the British establishment of the time, who exposed British moves for what they were, was Captain Joseph Davey Cunningham, brother of the famous explorer Alexander Cunnigham.

Palace Intrigues

Within days of Maharaja Ranjit Singh's death on 27 June 1839, his great empire began to flounder. Intrigues and conspiracies found its way in the palace, and the confidence and discipline of the famous Sikh troops started dwindling. The strength and power which was a hallmark of Ranjit Singh's Sikh empire was beginning to be destroyed from within.

The Raj Tilak was applied duly on Kharak Singh's forehead and he was formally recognised as the Maharaja of the Punjab. History has been unkind to Kharak Singh who was born in 1802 and died at the young age of thirty-eight. He has been universally written off, in some cases as an 'stupid', 'imbecile', as an 'incorrigible opium addict',[4] and yet in others as 'mentally unsound'. This may not have been true at all, but just a case of the writer's bias. He was ignored by the historians perhaps because of his short and lackluster rule, indecisiveness and closed mind which responded only to a shrewd courtier. Perhaps it was just a case of a mediocre son growing up in the shadow of a great father, and then for historians to judge him as such.

Victims of Conspiracy

Portraits of Prince Kharak Singh's younger days as the heir to his father is quite in contrast to later portrayals. A decade earlier, he had led armies in campaigns and had his father's ear on a number of subjects. Perhaps the constant usage of opium taken twice a day, impaired his mind and made him the weak, vacillating man that he has been described as. This was the beginning of the nineteenth century. One question to ask is, who gave the heir apparent and inheritor to such a vast and rich kingdom opium and ensured that he became an addict? The other would be, what was happening in the global theatre? Who was interested in gobbling up the Sikh empire?

When Kharak Singh became ruler, Russia was ruled by the authoritarian Tsar Nicholas I. Following Napoleon's defeat and overthrow, various rulers claiming to be inheritors of the dynasty before the French revolution ascended the French throne and left, until it was ruled by Louis Philippe, who had extended a hand of friendship to Ranjit Singh. Queen Victoria was on the English throne, but India was still not a British colony. Large part of the country was held by the East India Company, a trading company, through a Governor-General. This was before the 1857 Mutiny by EIC soldiers. Bahadur Shah Zafar II had just become the Mughal emperor.

By the first half of the eighteenth century, the East India Company was selling large quantities of opium grown in Bengal to China in exchange of silver. Punjab's immediate neighbour, Afghanistan and Iran, further north, were producing countries. That opium was extensively used in the Punjab is not surprising. Ranjit Singh himself consumed alcohol in large quantities and also opium at times. For all practical purposes, officials close to the princes may have actively encouraged them to addiction to further their own personal agendas and political ambitions. On hindsight, as the story unfolded in the Punjab two hundred years ago, there appears to be great scope for research and study also on the then British strategy for a Raj in the future. Here we look at how it played out.

Son Kharak Singh's Downfall

Immediately after ascending the throne, Kharak Singh came under the influence of a man called Chet Singh Bajwa, who soon established himself as the only advisor to Kharak Singh. Provoked by Chet Singh, Kharak Singh one day openly taunted Ranjit Singh's Dogra Prime Minister, Dhian Singh. The Jammu brothers, led by Prime Minister Raja Dhian Singh and his son Heera Singh, were intelligent and experienced and had led Ranjit Singh's cabinet for years.

Then Kharak Singh banned both, the Prime Minister and Heera Singh, from entering the *Zenana* (the women's quarter in the palace), a privilege accorded to the two by Ranjit Singh. The constant gossip of the women was considered an essential source of intelligence, and denying entrance to them, apart from being viewed as an insult, cut them off from this effective source of information on what went on in the palace.

Then, in a further attempt to insult the Raja Kalhan, who had been positioned in the durbar by Ranjit Singh as the most senior among the rajas, Chet Singh was elevated to the position of *Wazir*, with the same order of precedence as that of the Prime Minister. He then raised two battalions of bodyguards, with the object of using them, when required to eliminate the Prime Minister and whosoever he wanted to kill. Thus, even before he had consolidated his position, Kharak Singh had compromised his title and took on one of the most powerful of his father's men as enemy. Dhian Singh ignored the oath he had taken on his Maharaja's body.

Aware of the plan to discredit him, the Prime Minister, well-informed and ever shrewd, took corrective measures of his own. A story was soon discreetly circulated that Kharak Singh had established contact with the British. He was intending to accept their supremacy and, as a consequence, their protection. Six annas in a rupee (of 16 annas) had been agreed to, which would be paid for by the Durbar, to the British for this protection. All Sikh regiments would be disbanded and the Sardars deprived of their hereditary powers. The rumour swept the kingdom and the army.

At the same time, Dhian Singh urgently summoned

Prince Nau Nihal Singh, then stationed at Peshawar, to return immediately to Lahore. Dhian Singh's brother, Raja Gulab Singh, who was also in Peshawar at that time accompanied the Prince on the way and, having been thoroughly briefed by his brother, indoctrinated him so effectively during the journey that by the time he reached Lahore, Nau Nihal Singh had become an avowed enemy of his father.

Prince Nau Nihal Singh was incapable of distinguishing between the good and evil, which was perhaps responsible for his early end. Though he hated Dhian Singh for good reason, Nau Nihal connived with him in crudely removing his father from power and exercising all the ruler's powers himself. On 8 October 1839, he also connived with Dhian Singh in the killing of Chet Singh, his father's closest advisor. It was a chilling and brutal murder, carried out in the presence of a very ill Kharak Singh. Nau Nihal Singh himself, it has been written, was present. According to some accounts, Dhian Singh stabbed Chet Singh 'twice through the stomach with a long knife'.[5]

Ranjit Singh's Grandson, Nau Nihal Singh

Kharak Singh declined rapidly, both in body and mind, after witnessing the brutal end of his friend and callous disregard for his own dignity and sensitivity. Nau Nihal viewed his father's sad state as an opportunity to become the Maharaja of Punjab – a position to which he failed to bring his grandfather's qualities of statesmanship and leadership. 'His virtual assumption of power in the name of the titular monarch in December 1839', writes the modern historian Bikrama Jit Hasrat, 'was characterised with unwise political steps… he prevented the British political agent Claude Wade from meeting the Maharaja in December 1839, and made an attempt, so that Sir John Keane, the British General, should not have an interview with the Maharaja (Kharak Singh). He was also responsible for the recall of (the British political agent) Wade from Ludhiana for the latter's alleged overbearing and obnoxious conduct towards him and the Prime Minister, Dhian Singh'.[6]

Not content with these patently unwise moves against the British – in contrast to Ranjit Singh who had always made it a point to curb his own desires – Nau Nihal Singh opposed the various provocative moves the British made. Some of these moves were noted by the Governor-General in his minute dated 20 August 1839. Among other things the British 'proposed the establishment of a permanent British mission at Peshawar and a magazine at Rawalpindi, in the territories of the Durbar though they were not stipulated in the tripartite Treaty, signed on 26 June 1838, by Ranjit Singh with Shah Shuja and the East India Company, agreeing on a joint invasion of Afghanistan to put Shah Shuja on the Kabul throne'.[7]

Dhian Singh and Gulab Singh effectively played their part, and both Nau Nihal Singh and his mother Chand Kaur, and their loyalist Sardars, were all shown letters purportedly written and signed by the Maharaja (Kharak Singh) to the British. This so completely convinced them of the Maharaja's treachery that they agreed immediately to assassinate his chief advisor Chet Singh, to depose Maharaja Kharak Singh, and crown his son Nau Nihal Singh. As mentioned earlier, according to plan Chet Singh was stabbed to death on 8 October 1839, and Kharak Singh was transported under guard to his city mansion; where he had lived earlier, and was put under arrest while the 18-year-old Nau Nihal Singh was anointed with the Raj Tilak and proclaimed the new Maharaja.

Kharak Singh lived for another thirteen months and died on 5 November 1840, in his thirty-ninth year. He was administered a slow-acting poison under direction of the Prime Minister, a combination 'Safeda Kaskari (white lead)' and 'Rush Camphor (muriatic of mercury)'.[8] However, the

Maharaja, Nau Nihal Singh, thought that his father's death was natural. During these thirteen months he went to visit him just once, and that too towards the end, despite his father sending him innumerable messages.

When news reached him of the Maharaja's death, Nau Nihal Singh was out hunting in his favourite hunting ground at Shah Bilawal outside Lahore. According to those present, he received the news with joy and continued to sport for another two hours. His dislike for his father had reached such an extreme that there was wide-spread belief that the poisoning of his father, supervised by the Prime Minister, had his tacit approval.[9]

The funeral of Kharak Singh took place that very afternoon (5 November 1840), close to the Samadhi of his father. Two wives and eleven of his slave girls immolated themselves on his funeral pyre. A final salute of 180 gun fire was given from the ramparts and Nau Nihal Singh lit the pyre. Straight after doing so, he walked away towards the Ravi river, to bathe and change his clothes, as was the custom. He was, however, prevented by the Prime Minister from doing so immediately, as his leaving before all the rituals of the funeral would not be taken in good taste by the people who were present in large numbers at the funeral, along with all the Sikh generals and Sardars of the court.

Nau Nihal Singh is said to have waited for a while, but once again impatiently walked away, before the prayers ended, to take his bath and change his clothes before entering the palace. Having done so at the river, at a point of 120 yards away from the cremation site, he started walking towards the palace along with his friend Udham Singh, the son of Raja Gulab Singh and nephew of the Prime Minister.

The small northern gate (later known as *Khooni Darwaza*) of the Hazuri Bagh, through which he was to enter the palace, was about 40 yards from the Samadhi of Ranjit Singh. Both the young men entered it together, and as he was about to exit at the other end of the gate, a large chunk of the archway fell on him, perhaps loosened by the vibration caused by the large guns firing on the ramparts. Due to this accident, Udham Singh was killed on the spot and the young Maharaja was severely hurt. The Prime Minister, following at a distance, received an abrasion on his arm.

End of Ranjit Singh's Bloodline

Ironically, Nau Nihal Singh's own life also ended on the same day as his father's due to the fall of the archway on him, accidentally or deliberately. There are a number of versions of his death, one being that he did not die in the accident but was killed by Dhian Singh, a day or two later, during which time no one was allowed to see him on the plea that he was being treated for his injuries.

Accounts of Nau Nihal Singh's end by writers of the period leave little doubt of Dhian Singh's role in it. Major G C Smyth mentions: 'None of the female inmates (of Lahore Fort), not even his wives, were allowed to see him. Everything was kept locked up for a while… and the minister (Dhian Singh), with but two of his followers and chiefs remained with the prince.'[10]

An eyewitness account by Captain Alexander Gardener, an American serving in the Lahore Durbar's artillery, noted that it was some of Gardener's own men who put the injured Prince into a palki (palanquin) to take him to the fort. 'One of the palki bearers afterwards affirmed, that when the Prince was put into the palki, and when he was assisting to place him there, he saw that above the right ear there was a wound which bled so slightly as only to cause a patch of blood of about the size of a rupee… the blood neither flowed nor trickled in any quantity, before his being taken out. Now, it is a curious fact, that when the room was opened, in which his corpse was first exposed by the Raja (Dhian Singh), blood in great quantity, both in fluid and coagulated pools was found around the head on the cloth on which the body lay.'[11]

Whatever caused Nau Nihal Singh's death, the consensus among various accounts is that, the lives of the two men whom Ranjit Singh had hoped would ensure the continuity of his legacy came to an end within two days. Although there are other suspects, most fingers point not only at Dhian Singh but also at his brothers, Gulab Singh and Suchet Singh (although the last name of each was Singh, they were not Sikhs); they had sworn allegiance to Ranjit Singh, who knew how to retain their loyalty during his lifetime. An added edge to Dhian Singh's intrigues was provided by his obsessive desire to see his son Heera Singh ultimately ascend Ranjit Singh's throne. The conspiracies he hatched after the Maharaja's death to clear his son's way to the throne were phenomenal and as Prime Minister, he was in a position to arrange the bloodbaths necessary to attain his ends.

Aside from these Dogras and Brahmins, members of Ranjit Singh's own family were equally involved in their intrigues to capture power, indifferent to the fact that the British were waiting on the sidelines to exercise their skills in manipulation and subversion, which inexorably led to domination and subjection of the Sikh nation. The more active of these participants in the power struggle were Chand Kaur, Kharak Singh's widow and mother of Nau Nihal Singh, and Sher Singh, Ranjit Singh's second son, real or otherwise.

Chand Kaur & Sher Singh

After her son's death, Chand Kaur, widow of Kharak Singh and mother of Nau Nihal Singh, became the centre of struggle that now began in the Lahore Durbar.

There was another claimant to Ranjit Singh's throne. This was Sher Singh, supposedly Ranjit Singh's second son, born of Ranjit Singh's first wife Mehtab Kaur. It was accepted that Sher

Singh was not really his, but Ranjit Singh had given him the title of 'prince' under pressure from Sada Kaur, his powerful mother-in-law and honoured him in various ways. The man, in his early thirties now, had an impressive presence, but his degraded ways and lack of serious convictions earned him no respect, and as usual, the riffraff gathered around him for their own ends.

Two hours after the accident, Dhian Singh, the Prime Minister, told Nau Nihal Singh's mother that he wished her to be the next ruler. He then swore her to secrecy and warned her that any leakage of this decision would reduce her chances of occupying the *gaddi*. He then officially announced the Maharaja's death. He then also sent an urgent message to Sher Singh, informing him of Nau Nihal Singh's death. Sher Singh was then at his estate at Kanuwan, near Gurdaspur. He was urged to return immediately, as the Prime Minister wished him to be the next Maharaja. He was asked to come straight to the Shalimar Gardens where Dhian Singh would meet the heir apparent.

Nau Nihal Singh was cremated the next day, 6 November 1840, close to the Samadhi of his grandfather. Two of his young women committed Sati on his pyre.

The Prime Minister, knowing that a war of succession would now take place, had for the moment played safe by offering to make both Chand Kaur and Sher Singh the new ruler of Lahore. He had bought time, as he had no intentions of making Chand Kaur the new ruler. He knew Chand and her supporters – the Sandhanwalia Sardars – disliked him, and he would be their first victim, once they were well settled at Lahore. Not quite sure, however, of how the struggle for succession would end, he left his brother, Raja Gulab Singh, in Chand Kaur's camp to support her cause.

To ensure the support of the Dogra brothers, Chand Kaur then announced that one of Nau Nihal Singh's Maharanis was pregnant and if a boy was born he would be the new Maharaja and she the regent and that if it was a girl, she would adopt Heera Singh, Dhian Singh's son, who had been the late Maharaja Ranjit Singh's favourite, to be the new Maharaja. Thus, very intelligently, she managed to get herself installed as ruler of the Punjab. As to Sher Singh, she said that she did not acknowledge him as the legitimate son of the late Maharaja Ranjit Singh.

Shrewdly assessing the strength she had gathered by then, Dhian Singh thought it proper to remain quiet at the moment. He quietly advised Sher Singh not to precipitate matters at the moment but to wait for an opportune moment to press his claim. He asked Sher Singh to return to his estate at Batala. The Prime Minister then announced that he was unwell and required rest, and therefore, he was leaving Lahore for some time and returning to his estate in Jammu. Chand Kaur promptly appointed her ally, the Sandhanwalia Sardar, Attar Singh, as the new Prime Minister. A four-member council was formed to run the day-to-day affairs, and the council was presided over by the new Prime Minister. By now Raja Gulab Singh had firmly allied himself with the Maharani.

Dalip Singh

At this juncture Dhian Singh, unsure about Sher Singh's success in staking his claim to the throne, played his second card. He informed the British government that Rani Jindan, one of Ranjit Singh's wives, had given birth to a son, Dalip Singh, on 6 September 1838. This was the first time when the British government learnt of the existence of another heir to the throne of Lahore.

Khalsa Army becomes Kingmaker

While the new administration attempted to consolidate its precarious position, Dhian Singh set in motion monumental events to destabilise it. His directed his people in Lahore to play on the sentiments of those Chiefs, Sardars, and Generals of Ranjit Singh's famous army who felt disgruntled with the present establishment to rise in revolt. After making a thorough assessment of the situation, Dhian Singh's associates at Lahore suggested that Sher Singh march back to Lahore. Dhian Singh informed Sher Singh that he would meet him at Shalimar Garden, instead of the city camp. Sher Singh immediately left Batala and arrived at the Shalimar Gardens with around 300 of his followers. Dhian Singh, however, stayed safe in Jammu. He had, once again, decided to watch the incumbent Durbar's reactions and watch what happens to Sher Singh.

Dhian Singh was wholly aware of the support Chand Kaur was mobilising to consolidate her position and had played clever by stationing his brother Gulab Singh in her camp. It was a shrewd move. While his brother could subvert the state from within the Durbar, Sher Singh could be made to mount a frontal attack on it, given his own claim to the thrown. This would place both the Dogra brothers in a win-win situation because if things worked out in their favour, they would have got rid of both Chand Kaur and Sher Singh.

Sher Singh arrived at Shalimar Gardens in time. As described by a nineteenth-century historian, Syed Muhammad Latif: 'Sher Singh, according to previous arrangement, marched from Mukerian, at the head of about 300 followers, and posted himself at the Shalimar Gardens. To his great disappointment, however, he was informed that Dhian Singh had not, up to that moment, even left his hill territory in Jammu.

'This afforded an opportunity to Jawala Singh, an ambitious Sardar, and one of Sher Singh's principal councillors, who aspired to the Wazirship, to instill into the mind of the unsuspecting Prince the idea that Dhian Singh cared little for his (Prince's) interests, and that his real sympathies were with his brother Gulab Singh, who had openly taken up the cause of the maharani.'[12] Inevitably, the stage was now set for a showdown, with the subversion of the two camps by the Dogra brothers.

'For about thirty days', in the words of British historian, Major G C Smyth, 'Dhian Singh remained at Jammu, during which time, the emissaries he had left at Lahore secretly to play the Sikh Soldiery had so well played their part as to have received promises from the different corps that as soon as the minister and Sher Singh should present themselves at Lahore, they would place the latter upon the throne. These promises were given on the consideration that the army should receive an increase of pay, together with large presents – terms which were only afterwards partially fulfilled'.[13]

All this would soon prove fatal for Sher Singh, who lacked the intelligence to see that, by making the Sikh army take sides in palace intrigues, he was undermining the basic structure on which the supposedly-indestructible power of the Lahore Durbar rested. By foolishly drawing the army into the political decision-making process, he gave it the right to assert itself in decisions affecting the state – which was a right invested by the Gurus in the entire Khalsa community, and not just the army.

What aggravated the army still further were the feelers Sher Singh sent to the British, seeking their help in capturing Lahore. The move angered the Khalsa army – already ill-disposed towards the British – even more.

Dhian Singh, with his men, arrived at Shahdara not far from Lahore to join Sher Singh on the fifth day of the week-long siege of Lahore. Before his arrival, the Sikh soldiers had rallied around Sher Singh in numbers which are said to have been close to 70,000 infantrymen. The detachments stationed in the Lahore Fort were also mobilised to the fullest. The battle between the besiegers and the besieged was bloody. As for the Dogra brothers, while Gulab Singh oversaw operations within the fort, according to plan, Dhian Singh arrived outside it as an ally of Sher Singh. Sher Singh, on learning of Dhian Singh's arrival, offered to end the hostilities and negotiate with Gulab Singh, who refused to accept any overtures except through the mediation of his brother Dhian Singh.[14] What better outcome could the Dogras ask for?

The siege ended on the evening of 17 January 1841 with the surrender of Chand Kaur's forces. Negotiations now began between the two parties. Raja Heera Singh was deputed by Gulab Singh to negotiate on behalf of Maharani Chand Kaur. Heera Singh emerged on the seventh day, accompanied by the Sandhanwalia Sardars, and peace was agreed on the following terms: 1) The Maharani would surrender the Lahore Fort to Sher Singh and give up all the claim to throne 2) Sher Singh would give a jaagir providing her 9 lakh rupees annually, which would be managed by Raja Gulab Singh as her agent 3) Sher Singh would refrain from his wish to marry her by the Chadar Dalna ceremony 4) the Dogra troops would be allowed to leave the fort with their weapons, unmolested; and 5) security would be provided to ensure that the agreement was implemented.[15]

Gulab Singh Takes away Durbar's Wealth

The night before the agreement was finalised, Raja Gulab Singh took advantage of the confusion and collected all the jewels and other valuables of Maharani Chand Kaur on the pretext of keeping them safe. Then, without alerting anyone, he cleared out most of the treasury, taking sixteen carts filled with rupees and other silver coins. Each of his 500 horsemen were entrusted with carrying a bag of gold mohurs (gold coins), and other men were laden with quantities of jewellery and other valuables. He also took away twelve of Ranjit Singh's best horses from the stables, and quantities of the best pashminas and rich dresses from the Maharaja's wardrobe.[16]

Before leaving for Jammu, Gulab Singh met Sher Singh and paid his respects to him as the new Maharaja and told him that all that he had done was in good faith, as it was his duty to the late Maharaja Ranjit Singh's memory to protect his daughter-in-law. After professing unfaltering loyalty to Sher Singh, he pulled the Kohinoor diamond out of his bag and offered it to Sher Singh as a humble gift. Sher Singh had no problem in accepting it. Having, thus, put him in a happy mood, the shrewd Dogra then proceeded to pledge his abiding loyalty to Sher Singh just as he had to his old master Ranjit Singh. A happy Sher Singh immediately ordered that a royal *firman* (written order of the Durbar) be issued, making over 20 villages in the Bhimber district to Raja Gulab Singh forever.[17]

Sher Singh was anointed as the new Maharaja on 18 January 1841. All Sardars and Chiefs, except the Sandhanwalias, paid homage to him. Dhian Singh was brought back as the Prime Minister. The pay of the soldiers who put him on the throne was raised by one rupee a month. All the jaagirs and estates of the Sandhanwalias was regained by the state and orders issued for their arrest. Maharani Chand Kaur's Prime Minister, Attar Singh and his nephew Ajit Singh, escaped across the Sutlej to the British territory, while Attar Singh's younger brother Lehna Singh, was brought to Lahore in chains.

The Revolt of 1842

Sher Singh's becoming Maharaja emboldened the army to become increasingly intolerant and the soldiers began to take the law into their hands. The great Khalsa army had become extremely volatile. Maltreatment of officers became a routine affair. The houses of several officers were burnt and some suspected of harbouring an ill-feeling towards any of the troops were put to death. General Court managed to escape, while Colonel Faulkes was killed and so were Hast and Ford. In

Kashmir, the governor, Colonel Mihan Singh, who was second-in-command to Hari Singh Nalwa at the battle of Jamrud, was killed and his house plundered. In Peshawar, General Avitabile abandoned the town and escaped to Jallalabad to save his life. This was the mutiny of 1842 and discontent continued till British intervention was threatened.

The exodus of foreign officers from the Lahore army now began. In the matters of state, Sher Singh left the management of the government to Raja Dhian Singh. Sher Singh passed his days in hunting and other pleasures. The Jammu brothers, knowing that he still wished to marry Chand Kaur by the Chaddar Dalna ceremony, became instrumental in keeping them apart, by convincing each that the other was conspiring against him or her. Dhian Singh did not want Chand Kaur back in favour, as his own future was at stake. As for Gulab Singh, he believed the sooner she was off the scene, the better for him to become master of her wealth of which he had been appointed as custodian by the agreement.

The seed of bitterness was sown in Sher Singh's mind and nurtured to such an extent that finally he ordered for her execution. In early June 1842, when he went to Wazirabad on a routine trip, her maid servants were instructed to kill Chand Kaur. Each would be given 5,000 rupees to perform this task. One morning on the pretext of grooming her hair, they smashed her skull with a large stone, killing her on the spot.

Sher Singh and Dhian Singh Killed

After the death of Chand Kaur, the Sandhanwalia Sardars, her key supporters, fearing Sher Singh's anger, had fled across the Sutlej to seek British protection. In due course, however, all four were persuaded to return to Lahore. The British political agent at Ludhiana, George Russel Clerk did his utmost to plead and champion their cause with Sher Singh. Sher Singh had no reason to trust the Sandhanwalias but was swayed by Clerk's persuasive arguments. He pardoned them and allowed them to return to Lahore and had their estates restored to them. Attar Singh returned to his estate, Lehna Singh and Ajit Singh also in due course became the Maharaja's confidants to the extent that their views were solicited on all matters of state. Raja Dhian Singh encouraged this relationship and, in turn, befriended them himself.

In the meanwhile, the relationship between Sher Singh and Dhian Singh had also begun to sour. The Sandhanwalias, aware of this and desirous to see them both off the scene, began to play one against the other. They finally succeeded, by convincing Sher Singh that they had been promised a bribe of Rs 60 lakh by the Prime Minister to kill him. Sher Singh, already estranged from his Prime Minister, readily believed the story and eventually became so thoroughly convinced of Raja Dhian Singh's treachery that one day he gave permission to both Ajit Singh and Lehna Singh to kill Raja Dhian Singh. Sher Singh even gave them a firman for this purpose, thereby exonerating them from the act they were going to commit, which, it was written, was being done in the interest of the state.

This firman from the maharaja was a windfall for the Sandhanwalia brothers as it gave them a marvellous opportunity to finish both Sher Singh and Dhian Singh. The brothers promptly showed the prime minister this order. He, on the face of it, refused to believe it unless it had the personal signature and royal seal of the maharaja. This they soon procured. They now convinced Raja Dhian Singh that they had shown him the death warrant in good faith, as they only wanted to get rid of Sher Singh. Then they got his consent to kill the maharaja. Raja Dhian Singh told them that they would always have his support and promised them a great reward if they succeeded in their task. He then retired to his residence, pretending illness while the conspirators set about their task. It was decided to carry out this murder on the following Friday, the day Sher Singh was to be at his palace at Shah Bilawal.

On the appointed day, Sher Singh was sitting at the window of the *baradari* at Shah Bilawal, watching a wrestling bout when Ajit Singh Sandhanwalia entered and asked the Maharaja if he could show him a new shot gun he had just received. As Sher Singh stretched out his arm to take it, Ajit Singh emptied both barrels into his chest. With one blow of his sword, he then severed his head. The Maharaja's young son, Partap Singh, who was playing close by was also then hacked to pieces by Lehna Singh.

The conspirators now met the Prime Minister, who was outside the fort. Taking him by the hand, Ajit Singh asked him to return to the fort so that the new arrangements to run the government could be decided upon. He then asked the Prime Minister as to who he thought should be the new maharaja? Dhian Singh replied, 'Dalip Singh, of course'. To this, the retort was, 'he is to become the maharaja and you his wazir, what do we get for all this trouble?' The Prime Minister expressed his annoyance at these remarks and was about to ride away, when on Ajit Singh's cue, he was shot in the back and killed on the spot by one of his men. Another man then severed his head and hacked his body to bits.[18]

The First Moves on the Raj Chessboard

Dalip Singh was destiny's child. There was no proof that Maharaja Ranjit Singh had ever married his mother Jindan Kaur. But like many others, Ranjit Singh had accepted him too as 'son'.

During the seven years between the death of Ranjit Singh in 1839 and the start of the First Anglo-Sikh War in 1846, three maharajas – Kharak Singh, Nau Nihal Singh and Sher Singh – one maharani, Chand Kaur – four prime ministers

– Jawala Singh, Raja Dhian Singh, Raja Heera Singh, and Jawahar Singh – and twenty nine other leading figures of the state were assassinated; seven more died of natural causes. Of the thirty-seven mentioned above, five were killed on the orders of Raja Dhian Singh and twelve, on those if his son Raja Heera Singh. Virtually the entire leadership of the state built by the great Ranjit Singh ceased to exist at this point in time.[19]

The odds had been so strongly stacked in favour of an imminent and violent change of power that the British political agent at Ludhiana, George Russel Clerk and the British would have had to be blind not to know what was likely to happen, if the Sandhanwalias went back to Lahore. Were the British guilty of being accomplices or accessories to these treasonous murders? As the *British Friend of India*, published from London wrote in December 1843 of these murders: 'We have no proof that the Company (EIC) instigated all the king-killing in the Punjab since Ranjit Singh died.... We must say we smell a rat.'[20]

In any objective assessment of the extent of Sher Singh's responsibility for his own death, the only conclusion possible is that he himself was responsible. By actively participating in plots to assassinate political rivals, he completely reversed Ranjit Singh's policy of tolerance and non-violence even towards his vanquished foes. It was inevitable that he should pay with his life for the folly of failing to understand that once encouraged, political murders become a way of life.

The British knew how to take full advantage of their adversaries' weaknesses, but, in the ultimate analysis, far more serious was the effect of these palace intrigues on the army. Here again, Sher Singh gravely misjudged the dangerous implications of casting the Sikh army in the role of kingmaker, which he had done by winning over sections of it to help him attack Chand Kaur in Lahore, on 14 January 1841.

Bikrama Jit Hasrat pinpoints the situation: 'Sher Singh's

accession was unattended by any acts of violence; the army, which had enthroned him, had also become his master. It began to wreak vengeance on those whom it considered traitors to the Khalsa. It plundered the houses of several Chiefs, dismissed foreigners from state service, and declared its determination to punish those who sought foreign interference.'[21] Sher Singh's contact with the British stirred up further discontent within the army, which was utterly disapproving of the British. Sher Singh had been quite incapable of grasping the complexities of the unfolding situation.

When, inevitably, the army seriously split down the middle, the very fundamentals of the Khalsa's founding principles were affected, since it was the privilege of the entire Khalsa community to take decisions of profound importance to the faith. Even then, despite the serious dissension in its ranks, the army, whilst divided against itself and some of the key political players – was disapproving but not entirely against the Durbar. This, even the seasoned British failed to understand.

Their assumption that the restlessness of the Sikh forces was directed against the Durbar could not have been more wrong; their resentment was directed at the British who were trying to impose their will on the Khalsa. This misreading of the army's temper and the mood of the resurgent Khalsa would take a heavy toll not only of British lives in the battlefield but also of their pride and myth of invulnerability.

Destiny's Child Dalip Singh

The only aspirant left to the throne of Ranjit Singh, after Sher Singh's death, was the five-year old Dalip Singh, Ranjit Singh's son by Rani Jindan Kaur. Born on 4-September 1838, he will forever remain a tragic figure in history. He was ten-month old when his acknowledged father had died. His mother, Jindan Kaur, a soldier's daughter, was remarkably intelligent and an attractive woman with a 'ready wit and lack of sexual inhibitions, (which) made her well qualified to organise the more outlandish entertainments of the court'.[22]

Dalip may not have been Ranjit Singh's natural son but was very much an heir to his father's throne when the time came for him to claim his rights. He continued to live in the palace at Lahore with his mother through the reigns of Kharak Singh and Sher Singh, but she made sure he kept a low profile, which would help Dalip stay out of harm's way. In those unsettled times, anyone who was seen as a claimant to what others desired was in mortal danger. As the British historian C H Payne noted: 'Probably no one believed that Dalip was the son of Ranjit Singh; but, on the other hand, no one could prove that he was not; and that alone was sufficient to render him a dangerous weapon in the hands of such a master of intrigue as Gulab Singh.'[23]

The shrewd Jindan Kaur, seeing all the signs of trouble at the Lahore court, had taken her son Dalip Singh to stay with Gulab Singh at Jammu after Ranjit Singh's death. But she knew that Lahore was where she had to be to get her son on the throne. So, despite the relentless struggle for power which had become routine at the Lahore Durbar, it wasn't long before Jindan returned to it with her son. Her remarkable self-confidence and tenacity of purpose enabled her to weather the many ruthless plots and sub-plots that were being hatched all the time by the aspirants to power.

She not only managed to survive all of them but also became regent to keep the way to the throne open for her son. Dalip Singh was crowned on 18 September 1843, and at the age of five became the Maharaja of Punjab and its vast territories. The Kohinoor that Sher Singh had owned as part of the crown jewels, now belonged to Dalip Singh, the little Maharaja. Dalip Singh would never have made it to the throne without the astonishing skill with which his mother dealt with the shrewd ways of the Lahore Durbar and its key players. But even this forceful woman was to meet her match soon. Not in her own countrymen, whose ways were familiar to her, but in those from a distant land, who were waiting on the sidelines to acquire by whatever means they could the territories, treasures, natural resources and rare antiquities of this land, which did not belong to them.

They had not sailed thousands of miles to acquire wealth by signing treaties and such other documents. Treaties were fine as long as they served their purpose. The Sutlej Treaty of 1809 was no longer relevant with the East India Company's acquisition of Sind, and navigation rights on the Indus, along with many other advances made by the British. So, the 1809 treaty with Ranjit Singh had already been sidestepped through skilled manoeuvres.

If they had managed to get away with such tactics even in the time of Ranjit Singh – who was an equal match for them – the strife-torn, self-centred and short-sighted men who succeeded him were no match for the seasoned British, who now perceived that the time had come for them to annex Punjab. This was the most strategic State in India, with its rivers and mountains, which were crucial for them to control if the security of the subcontinent they had occupied was to be assured.

THE FIRST ANGLO-SIKH WAR

THE BRITISH WERE now ready to set up *their* Raj in India and play their geopolitical Great Game. The growing intrigues in the palace, treacherous behavior of the persons who mattered in the Sikh kingdom and increasing personal ambitions of the commanders were giving all indications that a showdown between the British and the Sikhs would soon be inevitable. There was no way Sikh pride and self-esteem could be reconciled with the obsessive British desire to bring the whole of India under their control.

[The Great Game began on 12 January 1830, when Lord Ellenborough, the president of East India Company's Board of Control for India, tasked Governor-General William Bentinck with establishing a new trade route to the Emirate of Bukhara. Historians are of the opinion that Britain intended to gain control over Afghanistan and make it a protectorate, and to use the Ottoman Empire, the Persian Empire, the Khanate of Khiva, and the Emirate of Bukhara as buffer states blocking Russian expansion. This is why, actually, the British had supported the Sikhs under Ranjit Singh in their wars against the Afghans. The British thought, the Russians were interested in India, at that time very rich and ripe for the picking by the first comer, and with no strong ruler anywhere. The British assumed their move would protect India and also key British sea trade routes by stopping Russia from gaining a port on the Persian Gulf or the Indian Ocean. Russia proposed Afghanistan as the neutral zone. The Sikhs were the strongest force between the British and Afghanistan. The results were the failed First Anglo-Afghan War of 1838, when Ranjit Singh was still alive, though ailing; the First Anglo-Sikh War of 1845, the Second Anglo-Sikh War of 1848, and later, the Second Anglo-Afghan War of 1878.]

British Provocation

By the time Dalip Singh ascended the Lahore throne, it was a free for all. The hawkish English Governor-General, Lord Ellenborough (in office till June 1844), who had taken over from the more moderate Lord Auckland, was already preparing to mobilise a sizeable army south of the Sutlej, from where Punjab could be invaded. He wrote to the Duke of Wellington on 20 April 1844, that, 'we can only consider our relations with Lahore to be those of an armed truce. I earnestly hope nothing will compel us to cross the Sutlej, that we may have no attack to repel till November 1845. I shall then be prepared for anything. In the meantime, we shall do all we can in a quiet way to strengthen ourselves'.[1]

The political agent of the Lahore Durbar at Ludhiana, a trusted *vakil* (authorised agent), sent some news on British troop movements to Lahore: 'About this time, a news was received... announcing that in view of the general disorder in the Punjab, the British said that the Sikhs all over Punjab had gone mad and had set their house on fire and that their neighbours feared their own house. Consequently, the English *Company Bahadur* (the East India Company) had decided to strengthen the frontier.'[2]

What the British did was to embed two of their mercenary soldiers, Lal Singh and Teja Singh, in the Khalsa forces. If the

British were to attack the Sikh State, 'since appearances had to be kept up, the British had to be shown as responding to improved aggression, their moves must convey a sense of noblesse oblige'.[3] As so often, accuracy was sacrificed for expediency.

The provocation came from Major George Broadfoot, the new British agent at Ludhiana, a man who could not tolerate the Sikhs and, in fact, had been hostile towards them for many years. His provocations included constructing cantonments at Ludhiana, Ferozepur, Ambala, and Kasauli; assembling materials for pontoon bridges along the Sutlej; and declaring the Cis-Sutlej possessions of the Lahore Durbar to be under British protection. These Cis-Sutlej States were a group of small States in Punjab region in the 19th century, lying between Sutlej river on the north, the Himalayas on the east, the Yamuna river and Delhi district on the South and Sirsa District on the west. Henry Hardinge, the Governor-General who was the next in line, was quite approving of Broadfoot and said, he was 'in his element on the frontier'.[4] [In the words of Ellenborough, the outgoing Governor-General, 'I will not fail to make him (Hardinge) acquainted with your merits and services'.][5]

The unrelenting Major's next daredevil act was to confiscate, in November 1845, two villages of the Sikh State south of the Sutlej, near Ludhiana, on the invented charge that they were sheltering criminals. All these British moves left Sikhs in no doubt of the intentions of their adversary. It was once again J D Cunningham who placed these developments in their true perspective. 'Had the shrewd committees of (Sikh) armies observed no military preparations on the part of the English, they would not have heeded the insidious exhortations of such mercenary men as Lal Singh and Teja Singh, although in the former days, they would have marched enquiringly towards Delhi at the bidding of their great Maharaja (Ranjit Singh)... (so) when the men were tauntingly asked whether they would quietly look on while the limits of the Khalsa dominion were reduced… they answered that they would defend with their lives all belonging to the commonwealth of Guru Gobind, and that they would march and give battle to the invaders on their own ground.'[6]

Hardinge Declares War

Broadfoot's scheming to precipitate an armed showdown between the two erstwhile allies was successful. This agent provocateur holding the rank of a Major, with the full support of Governor-General Hardinge, succeeded in provoking the Sikh army to cross the Sutlej, under the command of Teja Singh on 12 December 1845. Hardinge declared the Lahore Durbar as enemy on 13 December 1845.

Lord Hardinge recapitulated the friendly relations that had existed between the British and Ranjit Singh since the Treaty of 1809, the provisions of which, according to Hardinge, had been faithfully observed by the British but grossly violated by the Durbar in recent months. He claimed that British military movements were 'precautionary measure for the protection of the British frontier' and continued: 'The Sikh army has now, without a shadow of provocation, invaded the British territories.'[7] The Governor-General declared that the territories of the Durbar on the left bank of the Sutlej were being confiscated by the British and called upon the Chiefs and Sardars in the protected territories to cooperate with the British in 'punishing the common enemy' – which, according to him, were the Sikhs from the other side of the Sutlej.

Despite the forthright language of the proclamation of war, Lord Hardinge was full of doubts. Robert Cust, one of the political secretaries in his entourage, recalls that after announcement of war, Hardinge was thoughtful and silent and five days later, he eventually turned to his party and without addressing anyone, spoke at length: 'Will the people of England consider this an actual invasion of our territory and a justification of war? The Sikh army, after all, was camped just south of Sutlej in territory that, according to treaty of 1809, belonged to them.'[8] It would seem that Hardinge was having second thoughts about getting involved in a war against the wishes of the East India Company.

The Opinions of two other British officers closely connected with the Anglo-Punjab politics are worth noting. Major G Carmichael Smyth of the North-western Agency wrote: 'Regarding the Punjab war; I am neither of the opinion that the Sikhs made an unprovoked attack, nor that we have acted towards them with great forbearance… if the Sikhs were to be considered entirely an independent state in no way answerable to us, we should not have provoked them – for to assert that the bridge of boats brought from Bombay, was not a *casus belli,* but merely a defensive measure, is absurd; besides, the Sikhs had translations of Sir Charles Napier's speech (as it appeared in the *Delhi Gazette*) stating that we were going to war with them; and as all European powers would have done under such circumstances, the Sikhs thought it well to be first in the field. Moreover, they were not encamped on our territory, their own.'

'… and I only ask, had we not departed from the rules of friendship first? The year before the war broke out, we kept the island between Ferozepur and Punjab, though it belonged to the Sikhs owing to the deep water being between us and the island.

'… But if, on the other hand, the Treaty of 1809 is said to have been binding between the two governments, then the simple question is, who first departed from the "rules of friendship"? I am decidedly of opinion that we did.'

Even more emphatic on the subject is George Campbell, who was then posted at Kaithal (a Sikh State taken by forfeiture by the British). He wrote: 'It is recorded in the annals of history, or what is called history, which will go down to posterity, that the Sikh army invaded British territory in pursuance of a determination to attack us. And most people will be very much surprised to hear that they did nothing of the kind. They did not attack on our outlying cantonments, nor set foot in our territory; what they did do was to cross the river to entrench themselves in their own territory.'[9]

The Traitors, Lal Singh and Teja Singh

The Sikh army sent against the British mainly comprised Sikhs and Muslims. The Khalsa artillery had always been manned by Muslims. The Khalsa army also had small numbers of *Poorabias* and Gurkhas. Gulab Singh forbade the Dogras to join. The Sikhs started with the handicap of being led by traitors. There is enough evidence to prove that at different times, both, the minister Raja Lal Singh, the Commander-in-Chief, Teja Singh, and at a later stage, Gulab Singh Dogra, were in communications with British agents. Rani Jindan was also in liaison with the traitor Lal Singh, who had written a letter to the British 'to consider him and the *Bibi Saheba* as their friends'.[10] Nevertheless the feeling among many people was that the Durbar and Jindan were primarily responsible for pushing the soldiers into hostilities and then letting them down – the object being, to teach them a lesson for having executed her brother, Jawahar Singh. The Poet Shah Mohammad states in no uncertain terms that Jindan 'tore up the States from the floor'.[11]

As mentioned earlier, the first thing Lal Singh did on marching with his army across the Sutlej was to write to Capt John Nicholson, the British political agent at Ferozepur: 'I have crossed with the Sikh army, you know my friendship to the British. Tell me what to do.' Nicholson replied: 'Do not attack Ferozepur. Halt as many days you can, and then march towards the Governor- General.'[12]

Lal Singh carried out Nicholson's instruction. He detached Teja Sing with a force to march towards Ferozepur and took the rest of the army with him a few miles upstream, where he camped in a curved formation near the village of Pheru Shahr – (now described as Ferozeshahar) – with the river Sutlej behind him, and seven wells with good drinking water in their midst. Then, as Nicholson had instructed, he detached yet another force and marched it off to meet the main British army advancing under Lord Gough and the Governor-General.

Battle of Mudki

The force Lal Singh took with him was considerably smaller than the one the British were bringing up. According to Capt Nicholson, the Sikhs were no more than 3,500 men. Cunningham estimates it to have been about 12,000 men with twenty-two guns. Whatever their own strength, the Sikhs were unpleasantly surprised at the large size of Gough's army and its advanced position. Apart perhaps from Lal Singh, no one knew and no one was expecting to meet the enemy for another couple of days, when suddenly on the afternoon of 18 December 1845, they sighted the British encamped near the village of Mudki.

Instead of retreating to more suitable terrain, Lal Singh ordered his men to fall into the battle formation on absolutely flat ground, with little or no cover for his guns except some sandy hillocks and bushes. Sikh snipers took their landing place on branches of some tamarisk trees growing in the vicinity and before the enemy were within the range, Lal Singh ordered his guns to open fire – thereby betraying their position as well as wasting valuable ammunition.

Lord Gough waited patiently till the Sikh fire slackened. Then he got his guns in position and with intense bombardment, silenced the enemy. This is exactly how it had all been preplanned. Just before the sunset the British cavalry charged the Sikh flanks. Lal Singh promptly deserted his men and retreated to the camp at Ferozeshahar. The men, however, refused to give in. They fought a grim hand-to-hand battle against the more numerous enemies, led by the most experienced commanders of Europe, Lord Gough and Lord Hardinge. The battle continued with unabated fury till midnight (and came thereafter to be known as, Midnight Mudki). Then the leaderless Sikhs, who had lost more than half of their comrades and fifteen of their guns, withdrew from the battlefield. To note here is that 'the most experienced commanders of Europe' had to take help of deceit to win this encounter.

Mudki was a field action of not very great military significance. To the British, even this skirmish was an unpleasant surprise. Their casualties were 872 dead and wounded. Amongst those killed were their Quartermaster-General Sir Robert Sale, Sir John McGaskill and Brig Bulton. Sikh snipers had taken heavy toll of British lives. The British realised that they were up against the most determined fighters they had met on the Indian subcontinent. Gough sent word to Ferozepur warning John Littler, the garrison commander there, not to be drawn into any action with the Sikhs on his own, but to join him as soon as possible. More reinforcements were ordered from Ambala, Meerut and Delhi. Lord Hardinge relinquished his superior position of Governor-General and agreed to become second-in-command to the Commander-in-Chief.[13] A more detailed description of the battle tells us how well-trained and valorous the Sikh soldiers were.

Battle of Ferozeshahar, 1845

The game of deceit and betrayal were played out openly at Mudki: As detachments of the Sikhs attacked the British force, Lal Singh deserted his men. Though the outcome of this battle was a victory of sorts for the British, 'the success of the English was not so complete as should have been achieved by the victors in so many battles'.[14] The British at this point decided to join forces with John Littler, commanding Ferozepur.

Lal Singh, on his part, had persuaded his men that there was more glory to be won by delaying an engagement until they could do battle with the main body of the enemy, instead of the isolated garrison at Ferozepur.[15] Had the Sikhs gone ahead and neutralised Littler's force at Ferozepur, the outcome of not only the battle of Ferozeshahar, which followed, but also of the entire First Anglo-Sikh War would have been entirely different.

Lal Singh was safely positioned behind the camp at Ferozeshahar, while his men were grimly fighting at Mudki. On paper, the plan still was for Teja Singh to take Ferozepur from Littler and then join Lal Singh to fight the enemy coming up from Mudki. Far from accounting for Littler's force of under 8,000 men, Teja Singh, who had as many as 30,000 men under his command, did not even bother to keep a watch on enemy movement and allowed Littler to slip out of Ferozepur in broad daylight.

The battle of Ferozeshahar is not easy to describe. Even with the help of treachery, the British forces were shaken to the core by the punishment they received. Both, the treachery against the Sikhs and the drubbing the British received, was again described by Cunningham, one of the few objective historians of his time. Writing of the battle between the Sikhs and the British which began on 21 December 1845, he said, the confident English had at last got the field they wanted. '… (but) the resistance met was wholly unexpected…. Guns were dismounted, and their ammunition was blown into air; squadrons were checked in mid-career; battalion after battalion was hurled back with shattered ranks… the obstinacy of the contest plunged the English into confusion; men of all regiments and arms were mixed together; generals were doubtful of the fact or of the extent of their own success, and colonels knew not what had become of the regiments they commanded or of the army of which they formed part.'[16]

On the dawn of 22 December, as the Sikh and British forces once again took to the field of battle, Teja Singh also arrived with a well-rested reserve Sikh force, to the utter dismay of the enemy. 'The wearied and famished English saw before them a desperate and, perhaps useless struggle.'[17] 'The whole ground between Ferozeshahar and the latter place (Sultan-Khan-Wala) appeared indeed, covered with men; some running, others looking behind them with terror depicted in their faces, the dead of the Sikhs at their heels almost depriving them of the power of motion.'[18]

But Teja Singh, 'when the fate of India trembled in the balance',[19] refused to attack the dispirited and devastated British. The extent to which Teja Singh and Lal Singh – each driven by his own selfish agenda – went to ensure British victory and the defeat of the Sikh army is nowhere more graphically highlighted than by the events of 22 December at Ferozeshahar. Once again, had the two commanders who led the Sikh forces on that day been men of integrity, the outcome of the momentous engagement on the final day of the Ferozeshahar battle would have been profoundly different – as might have been the future of India.

Gough did not trust the mercenaries and, did not want to take the chance of Teja Singh coming down from Ferozepur to join Lal Singh at Ferozeshahar. He immediately ordered an assault on the Sikh camps. The battle commenced at 4 pm in the evening of 21 December (which was the shortest day of the year), with a charge by Littler's Cavalry and Infantry. 'The Sikhs repulsed Littler's Hindustanis with terrible slaughter. Sikh guns were well placed and fired with greater rapidity than the British. Gough threw in his Cavalry; the Sikh Infantry met the enemy charge with musket-fire and then in a hand-to-hand combat. When the light began to fail, Gough poured in all he had in one desperate advance of cavalry, infantry and artillery on all sides of the curve in which the Sikhs were entrenched.'

The battle raged with extreme intensity through the dust and gloom of twilight. A shell hit the Sikh powder magazine which blew up with a tremendous explosion and set many of the neighbouring tents on fire. The Sikhs turned this to their advantage by falling on parties of the enemy who had penetrated their camps. At midnight, the moon rose over the Sutlej and lit up the battlefield giving the Sikhs another opportunity to liquidate enemy pockets. There was no fight left in the British, their own men were dehydrated due to thirst as all the wells were in the Sikh camp – and it had turned bitterly cold. By 3 am (of 22 December) the last of the enemy advance units of Sir Harry Smith's brigade were repulsed and every inch of the ground that had been lost earlier by the Sikhs had been recovered.

On the night of the 21st and 22nd, the fortunes of battle were definitely on the side of the Sikhs. The British suffered terrible casualties, every single member of the Governor-General's staff had been killed or wounded; amongst the dead was the notorious Broadfoot. That frosty night, 'the fate of India trembled in the balance', Sir Hope Grant, one of the British Generals who fought the Anglo-Sikh wars, wrote. 'Truly that night was one of gloom and never perhaps in our annals of Indian warfare, has the British army on so large a scale been nearer to a defeat which could have involved annihilation. The Sikhs had practically recovered the whole of their entrenched camp; our exhausted and decimated bivouacked without mutual cohesion over a wide area….'[20]

Lord Hardinge sent his son, who was also his ADC, and the

Bavarian Prince Waldemar, who was his guest, back to Mudki with the sword which he had been given for his services in the Napoleonic campaigns, with instructions that in the event of a defeat, all his private papers were to be destroyed. An entry in Robert Cust's diary shows that the British Generals had decided to lay down their arms: 'December 22nd news came from the Governor-General that our attack of yesterday had failed, that affairs were desperate, that all state papers were to be destroyed, and that if the morning attack failed, all would be over: this was kept secret by Mr Currie and we were concerting measures to make an unconditional surrender to save the wounded, the part of the news that grieved me the most.'[21]

The British Commander-in-Chief, Lord Gough admitted that 'some brave men lost nerve and urged retreat upon Ferozepur' but he had resolved, as he said in his own words: 'rather to have my bones to bleach honorably at Ferozeshahar, than that they should not dishonorably at Ferozepur.'[22]

When at long last, the sun came up on the plains of Ferozeshahar the worst fear of the British were confirmed. Teja Singh arrived with his army from Ferozepur, fresh and eager for battle. The British guns had little ammunition left to fire and their men were too exhausted to fight. 'We had not a shot with our guns, and our Cavalry horses were thoroughly down up', wrote Gough. The British resigned themselves to their fate and expected the Sikhs to give them the *coup de grace*. The situation in the British camp at that time is described by Harry Smith in his autobiography: 'The ammunition for our guns was fully consumed, and our troops were literally exhausted, and we could not attack what would have been an easy prey under other circumstances.'[23]

Teja Singh's guns opened fire. The British artillery did not answer. Then without reason, the Sikh guns also became silent and a few minutes later, Teja Singh ordered the army to withdraw. The battle-eager soldiers were bewildered. A Nihang drew his sword, rushed up to Teja Singh and asked him to explain the order. Teja Singh, with folded hands and with great humility, said that he was doing this in the interest of the Khalsa as he wished to attack the enemy in the rear. The soldiers were mollified and followed Teja Singh. It was then that the men who had fought so gallantly at Ferozeshahar the preceding night discovered that their Commander, Lal Singh, had also decamped earlier. Argument and dissension broke out in the Sikh camp.

It did not take Lord Gough long to appreciate that Lal Singh and Teja Singh had fulfilled their treacherous undertakings and he ordered his troops to make one more charge on Ferozeshahar. The defenders, who had expected Teja Singh to relieve them, were taken by surprise. They fled from entrenchments, abandoning their guns, 80,000 lbs of guns-powder and all their stores.

This ended the battle of Ferozeshahar – a battle won by the Sikh soldiers but lost by the traitorous Commanders.

Soon after the debacle, Teja Singh visited the British camp and had an interview with Lord Hardinge. What passed between the two is not known; but from the subsequent treatment the British accorded the traitor, it is not hard to guess.

British won by Treachery and at High Cost

Even if the British won at Mudki and Ferozeshahar, their losses were unusually high. Amongst the senior British officers killed was Sir Robert Sale, Quartermaster-General, Sir John McCaskill, divisional commander, Brigadier Samuel Bolton, head of the First Brigade of Sir Harry Smith's division, Brigadier Newton Wallace, staff officers W R Herries and John Munro, and the warmonger, Major George Broadfoot, political agent at Ludhiana, Major Arthur William Fitzroy Somerset, Military Secretary to the Governor-General, and many others. The

British Prime Minister, Sir Robert Peel, placed this war in perspective when he spoke in the House of Commons about the mournfully large losses of British officers and men fighting with 'the most warlike (men) in India'. He was handsome enough to acknowledge the valorous conduct and courage of the Sikh soldiers so badly led and betrayed: 'We are astonished at the numbers, the power of concentration and the skill and courage of the enemy.'[24]

The last bastion of India's defence had fallen, and now the entire subcontinent was for the British to take. Realistic as always, the British took a far more serious note of the opening battle of the First Anglo-Sikh War in their inner councils, because it was soon clear to them that a high price indeed had been paid for what was drummed a victory but was 'not very far removed from failure'. Over a fifth of the British force had either died in the battlefield or been wounded, despite the fact that the largest body of armed men the British had ever assembled in India now faced the Sikh army on the Sutlej.

Inevitably, the situation, in a region of critical importance, led to urgent correspondence between the Prime Minister, Governor-General Hardinge and Commander-in-Chief Sir Hugh Gough on the handling of political, military and diplomatic affairs in India. One outcome of these high-level exchanges was very strained relations between the Governor-General and the Commander-in-Chief.

Continuing to employ his weapon of treachery, on Christmas Day 1845, Hardinge offered rewards and future pensions to all those who deserted from the Sikh ranks:

> *Hindostanee Proclamation* – Whereas the English Government is anxious to reward... bravery and fidelity... any non-commissioned officer or soldier of the Lahore Government who shall present himself before His Excellency the Governor-General, shall be immediately

> rewarded with the accustomed liberality, and shall have the benefit of invalid pension... In fact, every opportunity of favour and cherishment shall at all times be kept in sight by the Government.[25]

This raised double standards to a new high. The British would have shot their own troops out of hand had they succumbed to such offers.

On New Year's eve, the Governor-General issued another proclamation from Ferozepur, stating that he had been forced to take steps to punish the Lahore Government for their 'unprovoked aggression', and to prevent them from further act of treason in the future. 'It called upon all natives of Hindustan who had taken service under the Lahore Government to quit their service at once and place themselves under the orders of the Governor-General of India. They were ordered to flee to the British side of the Sutlej, and to report themselves to the British authorities. If they failed to comply with this order, they were to be considered as having forfeited all claim to British protection, and to be treated as traitors to their country and enemies of the British Government.'[26]

Battle of Aliwal and Budri, January 1846

With the opportunity to win the First Sikh War thrown away by the two traitors, Lal Singh and Teja Singh, at Ferozeshahar, the two sides again clashed between the villages of Aliwal and Budri on 28 January 1846. This time, the Lahore Durbar, the court that was directing the Khalsa forces in this war, told the troops to cut the British supply line. With about 12,000 troops sent by each side into the battle, it was bloody in the extreme. The Sikhs lost about 3,000 men compared to the British causalities, which were around 600. The Sikh losses were a result of the ferocity with which they fought.

The battle was fought on a Sunday morning. The Sikhs formed themselves into defensive triangles and as usual, started cannon fire before the enemy was within range. The British let the Sikhs exhaust their fire, discovered the exact location of their guns and then moved in to attack the weakest flank. At the crucial hour, the officers, including the commander, Ranjodh Singh Majithia, deserted their troops. The men refused to retreat and fought with desperate valour. When the British Cavalry charged, Sikh infantrymen drew the enemy's bayonet towards their bodies, to get close enough to hit the horsemen with their Kirpans. 'Although their leader, Ranjodh Singh, was the first to flee and quit the field, leaving his brave followers to conquer or lose, their courage was never quailed', wrote W W W Humbley, a British lancer. 'Again, they rallied and made one last and vigorous effort. Though defeat had made them desperate, they fought like men who jeopardised all.'[27] Large numbers were killed in battle, many were pushed into the river and drowned. Fiftysix Sikh guns fell into the hands of the British. The Sikhs lost the battle partly because of the river right behind them, which left them no room to maneuver; partly because they were totally outflanked and when they jumped into the river to swim across, it was under a 'tempest of shot and shell from the British guns'.[28]

Once again, the Sikh leadership in the field was lacking, Lal Singh ran away at Mudki, Teja Singh abandoned the field at Ferozeshahar, and as Captain J D Cunningham states in his *History of the Sikhs:* 'Ranjodh Singh Majithia abandoned the army after Smith's first charge at Aliwal, and left the army to its own resources.' This Ranjodh Singh had been in Teja Singh's wing at Ferozeshahar and had abandoned the field with Teja Singh on the second day of the battle. Once again, instead of being with his men, he chose the same path as he had done at Ferozeshahar. Major Mackeson, also of the same agency, commented in a letter to Frederic Currie, Secretary to the British government: 'However well a force without leaders may defend itself in its trenches, when required to move or maneuver in the plain without a directing head, it will be completely helpless and at our mercy.'[29]

Ranjodh Singh Majithia could not have known of the Lahore Durbar's conspiracy to decimate its own army. Knowledge of this decision was restricted to Maharani Jindan Kaur, the C-in-C Teja Singh, and the Prime Minister Lal Singh. In all probability, it was Ranjodh Singh's timidity that forced him to act in the manner he did. He was not an experienced or even a well-known Sikh general, and had not taken part in any previous battle. Why he was given the important task of cutting the British supply lines is not known. Perhaps his appointment fitted the larger game plan, to put a timid general in command, without an adequate force to carry out his orders.

Battle of Sobraon, February 1846

Aliwal may not have been as great a victory as was later made out by Sir Harry Smith, but it did take a heavy toll of Sikh armament. The British commanders could now bide their time till they had sufficient force to strike, whenever they wanted to, and at the most vulnerable point.

Which city would the British attack first, Lahore or Amritsar? That was the question uppermost in the minds of the Sikh military commanders. Once again, they made a foolish decision to defend both at the same time and divided their forces. The larger portion of the army was entrenched in a horse-shoe curve of the Sutlej near the village Sobraon, so as to block the enemy advance to Lahore. Lal Singh was posted a little higher up the river, at Harike to prevent a surprise move to Amritsar. The Sikhs still trusted him.

The pinnacle of treachery was reached at Sobraon during

the fourth and last battle of the first Anglo-Sikh War. The parties to the secret deals were Britain's Governor-General and the most selfish and greedy Gulab Singh of Jammu, who had now become Prime Minister at the Lahore Durbar. Sobraon, the last Sikh fortress on the Sutlej, was of critical importance to the two sides: to the Sikhs because its loss would lay the road to Lahore open for the British; to the British because without it, they could not establish their writ north of the Sutlej.

The British stakes were higher since without a decisive victory at Sobraon, the myth of British military superiority would be exposed. The battles they had won over the last few days had neither been convincing victories nor an endorsement of Britain's military might. The painstakingly-created self-image of the formidable British had been rudely shaken, which had not gone unobserved by a large number of Indians; the carefully-built image of the British would no longer be unquestionably accepted. With the help of Gulab Singh, the British made sure that the outcome of the battle of Sobraon would be in their favour.

Gulab Singh had outwitted the equally treacherous Lal Singh by managing himself into the good books of Maharaja Dalip Singh's mother, Rani Jindan Kaur. From this position of power, he was in close touch with the Governor-General on how best to turn the looming battle to their mutual advantage. Confidential records of the Government of India, which include the army Chief, Sir Hugh Gough's dispatches as also Henry Hardinge's papers, 'refer with staggering frankness to... the open and avowed treachery of Gulab Singh'.[30]

But this was just the beginning of the many treasonable acts that would follow. '(Hardinge) knew that time was pressing; that the speedy dictation of a treaty under the Walls of Lahore was essential to the British. A remedy had to be found out that would accomplish this and, at the same time, suit the ends of

Gulab Singh, Teja Singh and Lal Singh. It required a policy of discretion, allied to shameless treason.'[31]

Treason, this time, would be more than shameless. It would have a different face and would be orchestrated by a different conductor. Lal Singh and Teja Singh were once again given military commands, but this time, they would subvert the Sikh army under the direction of Gulab Singh. The subversion started from the very outset. The Sikh camps at Sobraon were on the left bank of the river, with a pontoon bridge connecting them with their base camp. Teja Singh had a brick tower built from which he could watch the actions; the tower was well behind the front line and close enough to the bridge for a quick escape. The bridge was also guarded by Teja Singh's personal bodyguards. All this could be ascribed to personal cowardice, but the way Teja Singh dispersed his force leaves no room for doubt that he wanted to ensure the defeat of the Khalsa army.

The big guns were placed behind high embankments and consequently immobilised for action. The infantry was also fixed and could not, therefore, be deployed to harass the invaders. The enemy was, thus, given complete freedom to move about and choose his time and point of attack. The greatest blunder that Teja Singh made was not to have learnt a lesson from Ranjodh Singh Majithia's defeat at Aliwal, namely that a river in the rear can be a death-trap, or, perhaps, he knew the lesson too well. What little chance the Sikhs had of holding out against an enemy superior in men, munitions and leadership, was lost by treachery.

In the first week of February, Lal Singh sent his emissary to the British camp with a map giving the disposition of the Sikh deployment at Sobraon. The British commander was not one to rely on the word of a traitor and hence sent a young peasant lad into the Sikh Camp. The 'Sobraon boy', as he came to be known, confirmed the information sent by Lal Singh.

The Khalsa army had traitors to lead it at the front and traitors in the rear to stab it in the back. Rani Jindan sent for Gulab Singh Dogra from Jammu and entrusted him with the task of negotiating with the British. The Punjabi Muslim regiments, which had been left behind to guard the capital, were ordered to proceed to the Sutlej, and Dogras occupied Lahore fort and the barracks in the cantonment. Gulab Singh refused to forward provisions of gun-powder to the army at Sobraon and opened communications with the Governor-General, Lord Hardinge.

The Sikhs' inactivity after Aliwal allowed the British plenty of time to get fresh reinforcements and ammunition. When all was ready, they decided to leave Teja Singh where he was at Sobraon and to cross the Sutlej lower down at Ganda Singh Wala. This plan was abandoned as the peasantry in the neighbourhood was found to be extremely hostile. Instead, Gough and Hardinge decided to make a frontal assault on the Sikh entrenchments at Sobraon and destroy their army at one blow. This was undoubtedly planned in the confidence that the Sikh commander was on their side.

On 7 February it began to rain heavily. For the next two days the sky remained overcast, and thc downpour continued unabated. The Sutlej river began to rise and within forty-eight hours rose more than seven inches, making all banks inaccessible; only one rickety pontoon bridge connected the army base on the left bank. Lord Gough was quick to seize the opportunity. On the evening of 9 February 1846, he marched out of Ferozepur, and under cover of darkness, surrounded the Sikhs at Sobraon.

On the morning of 10 February 1846, a heavy mist spread from the river over the rain-drenched fields and enveloped both the Sikh and British armies. When the sky cleared and sun's rays dissipated the mist, the Sikhs found themselves encircled between two horse-shoes: facing them were the British who covered their camps from one end to the other, and behind them was the Sutlej, now in spate.

This time the British artillery took the initiative. Sikh guns were quick to reply. Then both artilleries ceased fire. There was half-an-hour of nerve-wracking silence and then the guns began barking again. British Cavalry made a deceptive charge and withdrew after confirming the exact location of the Sikh guns. The shelling was resumed by the British with better results. In two hours, the British guns put the Sikh artillery out of action. The Sikhs had, in any case, run out of gun powder and shell. The British Cavalry charged the Sikhs camps from three sides.

The Men from Attari

At this moment, the Sikh C-in-C Teja Singh was seen once again deserting his command. He crossed the boat bridge to the north bank and to safety, damaged the bridge, either by mistake or intentionally, leaving his command to their fate.

Sham Singh Attari, the Commander of the Sikhs, who was left in the battle and opposing Harry Smith's Ist Division and was in his first battle, realised the desperate situation they were now in. He had volunteered to be part of Teja Singh's army after the Sikh defeats at Mudki, Ferozeshahar and Aliwal, and had left his village of Attari, having taken a vow in his gurdwara, along with the followers of his feudal levy, to either return victorious from Sobraon or to die in the attempt. He now came forward on the ramparts, in a white robe (the colour of sacrifice) over his clothes, calling to his troops to rally around him. There followed a hand-to-hand battle, the bayonet against the sword, until Sham Singh fell mortally wounded and died on the ramparts. There his body lay alongside those of his men until it was taken back to Attari the following day – 53 other men from his village who had taken vow with him were also cremated at the same site.

Witnessing the extreme gallantry of Sham Singh and his men, General Gough was to later record his feelings: 'Policy, however, precluded me publicly recording my sentiments on the splendid gallantry of our fallen foe, or to record the acts of heroism displayed, not only individually, but almost collectively by the Sikh Sardars and army; I declare, were it not from a deep conviction that my country's good required the sacrifice, I would have wept to have witnessed the fearful slaughter of so devoted a body of men.'[32]

As the fighting penetrated deeper into the Sikh defences, the British guns and men were able to pour through the gaps now prepared by the engineers. The military historian George Bruce writes: 'Lashed by a merciless fire, attacked by Cavalry and Infantry on three sides, the Sikhs only stubbornly yielded, fighting bitterly to the death, until at last they could take no more. First a few, then all gave way, until a retreat became a rout and finally a desperate stampede. Soon they were hemmed in a mass at the head of the bridge, there to be shot down or hurled into the river below, which the heavy rains had made no longer fordable.'[33]

The Governor-General's son, Arthur Hardinge, who was his father's ADC, later wrote: 'I saw the bridge at that moment over-crowded with guns, horses, and soldiers of all arms, swaying to and from, until at last with a crash it disappeared in the running waters, carrying with it all those who had vainly hoped to reach the opposite shore. The river seemed alive with the struggling mass of men. The artillery, now brought down to the water's edge, completed the slaughter. Few escaped; none, it may be said, surrendered.'[34]

There could not have been a more do-or-die situation and the Sikhs, not given the choice, chose to do and die. Cunningham adds: 'No Sikh offered to submit, and no disciple of Gobind asked for quarter. They everywhere showed front to the victors, and stalked slowly and sullenly away, while many rushed singly forth to meet assured death by contending with a multitude. The Victors looked with solid wonderment upon the indomitable courage of the Vanquished, and forebore to strike when the helpless and the dying frowned unavailing hatred.'[35]

Gough describes the last moment as: 'In their efforts to reach the right bank through the deepened water, they suffered from our horse artillery a terrible carnage. Hundreds fell under this cannonade; hundreds upon hundreds were drowned in attempting the perilous passage. Their awful slaughter, confusion and dismay were such as would have excited compassion in the hearts of their generous conquerors, if the Khalsa troops had not, in the earlier part of the action, sullied their gallantry by slaughtering and barbarously managling every wounded soldier whom, in the vicissitudes of attack, the fortunes of war left at their mercy.'[36]

The battle was over by noon of 10 February. Cunningham puts the Sikh losses at 5,000-8,000, out of the 15,000 effective fighting force in the defensive enclave, the remainder being camp followers. These casualties amount from one-third to a half of the troops committed to battle. The Sikhs took the maximum casualties during the withdrawal across the river, the Sikhs lost their great general, Sham Singh Attari, and the Sardars of the *Jaagirdari Fauj*, Gulab Singh Koopta, Heera Singh Topee and Kishan Singh (the son of late Jamadar Kooshal Singh) and the Commanders of the Sikh artillery, generals Mubarak Ali, Ilahi Baksh, who had been part of Ranjit Singh's army from its inception, and Shah Nawaz Khan (the son of Fateh-u-Din Khan of Kasuri).[37]

The cost of the First Sikh War to the British was 105 officers killed and 315 wounded. Those killed included three Major Generals, Sir Robert Sale, Sir John McCaskil and Sir

Robert Dick; and Brigadier Wallace and the wounded included Major-General Gilbert and 3 brigadiers, Taylor, White and McLaren. As many as 1,290 other ranks were killed and 4,547 were wounded.[38]

BRITISH PLAN TO ANNEX PUNJAB IN TWO STAGES

HUGH GOUGH LOST little time in putting his troops across the Sutlej, after Sobraon. Wilkinson's 6th Brigade marched 25 miles and crossed the river via Harike that night. Part of the army crossed by the repaired bridge of boats that evening and still more were sent via Ferozepur to Kasur, 16 miles into Lahore territory, which they reached on 12 February 1846. The remainder of the army moved up the next day.

Governor-General Hardinge now sent a message to Prime Minister Gulab Singh to say that, if Ranjit Singh's kingdom was to survive as an independent State, it was necessary for him to come for negotiations without delay. On 15 February, Raja Gulab Singh and a deputation of Sardars came to Kasur to discuss terms. Also, on the same day, the Governor-General issued a proclamation that the British objectives had been achieved.

Gulab Singh, accompanied by a number of chiefs and nobles, each on his own elephant and with his own entourage, had arrived at Kasur for negotiations. He was regarded as the most shrewd person in the Durbar and was now the most powerful man in the Punjab. He had distanced himself during the First Sikh War and was now going to claim his reward. He went into the Governor-General's durbar tent alone, to hear and discuss the surrender terms. The other chiefs were left sitting on their elephants. Occasionally, he would come out to confer with the other chiefs. It was well past midnight when he finally agreed to the terms.

Lord Hardinge wanted to annex the Punjab outright; but he realised that this could not be done in the spring of 1846.

Although the Sikhs had been defeated on the Sutlej, they still had considerable forces in other parts of the State. Besides 25,000 armed men at Raiban, there were 8,000 more at Peshawar and an equal number in the south near Multan. Hardinge's own force was 20,000 men, of which only a small proportion were Europeans; and the Hindustani sepoys had shown up very poorly against the Sikhs. All-out campaign would require more reinforcements which, in turn, would put a severer strain on the exhausted treasury. In any case, the campaigning season was almost over and the English soldiers were most reluctant to fight in the intense heat of summer.

For these reasons, Lord Hardinge decided to annex the Punjab in two stages, taking half each time.

In the first stage, he would take the Jullundur Doab, separate the hills (Kashmir and Hazara) from the plains and weaken the Sikh State by limiting the size of the Sikh army, to facilitate the final takeover. In an official minute he wrote: 'A diminution of the strength of such a warlike-nation on our weaker frontier seems to me to be imperatively required. I am, therefore, determined to take a strong and fertile district between the Sutlej and Beas. This will cover Ludhiana and bring us within a few miles of Amritsar, with our back to the Hills. In a military sense, it will be very important – it will weaken the Sikhs and punish them in the eyes of Asia. I shall demand (in rupees) one million and a half money as compensation and if I can arrange to make Gulab Singh and the hill tribes independent, including Kashmir, I shall have weakened this warlike republic.

Its army must be disbanded and reorganised. The numbers of the artillery must be limited. The Maharajah must himself present the keys of Gobindgarh and Lahore, where the terms must be dictated and signed.'[1]

Lord Hardinge wanted the ruling clique to remain Sikh so that it could keep a balance of power with the Muslims, who formed the majority of the population. The British were at the time highly distrustful of Muslims. These were the terms which Hardinge instructed his agent, Major Henry Lawrence, to impose on the Durbar.

On 15 February 1846, Gulab Singh Dogra, Fakir Nur-ud-Din and Dina Nath, along with Sultan Mohammad Barakzai and other Sardars, waited on Lord Gough at Kasur. The Commander-in-Chief refused to accept nazars (presentations) from them as they represented a nation still hostile to the British. He strongly warned them of the fate that awaited them. Gough had, however, showed special favour to Gulab Singh. He praised the Dogra in front of the Sardars for the wisdom, prudence and good feeling shown by him in having kept himself aloof from these unjustifiable hostilities of the Sikhs.

Treaty of 1846 and handing over of Dalip Singh

The representatives of the Lahore Durbar spent the whole night discussing the terms of the treaty with Frederick Currie, Chief Secretary of the British Government (with the EIC), and Major Henry Lawrence, and in the end conceded all that the victorious British required of them. They agreed to relinquish in full, the sovereignty of the territory, hill and plain, lying between the Sutlej and the Beas (the Jullundur Doab at the time yielded a revenue of £400,000); to pay Rs 1½ crore as war compensation (which the British knew the Durbar could not pay); and to surrender all guns that had faced the British, pay off the army and limit its strength to the number at that time of Ranjit Singh.

Three days later, Maharaja Dalip Singh was escorted by Gulab Singh Dogra and Bhaia Ram Singh to the British camp, to make his submission to the Commander-in-Chief and the Governor-General at the village of Lulliani. The Dogra acted as Master of Ceremonies for the Durbar. 'Gulab Singh's oriental form of expression was rather fine', wrote General Hope Grant, who was present at the meeting. 'If', said Gulab Singh, 'my son or dearest friend were taken ill, I should immediately send for the most eminent physician and throw into his hands, request his advice, and make the patient swallow the physic prescribed. I now place the Maharaja in the hands of the Governor-General as that skillful physician. I know everything he will do with regard to him will be for the best and for his advantage'.[2]

Lord Hardinge replied with a speech praising Ranjit Singh and expressed hope that the relations between the two states would return to friendly normality. Presents were exchanged and British guns fired a salute to the Maharaja.

The Governor-General resumed his march to Lahore, with the vanquished Maharaja in his cavalcade. British troops were stationed at Mia Mir just outside the Capital. The Maharaja's guardians were nervous of the reaction of the populace, and asked for a British force to guard the fort. The request was granted, and British troops were posted round the palace and at the Hazuri Bagh entrance to the fort.

The Sale of Kashmir

On 9 March 1846, the Treaty of Lahore, embodying the clauses of the partial annexation of the Punjab was signed. General Hope Grant gives a vivid description of the scene: 'The hall of the Durbar was inlaid throughout with looking-glass; lusters and chandeliers were suspended from the ceiling; in front of the hall was an open court with lofty arches, beneath which a fountain was playing, and in the adjacent wide extent of water lovely water-birds were disporting themselves – amongst them a beautiful scarlet flamingo luxuriated in the spray. Hanging silk drapery and shawls screened off the sun, and beautiful rich-coloured carpets were spread over the floor. Inside the hall were young Maharaja, Dalip Singh, a pretty boy, and the Sikh Chiefs, Raja Lal Singh, a fine jovial looking fellow, Raja Teja Singh, one of the Generals, with a most disagreeable countenance, strongly marked with small-pox, and presenting a disgusting drunken aspect, Raja Ranjodh Singh, who commanded at Aliwal, a handsome but an effeminate-looking fellow and innumerable chiefs.'[3]

The signatories for the Durbar were Lal Singh, Teja Singh, Bhaia Ram Singh and Dewan Dina Nath. Two clauses of the agreement drawn up at Kasur were amended. Since the Durbar was unable to pay more than 50 lakh rupees of the total war indemnity of 1 crore, Hazara and Kashmir were taken away from the Punjab (just as Hardinge had planned) and Kashmir sold to Gulab Singh Dogra for 7,500,000 rupees.

Unlike Ranjit Singh, the Dogras found it impossible to take Hazara from the Pathan tribes who had availed of the Sikh pre-occupation in the Sutlej campaign to free themselves and had captured all the forts in the region. The British came to the rescue of the Dogras by taking over Hazara, and compensating Gulab Singh by giving him additional territory adjoining Jammu. Thus was the State of Jammu and Kashmir formed, and treason rewarded by the grateful British who made Gulab Singh a 'Maharaja'.

On 16 March, another ceremony took place in Amritsar. This was to ratify the treaty with Gulab Singh and formally give him the title to Jammu and Kashmir. The treaty was signed by Hardinge, Currie and Lawrence. He was recognised as the Maharaja of Jammu and Kashmir in this treaty. The Dogra, who had been just one of the many chiefs in this region, had only hoped to be the Chief Minister of truncated Punjab. He became, instead, the Maharaja of a State about the size of Italy. Thus, the *reech* (bear), as he was known amongst the people, got the best honey out of the Lahore Durbar's honeycomb. Cunningham describes Gulab Singh's investiture as sovereign of his new territories in these words: 'On this occasion "Maharaja" Gulab Singh stood up, and, with joined hands, expressed his gratitude to the British Governor General – adding, without, however, any ironical meaning, that he was indeed his *zurkharid*, or gold-boughten slave.'[4]

After setting the frontier between Kashmir and the Punjab, Captain James Abbott was put in charge of Hazara. The Lahore Durbar's Khalsa army was reduced to 20,000 infantry and 12,000 cavalry.

At the request of Lal Singh and other Sardars, a British force was kept for the protection of the Maharaja till the end of the year at a payment of £22,000. A Council of Regency was set up to administer the State on behalf of the Maharaja till he came of age. Rani Jindan became Regent with Lal Singh as her Chief Advisor. Major Henry Lawrence was posted at Lahore as agent of the Governor-General.

The British did well out of the entire deal. 'Half a million, the total expenses of the war to the East India Co', read a cryptic comment by Hardinge to Ellenborough when he submitted the statement of War Charges to London. The figure was arrived at thus: the cost of the 60 days' Sutlej campaign was two million pounds, of which a million was earned by selling Kashmir to Gulab Singh and another half a million came in the form of indemnity from the Lahore Durbar. 'From a financial point of view, the first Sikh War was one of the cheapest....' What this arithmetic did not indicate was how high the East India Company's profit was. It was clearly a great deal, since the First Treaty of Lahore gave the British more than one-third of the Sikh empire's territory, and added an annual revenue of three million rupees to the revenues of the company, and good deals were what trading companies – and empire builders too – revelled in.[5]

The British Annex the Punjab

The unstated aim of the First Treaty of Lahore was to consolidate British control of the Sikh State, to be followed in time by outright annexation. Once this was achieved, they would be masters of the entire subcontinent, their next step Afghanistan. The principality of Hazara was already in their grasp. The British now became busy entrenching themselves in Punjab. Relentlessly, and with a clear sense of purpose, they began to tighten their hold on the Punjab; familiarising themselves with every stratum of this region with its extraordinary diversity of people, religions, languages, natural resources and beliefs. To make their hold more secure, the British wanted some more power to make the once-powerful Sikh empire a virtual protectorate of the British.

The Holy Cow

However, a row between the British and their 'protected' people, indicated the state of mind of the 'protectors' and their attitude towards the natives. It so happened that an English sentry, irritated by an obstruction caused by a herd of cows, slashed some of them with his sword. This outraged the religious feelings of both, the Sikh and Hindus, and people pelted stones on British agents and officers across the land. This infuriated the British, who demanded severest punishment for the insult. The next day Maharaja Dalip Singh was taken by Lal Singh to make apologies to the agent. This further enraged the sentiments of the natives; it caused a riotous situation in which many houses in the Lahore bazar were razed to the ground. However, within a short time, the situation was brought under control.

Not all the Sikhs had accepted the terms of the Treaty of Lahore, and at least two commanders expressed defiance in no uncertain terms. The commander of the fort of Kangra refused to obey the order of the Durbar to hand over the citadel to the British; he replied haughtily that he would not open the gates until Maharaja Ranjit Singh ordered him to do so. In May 1846, Henry Lawrence proceeded to Kangra with a combined British and Sikh force to compel the fort to surrender – which it did on 28 May 1846.

A somewhat similar defiant situation was exhibited by Sheikh Imamuddin, the governor of Kashmir, who felt let down by Gulab Singh's deal with the English. In such a frustrating situation, Imamuddin got emboldened when he received a secret message from Lal Singh, extending all support to him if he inflicts injury to and punishes the Raja.

Seeing the hostile attitude of governor Imamuddin, Gulab Singh appealed to the British agent to fulfil its obligations under the Treaty. In October 1846, Henry Lawrence again took 17,000 Durbar troops along with Gulab Singh and his Dogras and proceeded to Kashmir. Sheikh Immamuddin surrendered without any resistance, and, in addition, he handed over three secret correspondences received from Lal Singh exhorting him to resist Gulab Singh.

The British took immediate action against Lal Singh; he was tried by a British court and found guilty of duplicity and sentenced to be exiled from the Punjab. Thereafter Lal Singh lived in peaceful anonymity in Dehradun and Mussoorie, till his death in 1867.

Meanwhile, there were resistance against the British in many places in the annexed Jalandhar Doab, but all such incidents were contained successfully by the agent. For proper governance of the State, the Council of Regency was reorganised with four new members: Teja Singh, Dina Nath, Fakir Nur-ud-Din and Sher Singh Attariwala.

In December 1846, Lord Hardinge again visited Lahore to review the working of the Treaty and to revise it in such a way as would facilitate the complete annexation of the Punjab.

Under the terms of the Treaty, the British force for the protection of the Maharaja had to be withdrawn by the end of the year. Hardinge did not want to withdraw this force; instead, he wanted to get the Durbar to ask for its retention. The Durbar was somewhat reluctant to make the request. In a letter dated 10 December 1846, Hardinge wrote to Currie: 'The coyness of the Durbar is natural; but it is very important the proposal should originate with them; and in any documents proceeding from them this admission must be stated in clear and unqualified terms; our reluctance to undertake a heavy responsibility must be set forth.'[6]

In another letter, Lord Hardinge instructed Currie to 'preserve in your line of making the Sikh Durbar propose the condition or rather their readiness to assent to any conditions imposed, as the price of the continuance of our support'.[7]

Rani Jindan, who had been most anxious to have British troops in the capital, had had second thoughts after the fall of Lal Singh. She now wished to assert her own rights as the Queen Mother and get the foreigners out of the kingdom. This was easier said than done.

Hardinge decided to get rid of Jindan and make the British Resident (the agent's new title) *de facto* ruler of the Punjab.

The British did not find it too difficult to overcome the ministers. Their jaagirs were confirmed, two leading Sardars, Sher Singh Attariwala, whose sister was engaged to the young maharaja, and Teja Singh were handsomely rewarded – the former being made a deoridhar and the latter a Raja. A false sense of security was created at Lahore. The English garrison packed up and made noisy preparations to leave; the ministers made an earnest appeal for it to stay; and the British EIC government reluctantly acceded to the request. The garrison returned to their barracks and unpacked their kits.

The Second Treaty of Lahore

To strengthen the British grip on the Punjab, Hardinge required the Treaty of Lahore of March to be amended, to incorporate changes. In so doing, he desired that it be made clear to the Sikhs that apart from paying for the upkeep of the British force (which the Durbar was already doing), the Durbar should agree that until Dalip Singh was sixteen in September 1854, the British EIC government would undertake 'the maintenance of an administration, and the protection of Maharaja Dalip Singh during the minority of His Highness'. The Resident was given full authority over all matters in every department of the state and the Governor-General was 'at liberty to occupy with British soldiers, such position as he may think fit for the security of the capital, for the protection of the Maharaja, and the preservation of the peace of the country'.[8]

According to the second Treaty of Lahore (which is also known as the Treaty of Bhairowal because Hardinge ratified it in his camp on 22 December 1846), the British Resident became the governor of Punjab and was quite independent of the Council of Regency of eight ministers that Dalip Singh's court ostensibly had. Hardinge clearly stated:

> 'It is politic that the Resident should carry the Native Council with him, the members of which are, however, entirely under his control and guidance; he can change them and appoint others, and in military affairs his power is unlimited as in the civil administration. He can withdraw Sikh garrisons, replacing them by British troops,

> in any and every part of the Punjab. In all our measures taken during the minority, we must bear in mind that by the Treaty of Lahore, March 1846, the Punjab never was intended to be an independent State. By clause I added, the Chief of the State can neither make war nor peace nor exchange nor sell an acre of territory, nor admit an European officer, nor refuse us thoroughfare through his territories, nor, in fact, perform any act (except its own internal administration) without our permission. In fact, the native prince is in fetters, and under our protection, and must do our biddings.'[9]

Jindan Exiled

Governor Currie's bad judgment in sending Maharani Jindan Kaur into exile became the catalyst in Punjab in 1848, to cause thousands of Sikhs, both demobilised soldiers and others, to flock together to raise a banner of revolt. Had Lawrence been the resident, it is most likely that he would not have taken this step. The new Resident of Lahore, Sir Frederick Currie had taken over from John Lawrence on 6 March 1848.

For the Maharani, those who had considered her a traitor at the end of the first war, saw in her a rallying point at the start of the second, because of her confinement by the British and their hostile attitude towards her. In 1846, the situation could not have been worse. She had conspired along with Raja Lal Singh and Raja Teja Singh to get her belligerent army cut to seize. The British played their part to perfection in this conspiracy and helped her in achieving her goal, which fitted in admirably with their own.

Three years later, in 1849, the same British sent her into exile, from which she would never return. On her death, her ashes too had to be immersed in the river Godavari at Nasik in Central India, and not in Lahore. Ironically, one of her intimate confidants in the conspiracy of 1846, her former Commander-in-Chief during the first Sikh War, Raja Teja Singh, who was now a member of the British-set up Council of Regency, was one of the three signatories, who signed the order exiling her to Benares.

The British adherence to the various articles of the second treaty were also on a selective basis. The Treaty of Bhairowal deprived Rani Jindan of all powers. Article 10 of the Treaty provided for her to receive an allowance of rupees 150,000 (15,000 pounds sterling) per year. When she was first moved to Sheikhupura from Lahore in 1847, it was reduced, despite the Treaty, to rupees 48,000. After her deportation to Benares, it was further reduced to rupees 12,000. At Benares, her jewellery and other valuables were taken from her (she sent letters to her son, hidden in bejeweled amulets).

Though the reason given for exiling the queen mother first to Sheikhupura on 20 August 1847, and then to Benares on 16 May 1848, was her continuing role in inciting revolt and attempt to get the British Resident and others poisoned at Lahore, but the more compelling reason, however, was the refusal of the nine-year old Dalip Singh to put the Raj Tilak on the forehead of Raja Teja Singh, in full Durbar, whom Lawrence had decided to appoint as the Raja of Sialkot for his services rendered during the first Sikh War.

Dalip Singh's consistency in refusing to do as he was asked to, was attributed to the instructions he had from his mother. The maharani was under a strict military guard at Sheikhupura and visitors to her were regulated as was her correspondences. Nevertheless, in view of her influence over her son, she was now transferred to Benares. Mother and son would now meet in 1861, fourteen years later.

Maharani Jindan arrived at Benares on 2 August 1848, and her escort handed her over to her warder, Major George

MacGregor, who kept her and her twelve servants confined to her apartment. They were under heavy guard and could not cross the sentry posts. Four of her servants, including her munshi Ram Kishan, were allowed access to her as they carried in food and other items ordered by her. The guard was composed of one subedar and sixty men. Most of her jewellery was taken from her on arrival at Benaras, and her allowance reduced, on the pretext that she could save money to engineer her escape.

Her current attitude and the fact that an escape route had been tested by her, by sending one of the maids through, convinced Major MacGregor that the maharani intended to escape. He immediately transferred her under heavy escort, provided by an entire battalion, and a troop of the 8th Irregular Cavalry, to the fortress of Chunar, where he handed her over to the Commander, Captain Rees and his adjutant, Lt Nelson. Major MacGregor stayed on as her personal warder. By 30 March 1848, the British had annexed the whole of the Punjab and Dalip Singh, Jindan's son, was exiled and had become a pawn in Britain's game. Jindan had nowhere to go.

Every day, both in the morning and evening, the duty officer called on her, and because she was in *purdah,* spoke to her to ensure her presence. She had a variation in her voice which made it easily distinguishable. On 15 April 1849, it was reported her voice was harsh due to a bad cold. On the 16th and 17th, her cold got worse and on 19 April, she was found missing from her apartment. A massive search was launched but there was no trace of her.

The resourceful maharani had requested for a woman tailor, and one had been chosen for her by Major MacGregor. This seamstress came daily and eventually, the sentries, quite used to her, let her go without checking her identity. On 15 April, the maharani had changed clothes with the seamstress and walked out of the fortress. She then dressed as a *sanyasin* in saffron clothes and carrying on her own person whatever jewellery she could, walked for thirty-four days to Nepal. At night she would stay at temples, where she would be fed and given a bed to sleep on.

On reaching Nepal on 21 May 1849, and disclosing her identity, Prime Minister Rana Jung Bahadur gave her refuge, a house next to his own to live in and an allowance of a thousand rupees a month. She lived in Nepal for twelve years.

Last Days of Maharani Jindan

When Maharaja Dalip Singh was exiled from India, the situation changed for Maharani Jindan. Dalip Singh sailed for England on 19 April 1854. After staying in England for about seven years and, with the support of Victoria, the Queen of England who was his guardian, Dalip Singh decided to bring his mother back from Nepal to a suitable place in India and towards that end he sent Pandit Goreh to Kathmandu. After the Sepoy Mutiny of 1857, the East India Company no longer governed India. Queen Victoria ruled India, through her government.

Dalip Singh was by now a loyal British subject, as British as any Indian could ever be. With a plan to meet his mother, in England he gave out that he intended to go to India to shoot tigers. Victoria did not want him to go to India at all. For her, Dalip Singh was like a prized pet. Nevertheless, in early February of 1861, Dalip Singh reached Calcutta where he was received with a twenty-one-gun salute and Lord Canning, the Viceroy at the time, sent his ADC to receive him. Dalip Singh was looked after in Calcutta extremely well but was not permitted to visit the Punjab. Mother and son met for the first time since 1848, on 16 January 1861, after a period of thirteen years, at the Spence's Hotel in Calcutta.

In view of the Government of India's continued animosity towards his mother, Dalip Singh decided to cut short his trip to India and to take Jindan Kaur back with him to England. To this request the government readily agreed. The British Indian government was delighted with Dalip Singh's decision to take his mother to England, and offered to return her all the jewellery which had been confiscated from her at Benaras and Chunar. In addition, she was offered 3,000 pounds sterling as an allowance for her in England. Mother and son arrived in England in early summer of 1861. The Government in India wanted Jindan Kaur as far away from the Punjab as possible. Merry ol' England was even farther than anywhere in India.

Over the next few months mother and son would sit together for hours on each day when she would narrate to him the events of the past. She told him of a prophecy which had been written in a Sikh book called *Sakheean*, which had clearly stated that he would return in glory to rule Punjab.

Maharani Jindan, however, was not happy in England. She did not like to stay with the white people, whom she considered as firangis and *mlechcha*s and therefore, Dalip Singh suddenly, in June 1862, informed his caretaker Login that, 'I have decided to arrange for my mother's return to India and will see Sir Charles Wood on the subject at once, to have a place of residence fixed for her'.[10] Everyone in London was delighted at this development but that was not the case in Calcutta.

Sir John Lawrence, who was now a member of the Indian Council, vehemently opposed her return. While objections and counter-objections flew between London and Calcutta, Maharani Jindan Kaur, partially blind by then, suddenly died on 1 August 1863, at the age of forty four, in the Maharaja's residence, at Abingdon House in Kensington. Dalip Singh, who was at Loch Kennard Lodge in Perthshire, up in Scotland, hurried down to London. Her body was held in a vault in the

Kensal Green Cemetery, until she could, as per her wishes, be taken to India for her last rites.

Maharani Jindan Kaur's body was brought by Dalip Singh to India. Her cremation took place at Nasik on the west bank of the river Godavari, as Dalip Singh was not permitted to perform the last rites in the Punjab. A part of her ashes were immersed in the river and others were buried in an urn, in a small memorial and monument which was erected at the site. The maharani wanted her ashes to be buried at the memorial erected to Maharaja Ranjit Singh at Lahore. They were, therefore, kept at Nasik till the time for that became possible. This was finally done on 17 March 1924, when her granddaughter, Princess Bamba Sutherland brought the ashes from Nasik and buried them in the memorial of Maharaja Ranjit Singh, after Sardar Harbans Singh, a descendent of the late brave and loyal Sardar Sham Singh Attari offered prayers and performed *ardas* for her.[11]

THE SECOND ANGLO-SIKH WAR

THE GOVERNMENT OF the Sikh empire was now effectively in the hands of the British. In the very year of the fall of the Sikh empire, a British writer gave this assessment of the situation in 1847: 'The Government of Lahore may be said to be annihilated. In appearance, it exists: there is a king, a prime minister, and an army. But one and all are dependent on the British power. The capital of the country (the Punjab) is not garrisoned by the Sikhs. It is entirely in the hands of the paramount power, whose soldiers are lent for a time to preserve the semblance of a government, but, in reality to keep possession of the advantages already gained, until the season of the year shall enable the Governor-General to annex the whole country to the British possessions.'[1]

As the various accords began to be revised to suit Britain's colonial needs, terminologies too began to be changed. Political agents became Residents, the East India Company's Governor-General began to be called the Viceroy. Considering the mixed bag of district administrators, revenue collectors, political agents, engineers, troop commanders and traders who had fanned out across the sprawling Sikh domain, sparks could be expected to fly given the volatile nature of the Sikhs and the domineering ways of the British. And so it transpired in Multan, at the end of 1847, where by April 1848, a small disturbance developed into a major rebellion.

Dewan Mulraj, the able governor of Multan whose father Diwan Sawan Mal had also been a capable and admired governor of this strategically important region, was for various reasons eased out by the British. The troops of Lahore Durbar did not take kindly to this move, and a flashpoint was reached on 19 April 1948, when the two British officers who were accompanying Mulraj's replacement were killed by resentful Sikh soldiers. The killing coincided with or triggered off a major rebellion in Multan.

The Maharaja, Dalip Singh, was still too young to be able to quell such dissention. His mother Jindan, the only one he could turn to for advice, had been removed from the scene. Her place had been taken by his prospective father-in-law, Sardar Chattar Singh Attariwala and his son Sher Singh Attariwala. The old Sardar was governor of the North-West-Frontier districts. British officers were posted in close proximity to keep a watch on him. These officers were Major George Lawrence at Peshawar and his deputy, Captain James Abbott, at Hazara. Sher Singh assumed pre-eminence in the Lahore Durbar by virtue of the fact that his sister was engaged to marry Dalip Singh.

The Attariwala family were particularly cautious in their dealings with the British because they did not want to jeopardise the prospects of Dalip Singh becoming sovereign (or even a titular sovereign) of the Punjab. They were determined to support the new Resident at Lahore, Sir Frederick Currie, in all measures he wished to take during the minority period of the Maharaja. Up till now, there was complete harmony between the Durbar and the Resident.

Flashpoint Multan

Currie, who had taken over from John Lawrence, held the

Lahore Durbar responsible for the 1848 mutiny, whereas the Sikh view was that it had been precipitated by the East India Company's clumsy handling of the situation in the early stages. But the British would not take the blame for it. Currie continued to hold the Durbar responsible for events at Multan, and, furthermore, demanded that its Sikh troops put it down. The result of this mindless order was that the rebellion began to spread, with more and more Sikh soldiers rallying around Mulraj, to be joined even by those who had been earlier disbanded from the Sikh army.

A second point of British transgression for the Sikh troops was Captain Abbott dealing very stupidly with the old Sardar, Chattar Singh Attariwala. Abbot was not only arrogant in his behaviour but became outright insulting as days passed. It is hard to tell whether Abbott by nature was ill-bred and ill-tempered or was acting under instructions. He did, however, succeed in driving the Sikhs to desperation.

From the time the two British officers were killed, the situation at Multan deteriorated to the point where many felt it to be a principal cause of the Second Sikh War. By June 1848, the Sikhs were forced to pull back inside the Multan fort. On 4 September, Sher Singh Attariwala, who so long had been a good friend of the British, was then sent to Multan with a contingent of Durbar troops to help quell the rebellion. The Resident instructed Sher Singh and two other Durbar officers, Imamuddin and Jawahar Mal, to accompany General William Whish on the expedition against Mulraj. The plan was to make a three-pronged attack on Multan: the Lahore troops from the north, the Bahawalpuri Daudputras from the east and the combined forces of General Van Cortlandt and Lt Edwards from the west or south. Now, a large pro-British contingent was gathered on the west of the Sutlej, and an attack on the city was launched five days later.

Within days of Sher Singh Attariwala's arrival in Multan, however, things got out of hand. Rebellious Sikh troops of Multan not only turned the Durbar troops to their side, but also brought out Sher Singh's simmering anger which had been ignited by Abbot's insults of his father, Sardar Chattar Singh Attariwala, a long-time and much-respected chieftain of the NWF provinces and Hazara, a man highly regarded by both the Sikhs, and also the British Resident.

Chattar Singh was an old bespectacled and bleary-eyed man who walked with a bad posture and was in bad health. He was looking forward to getting his daughter married to the Maharaja and then retiring to his village, Attari. He did not want, nor was he fit enough to lead a rebellion. But the treatment he received at hands of Abbott and Capt Nicholson forced him to draw the sword with his feeble hands. He wrote to his son, telling him the way he had been insulted by upstart foreigners and exhorted him to join his countrymen in fighting them to a finish. Until then, Sher Singh Attariwala had stuck resolutely to his British allies and ignored the pleas of his soldiers and Mulraj's emissaries.

His father's letter had made Sher Singh extremely uneasy, however. There were even rumours afloat that Chattar Singh had been killed by a British mercenary Fateh Khan Gheba. But Sher Singh had so far not taken notice of these rumours. On 13 September events took a dramatic turn, which finally convinced Sher Singh of the dishonesty of the British. That night he had visited the British officers' mess after dinner, as he had done every day and took his seat next to Lt Edwards. He noticed General Van Cortlandt slip out of the tent. A little later, an officer of Sher Singh's regiment came in and whispered in the Sardar's ear that Cortland had ordered the mess tent to be surrounded by Pathan mercenaries. Sher Singh took a hurried leave and got away before Van Cortlandt's men could apprehend him. Next morning, Sher Singh Attariwala and his troops left the British camp.

Enraged, Sher Singh issued a proclamation, asking all Sikhs to rise against the foreign oppressors. The proclamation issued under his seal declared: 'It is well known to all inhabitants of the Punjab, to all the Sikhs, and those who have cherished the Khalsa, and in fact, the world at large, with what oppression, tyranny and violence the feringhis have treated the widow of the great Maharaja Ranjit Singh and what cruelty they have shown towards the people of the country.' The proclamation further stated: 'In the first place, they (the English) have broken the treaty by imprisoning, and sending away to Hindostan, the Maharani (Jindan Kaur), the mother of her people. Secondly, the race of Sikhs, the children of the Maharaja (Ranjit Singh), have suffered so much from their tyranny, that our very religion has been taken away from us. Thirdly, the Kingdom has lost its former repute. By the direction of the holy Gooroo, Raja Sher Singh and others, with their valiant troops, have joined the trusty and faithful Dewan Moolraj, on the part of Maharaja Dalip Singh, with a view to eradicate and expel the tyrannous and crafty feringhis.'[2]

For three weeks, Sher Singh Attariwala tried to convince Mulraj that he had broken with the firangis but the Dewan refused to believe him. His suspicions had been further roused by a forged letter which Edwards had planted and let fall into Mulraj's hands. In this letter, Edwards pretended to be a privy to a plot by which Sher Singh was to take the fort by action. The gates of Multan fort remained firmly shut against Attariwala. Sher Singh lost patience with Mulraj and on 9 October 1848, got out of camp to go north to join his father. Thus, the Sikh nation began to rise in arms once again.

Sikh Victory at Ramnagar

The new EIC Governor-General who arrived in India in January 1948 was the Marquis of Dalhousie, variously described as 'ever-excitable and over-strung'. He was hardly of a temperament suited to implementing statesman-like policies to sustain a sensible relationship with the most turbulent part of the subcontinent. Instead of showing serious concern at the way things were going, Dalhousie promptly announced that, 'We have, without hesitation, resolved that Punjab can no longer be allowed to exist as a power and must be destroyed'.

Not content with this shocking statement, even more coarsely he wrote a letter to London on 8 October 1948: 'I have drawn the sword and have this time thrown away the scabbard. If the Sikhs, after this is over, arise again, they shall entrench themselves behind a dunghill, and fight with their finger-nails, for if I live twelve months, they shall have nothing else to fight with.'[3]

As the fighting in Multan escalated, on 16 November 1848, the British Commander-in-Chief, Sir Hugh Gough, crossed the river Ravi to confront Sher Singh. A week later, at Ramnagar on the river Chenab, a major battle was underway. The Company's force 'of over 104,000 men, about 60,000 supported by 45 guns, converged to give battle to the Sikhs, whose strength was around 23,000 men, drawn from the Hazara, Peshawar, Tank and Bannu garrisons, and including Sher Singh's own contingent. Because the British had for over two years systematically dismantled the Sikh army, sending some of its finest fighting men back to their villages, disbanding its generals and appropriating or destroying its guns, a force of 92,000 men, 31,800 Cavalry and over 384 guns was now reduced to a few thousand. Moreover, unlike the British, the heavily outnumbered Sikhs had no reinforcements to fall back upon, as even their unarmed comrades from the Majha and Malwa regions were stopped at river crossings and fords and prevented' from joining them. After the British – helped by Pathan horsemen – had taken over the lightly-defended fort at Attock, the prospects of Sikh troops from Peshawar joining

Chattar Singh's force at Hazara became slim.[4]

Nevertheless, in this, the first battle of the Second Anglo-Sikh War at Ramnagar on the river Chenab, on 22 November 1848, the British were decisively defeated.

The heavily outnumbered Sikh forces under Sher Singh wreaked havoc on the British, who lost two Cavalry Commanders, Brigadier Curteon and Colonel Havelock. Havelock, a hero of the Peninsular campaign, had walked straight into Sher Singh's trap and 'when last seen he was in the thick of battle – with left arm dangling, virtually cut off by a sword stroke. His badly wounded body was recovered a few days later. The British troops finally managed to withdraw', but had also lost their Commanding Officer, another 6 officers and 43 troopers. When the fight at Ramnagar ended, most of the Sikhs withdrew to the north bank, but groups of Ghorchurras were still around, which kept the British on their toes.

Gough established camp at Ramnagar and waited for supply convoys to catch up. However, the records show that on the first night, the British supply position was completely disorganised. His own bosses laughed at Gough's attempts to make this defeat appear as a victory. While the Governor-General said that he would rather 'reserve salutes for real victories which this is not',[5] The president of the East India Company's Board of Directors said that: 'It is no wonder that all confidence in Lord Gough, if it was ever entertained, should have been entirely lost.'[6]

Sikh Victory at Chillianwala

The second major battle of the Second Sikh War was fought at Chillianwala on 13 January 1849. Once again, the Sikhs were outnumbered in the field when their force of 10,000 men faced a far bigger army. But even then, the enemy lost 2,446 men, including 132 officers.

A British Subaltern wrote: 'The Sikhs fought like devils… fierce and untamed even in their struggle…. Such mass of men I never set eye on and as plucky as lions: they ran right on the bayonets of the 24th (Regiment) and struck at their assailants when they were transfixed.'[7]

The bloody battle lasted till darkness fell. The Sikhs captured four British guns. The night was one of great terror for the British. General Thackwell wrote: 'Confusion pervaded in the whole army. Fears were generally entertained that the enemy (the Sikhs) would attempt a night attack. If they had been enterprising and could have perceived the extent of their advantage, they would assuredly have thrown themselves on us… the jungle which had befriended them in the commencement of the action now formed a protection to us.'[8]

Few historians have tried to gloss over the devastating defeat suffered by the British at Chillianwala:

> '… advancing British infantry men were mowed down by the terrific fire of the Sikh musketry. The Sikh ghorcharas… in successive onslaughts broke up the British Cavalry line and cut down their horsemen… suddenly to their amazement, the enemy took to their heels… galloping over their own horse artillery and turning it topsy-turvy, leaving their comrades to be slaughtered by the Sikhs. At another site from within the Jungle, the guns opened up with devastating effect. Lieut Col Brookes, leading 24th foot (soldiers), was killed between the enemy guns. Trapped, the brigade turned to flee in the face of destructive fire of shot and shell. In yet another engagement, a large body of Sikhs surrounded the Second Infantry Brigade. Now Gilbert's Force (Sir Walter Gilbert was divisional commander) had neither the cover of guns nor support of Cavalry. In the hand-to-hand fight, the brigade was repulsed and driven back with loss.'[9]

Thus, Chillianwala became the worst defeat the British had suffered since their occupation of India. Gough was superseded and General Charles James Napier was asked to come from England to take over the Command.

Sher Singh Attariwala again sent a proposal for settlement. Since the Maharaja was in British hands, all he asked for was the reinstatement of Dalip Singh and the evacuation of British forces from Lahore. Sher Singh sent George Lawrence, who was a prisoner in his hands, as an envoy. The terms were rejected. More reinforcements were sent up from then British India.

It may be mentioned here the Sikhs behaved with the British prisoners in a most commendable manner. It was always commended by British soldiers – though not always by British historians. The same British Subaltern wrote: 'Two of 9,000 lancers who were taken prisoners the other day were sent back this morning with Sher Singh's compliments. They seemed rather sorry to come back as they had been treated like princes, and sent away with Rs 10 each in his pocket.'[10]

The Disaster at Gujrat

Dalhousie was planning to turn the Chillianwala defeat to his advantage. He would use it to demand the complete annexation of Punjab, erase the Sikh State from the face of India and establish British rule over the entire subcontinent. 'As he knew himself to be always in the right and those who differed from him always in the wrong', a late nineteenth-century English historian, S S Thorburn writes, 'he naturally desired to shape the growth towards a restricted autonomy of the province, which was the first fruit of his policy of all India for the English'.[11] Since expansion was very much in vogue in the higher echelons of power in Britain at that time, Dalhousie's was a welcome assertion of his country's sense of its own destiny, even though there were men of influence in

London, including Auckland, Ellenborough, Hardinge and Henry Lawrence who were against the annexation of Punjab.

Thorburn further observes: 'It was Henry Lawrence's refusal to recognise that (the battle of) Gujrat had destroyed all old title-deeds, and given us a clean slate whereon to inscribe our own sovereign will and pleasure, which soon afterwards caused the final breach between him and the self-willed autocrat (Dalhousie) then guiding our destinies in India.'[12]

But, Dalhousie was not to be deterred easily, and since he was the man on the spot, he decided to make the Battle of Gujrat the clincher of the second Sikh War. Many historians hold that for no other single battle had the British assemble such a formidable force of infantry, horseman, armour and field artillery of every size, range and destructive power. As for the number of men who confronted each other at 7.30 that morning of 21 February 1849, the British had 56,636 infantry and 11,569 cavalry, while the entire Sikh force facing them consisted of just 20,000 men.

The battle was fought with unbelievable ferocity since each side knew what the ultimate significance of the battle of Gujrat was; if the British won, they would control entire India. Thus, even though the Sikhs were outnumbered, outgunned and unable to restock their supplies as the British could, they fought with passionate intensity for the honour of the Sikh empire, the holy teachings of their Gurus and for the sanctity of the very soil of Punjab. The gunners, both Muslim and Sikh, literally stuck to their last. General Thackwell remarked: 'The fidelity displayed by the Sikh gunners is worthy of record: the devotion with which they remained at their posts, when the atmosphere around them was absolutely fired by the British guns does not admit description.'[13]

Against such firepower, the Sikhs soon began to retreat. By noon they had evacuated Gujrat. The British occupied the town and pressed home their advantage by relentless pursuit. The Sikhs were hemmed from all sides. Gough in front, Dogras on their right, Imamuddin on their left and Abbott's Pathan mercenaries behind them. The Commanders (except Sher Singh Attariwala) fled, leaving the common soldiers to fight. The men fought late into the night; their bodies were found scattered for many miles beyond the field of battle. The night was made more fearful by explosions of unfired Sikh ammunition dumps and the thunder and rain which followed. The British Subaltern wrote with perspective: 'Little quarter, I am ashamed to say, was given – and even those we managed to save from the vengeance of our men, I fear, were killed afterwards. But, after all, it is a war of extermination.'[14]

The Battle of Gujrat was a disaster from which the Sikhs could scarcely hope to recover. A decisive finishing blow was, however, delivered by the arch-traitor Gulab Singh Dogra. He helped Abbott to cut off Sher Singh Attariwala's retreat towards the frontier. The prospect of continuing the fight with Afghan help was thus prevented. He also arranged for the supply of boats for the British army to cross the Jhelum. Sher Singh tried to negotiate terms, but the British insisted on unconditional surrender.

On 14 March 1849, both the Attariwala Sardars, father Chattar Singh and son, Sher Singh came to the British camp at Hurmel near Rawalpindi with their faces covered under their shawls and gave up their swords to General Gilbert. They were followed by batches of hundreds. 'The reluctance of some of the old Khalsa veterans to surrender their arms was evident, some could not restrain their tears; while on the faces of others, rage and hatred were visibly depicted', wrote General Thakwell.[15] It was the saddest day in the history of a proud and zestful people who had lived with a rare sense of confidence and self-esteem.

There is a moving account that captures the moment of

Sikh grief and deep inner hurt when an old veteran of the Sikh army threw down his sword in disgust at the surrender ceremony with the words: 'Aaj Ranjit Singh mar gaya.' (Ranjit Singh has finally died today.)[16]

Grabbing the Kingdom and the Kohinoor

On 29 March 1849, Eliot, Lord Dalhousie's Secretary, called a *durbar* in the fort of Lahore where a formal annexation ceremony was held, and the EIC's Governor-General's proclamation was read-out. It was attended by the eleven-year-old Maharaja Dalip Singh, and all the nobles of the State who had not taken part in the rebellion. Thus, Dalhousie's oft-repeated policy of encompassing the Punjab into the Indian empire was announced to those who never took part in the Wars. As Major Evans Bell puts it, 'It was Lord Dalhousie who converted our protective occupation into a so-called conquest'.[17]

After the proclamation, Dalip Singh was informed of his future:

1. His Highness the Maharaja Dalip Singh shall resign for himself, his heirs and successors all right title and claim to the sovereignty of the Punjab or to any sovereign power whatever.
2. All the property of the State, of whatever description and wheresoever found, shall be confiscated to the Honourable East India Company, in part payment of the debt due by the State of Lahore to the British government and expenses of the war.
3. The Gem called Koh-i-noor, which taken from Shah Sooja-ul-Moolk by Maharaja Ranjit Singh, shall be surrendered by the Maharaja of Lahore to the Queen of England.
4. His Highness Dalip Singh shall receive from the Honourable East India Company, for the support of himself and his relatives and the servants of the State, a pension not less than four, and not exceeding five, lakhs of the Company's rupees per annum.
5. His Highness shall be treated with respect and honour. He shall

> retain the title of Maharaja Dalip Singh Bahadur, and he shall continue to receive during his life such portion of the above-named pension as may be allotted to him personally, provided he shall remain obedient to the British government and shall reside at such place as the Governor-General of India may select.[18]

After the Maharaja was informed of his future and terms granted to him, the Kohinoor diamond was handed over by the young Maharaja and he stepped down from his illustrious father's throne – never to sit on it again. Indeed, Maharaja Ranjit Singh was dead.

HOW THE BRITISH SUBVERTED THE SIKH STATE

THE ONE OUTSTANDING example in the British establishment of the time who exposed British moves for what they were was Captain Joseph Davey Cunningham, whose father was the well-known Scottish poet, Allan Cunningham. Joseph was a mathematician who wanted to be a soldier. After a brilliant career at Addiscombe Military Academy, on the recommendation of the famous writer, Sir Walter Scot, he came to India in 1834 and joined the staff of the chief engineer of the East India Company's Bengal holdings.

His younger brother was Alexander Cunningham. Both the brothers came to India together and joined the services of the East India Company. In 1837, Joseph was appointed assistant to Colonel Claude Wade, the political agent in the Sikh Empire. For the next eight years he held and occupied several political positions in this area under Colonel Wade and his successors until 1845. At the time of the outbreak of the first Anglo-Sikh War (December 1845), he was himself the political agent in the State of Bahawalpur.

From 1836 to 1840, brother Alexander was ADC to Lord Auckland, the Governor-General of India. In 1845-46 he was called to serve in Punjab and helped construct two bridges of boats across the Beas river, prior to the Battle of Sobraon.

In 1846, Alexander was made commissioner, along with P A Vans Agnew, to demarcate boundaries for the British EIC. The commission was set up to delimit the northern boundaries of the then British holdings, after the First Anglo-Sikh War concluded with the Treaty of Amritsar, which ceded Kashmir as war indemnity to the British. Letters were written to the Chinese and Tibetans by Lord Hardinge, but they did not join the survey. A second commission was set up in 1847, which was, again led by Alexander Cunningham to establish the Ladakh-Tibet boundary. His early work *Essay on the Aryan Order of Architecture* (1848) arose from his visits to the temples in Kashmir and his travels in Ladakh during his tenure with the commission. He was also present at the battles of Chillianwala and Gujrat in 1848-49.

Stationed in Bhawalpur, Joseph Cunningham was writing his own account of the disgraceful British acts of annexation of the Sikh kingdom from the minor Dalip Singh. In the battle of Sobraon, and the fourth and last battle of the First Anglo-Sikh War, fought on 10 February 1846, the British used secret deals and every conceivable form of deceit to help them to emerge victorious over the Sikh forces. The methods they used led Cunningham to record them in disgust in his book, *History of the Sikhs* (1849).

What this young officer found utterly distasteful was the understanding Governor-General Hardinge had reached with Gulab Singh, whereby the later would *ensure the defeat of his own side* and facilitate the victory of the British. Cunningham found it unbecoming, if not indecent. '...that the Sikh army should be attacked by the English, and that when beaten, it should be openly abandoned by its own government; and further that the passage of the Sutlej should be unopposed and the road to the Capital (Lahore) laid open to the visitors. Under such circumstances of discreet policy and shameless treason was the battle of Sobraon fought.'[1]

Joseph Cunningham's exposé infuriated his bosses. They punished him by transferring him from the Punjab to the public works department in Meerut. This vilification hurt Cunnigham deeply. The former additional aide-de-camp to the Governor-General during the Sobraon battle died within two years of being removed from office, not even 40 years old. It is said, his heart was broken. He died in the city of Ambala, Punjab in 1851. His grave is still there in the Ambala Christian cemetery. The second edition of the book was published in 1853 after Joseph's death, by his brother Peter Cunningham, who was also a writer. The British, thus, took victims from among their own.

What the British did to the Sikhs can hardly be the line of action enjoined upon the East India Company's various governors-generals selected to serve in India, or the advice that the chairman of the Company's Board of Directors gave to Lord Hardinge at his farewell dinner before he left for India. Yet, it was the same Hardinge who entered the infamous understanding with Gulab Singh before the battle of Sobraon. And, of course, it is not wrong to conclude that Britain's Queen was kept ignorant of the ways it annexed India, the jewell in her crown. Even after Sobraon, which opened the road to Lahore, there was no change in the unbecoming conduct of the English. Unequivocal evidence exists showing how Gulab Singh was persuaded by the British to betray the Sikh government – of which he was the prime minister – in return for many British favours like the sale of Kashmir to him. And investing him with the title of Maharaja.

Main Traitors

The one man with ideal qualifications to fit the British bill was Gulab Singh. He had been Ranjit Singh's confidant when the young Maharaja had won Jammu and attached it to his expanding kingdom. Gulab Singh and his brothers were known as the Dogra brothers. His brother, Dhian Singh, was Maharaja Ranjit Singh's prime minister since 1818.

To begin with, Gulab Singh was a great survivor. While his brothers Dhian Singh and Suchet Singh were no less treacherous than Gulab Singh, they had failed to utilise many opportunities in their favour after the death of Ranjit Singh. Gulab Singh utilised them all. He also managed to amass an immense fortune during these turbulent times, in addition to lands and estates in Jammu. At the zenith of their power, the Dogras of Jammu held jaagirs worth an annual revenue of 1,897,379 rupees: Gulab Singh 737,287 rupees; nephew Heera Singh 462,115 rupees; Suchet Singh 306,865 rupees, and Dhian Singh 291,112 rupees, of the kingdom's approximate total revenue of 32,475,000 rupees at Ranjit Singh's death in 1839. The Jammu brothers earned about one-third from farms, tributes and free trade.[2]

Gulab Singh was aptly described as a man 'whose aspirations left no room for pangs of conscience or purity of ideals'.[3] It did not take the British long to identify him as their *most likely instrument of policy* so far as the annexation of Punjab was concerned, even though they were mistrustful of his ambitions. Wedded to their old proverb of there being no permanent friends or enemies but only permanent interests, however, they were quite prepared to continue to deal with him. He was to prove a highly successful choice as he helped them dismantle the State, which Ranjit Singh had so single-mindedly built.

Two other men now occupied centre stage but had not held any significant office during Ranjit Singh's time were the two Brahmins, Lal Singh and Teja Singh. While Teja Singh was from Meerut, Lal Singh came from the Gandhara Valley; both had risen in the Lahore Durbar through devious means. Yet, in November 1845, at the most crucial period of the Khalsa army, in a supremely ironic twist of fate, Lal Singh was chosen as Prime Minister and Teja Singh as Commander-in-Chief of the Sikh army. Both these traitors totally betrayed the Sikh State. There were a number of others whom the British had skillfully lined up to help them subvert and put an end to the Sikh empire, but the roles of these three traitors were crucial to the realisation of British goals.

Ranjit Singh's death, and self-destructive moves and betrayals of his successors, not only subverted his dream of a strong, secular and invincible Sikh State, but also made a mockery of a supremely confident and proud people inspired by ideals of their faith. Unheeding of those who were pressing on Punjab's border, eager to lay hands on its riches, the Sikhs, already vulnerable because of their infighting, were made even more so by the traitors in their midst. The real tragedy for them was the lack of character shown by Ranjit Singh's own kin.

Destruction of the Invincible Sikh Army

After Ranjit Singh's death, the highly disciplined Khalsa army that had helped him build and secure his kingdom began to crumble. Throughout history, Sikhs have always responded to good leadership, a characteristic that was missing in Kharak Singh, Ranjit Singh's son. His reign lasted only four brief months, a period during which the new maharaja, despite his previous active command in the army, spent his days in an opium-induced slumber.

His son, Nau Nihal Singh deposed him, and together with his prime minister Raja Dhian Singh, spent much of his time with the army, continuing his grandfather's policy of troop reviews and regular training exercises. Although keen and considered to be the closest in temperament to the late Ranjit Singh, Nau Nihal Singh at eighteen, lacked experience and did not receive the complete respect and support of the army as had his grandfather. Ranjit Singh had been the last to exercise control over the brave but unruly Sikhs of the Punjab.

It was during Maharani Chand Kaur's reign that the real breakdown in command began. She occupied the throne for only two months – from November 1840 to January 1841 – and can hardly be blamed for this situation, yet historians attribute the independence of the army from the durbar to have started during her reign. The army began to act in all matters of the state, overthrowing Chand Kaur and bringing the usurper Sher Singh to the throne. The one important aspect during Sher Singh's reign which deserves a mention and which later had a bearing in the battle of Gujrat during the second Sikh War, was the visit of Ranjit Singh's old enemy, the former king of Afghanistan, Dost Mohammad. He arrived in Lahore in February 1843 and signed a treaty of friendship with Sher Singh.

Being indebted to the army for his position, Sher Singh satisfied it in every way. He raised its strength, increased its pay and allowance, and submitted to it on all other matters. In 1842, for instance, Sher Singh increased the pay from 8 rupees to 12 to buy peace during a crucial Khalsa meeting. During Maharani Jindan's rule, she raised it to 14 rupees. In 1845, Peshora Singh, yet another so-called son of Ranjit Singh, promised the army to increase pay to 15 rupees for an infantryman and 40 rupees to a cavalry trooper. In addition, a further 100 rupees and a gold bracelet would be given to every soldier who helped him seize the throne. Appeasing the army had now become routine.

It was during this period that the panchayat system took root in the Khalsa army. With a history of the Panj Piyares, this system had evolved in the villages, being a council of five elders who decided on matters that needed attention for the collective benefit of the whole. This was a concept that the troops both understood and trusted, and was therefore, adopted by them. While this democratisation worked as a village system, it caused havoc in the army. What should have been a disciplined force under a strong and effective leadership was now one that was controlled by voting. And mercinaries planted by the British carried the vote because of their ability to pay and became leaders of the men.

The council would decide what was right or wrong, or what should or should not be done in the battalion. Each company elected two members to the panchayat, putting an end to the disciplined force that Ranjit Singh had so painstakingly created. Commanding officers would henceforth exercise command on parade and, for whatever they were worth, lead their units in battle, but for administrative matters, they had to abide by the decision of the panchayat. The British C-in-C Lord Gough describes the panchayats as 'Guiding the united action of the soldiery, were able to dictate to their officers, and later on found themselves able to appear to be representing the Khalsa in arms, and to dictate to the durbar or court itself'.[4]

Maharaja Sher Singh should have been the last person to accept such a system. He had been a general, had led successful campaigns during the days of Ranjit Singh, and knew the importance of being able to command. However, Ranjit Singh was aware that Sher Singh and Tara Singh were not his sons. It was only towards the end of Ranjit Singh's life that Sher Singh was permitted to be seated in the Maharaja's presence – Tara Singh was never given this honour. Perhaps because of this background, he turned a blind eye to the functioning of the army and let matters drift. The army realised its strength and now knew, as did the Durbar, that if anyone wanted to rule the State s/he had to gain the army's approval. Consequently, the army soon declared itself the representative of Sikh aspirations and called itself Sarbat Khalsa (Sikh Nation) – the Supreme body of the Sikhs – whose decision was binding on all.

The army mutinied soon after Sher Singh's accession in 1841. One of its demands was the removal of its foreign officers – a demand also supported by the Sardars who had, even in the days of Ranjit Singh, felt threatened by them. These were trained men from European armies, including Napoleon's army. A few of these foreign officers were killed during the meeting and most left the army during Sher Singh's reign or later, during the prime ministership of Heera Singh. Only four remained on the eve of the First Sikh War. None of those who had built the Sikh army – Allard, Ventura, Avitabile, Court – all Ranjit Singh's friends and trusted Generals, were amongst them.

Sher Singh was indifferent towards the events taking place around him. He isolated himself from the reality and left the affairs of state to his prime minister. He became negligent, enjoying his pleasures of dance, music, sports and hunting, and has been described by some historians as completely perverted. Had Raja Dhian Singh not exercised some control over events, the government would have collapsed then. The army now dictated its strength and its pay – even to the extent of telling the Durbar who its leaders should be. The Jaagirdari Fauz fared better, as they continued to respond to their traditional leadership. On their own, these leaders increased the strength of their levies. This was done by the Chiefs and Sardars more for their own security than necessity, as a consequence of the anarchy that was then prevailing in the army.

Because of the Panchayat system, discipline and training suffered in the regular army. Even at the level of the Durbar, bribes and money, rather than merit, became the order of the day. However, despite this gloomy state of affairs the troops themselves looked forward to fight with the British.

Selfish Maharani Jindan Kaur

Following Sher Singh's death, ever fearful of the army's takeover of the State, the regent, Maharani Jindan Kaur, devised means to minimise its authority. The soldiers were constantly demanding a raise in pay, the treasury was empty and the army panchayats were becoming more and more belligerent. A war with the British was a scheme that Maharani Jindan Kaur finally settled upon, hoping it would end the menace from the army once and for all. If the British won, the army's constant threat to her and her son Dalip Singh would be over. She was naïve, to say the least, she assumed that the British would permit her to stay on as regent with Dalip Singh as the maharaja. If the Sikh Army won, Jindan thought, they could plunder the whole of India, leaving her in peace. This would also make her a very powerful ruler and she thought she had a win-win situation either way.

To execute her plans, she needed two trustworthy leaders and she found them in Lal Singh and Teja Singh. She realised that both would be unacceptable to the army and to the Sardars unless she created the right situation. To this end, reports were circulated of the intention of the British to take possession of the Sikh territories to the south of the Sutlej river. On several occasions in open durbar, Lal Singh produced and read papers purporting to be letters from Kardars or administrative officers, of the country beyond the river. These fake letters stated that the British army was already advancing, creating disturbances and annoyance in the Sikh State. This seemingly authentic intelligence created considerable excitement among the troops and people of Lahore, and soon it became almost the only topic of discussion.

When these rumours had worked their intended effect, Lal Singh summoned a council of Sardars, officers and deputies at Shalimar. During this assembly, Dewan Deena Nath read a letter, that he claimed, had been sent to the Durbar by the Kardars of the States beyond the Sutlej. The contents of the letter stated that British authorities really meant to seize that part of the country, that they were causing great annoyance to the servants of the Durbar and had actually given orders to people of several villages to pay tributes only to the British government, which now claimed sovereignty. Dewan Deena Nath also claimed that great disturbances existed in Kashmir, Peshawar and elsewhere, and that for a long time not a rupee of revenue had been paid by the Kardars.

Having thus created alarm and concern in the assembly, the wily Dewan went on to remind them that their sovereign was a child, that there was no recognised head of state and that unless arrangements were made for the governance of the country, ruin must speedily ensure. He then informed them that it was the wish of the Maharani that Raja Lal Singh should be Wazir and Sardar Tej Singh the Commander-in-Chief. It was also stated that she was willing to sanction the march of the army across the Sutlej for the protection of the national honour and would, if they thought proper, order all necessary preparations to be made. The Council unanimously confirmed Her Highness's choice.[5]

Earlier, General Avitabile, Court and Pouvindia, aware of future events, had sent a delegation to Raja Gulab Singh, who had returned to Jammu after his forced visit to Lahore. In it, they offered him the position of Commander-in-Chief, an offer he politely declined. He had also declined the post of prime minister when it had been offered by the regent during his enforced visit to Lahore, commenting to his well-wishers that, he 'wished to live longer than six months'.[6]

The army's acceptance of the regent's decision, when they had no confidence in Tej Singh and Lal Singh, as even the British were aware, shows the devious and clever manner in which Maharani Jindan managed the issue through her Dewan and courtiers. They played on the sentiments of the army to the extent that her decision to allow them to cross the Sutlej to get to grips with the British became the overriding factor. Once this decision was taken, it did not matter who led them: their objective had been achieved.

By this time, Raja Gulab Singh was already in touch with the Governor-General, offering his assistance in the event of hostilities breaking out between the British and the Lahore Durbar and always assuring his support and promising that whenever he saw the opportunity, he would throw the whole weight of his influence and power into the scale on the British side.

Jindan had been, for some time, thinking of making Lal Singh the prime minister. He had already crossed the Sutlej with a few followers at the end of August 1845, and had moved along the river on what was obviously a surveillance mission. It was also clear by then that her intentions were to cross the river Sutlej and to provoke British retaliation in a war that would destroy her army. Subsequent statements (by Jindan) of marching to Ludhiana, Ambala or even Delhi, were meant to indicate to the army that the Durbar had every intention of defeating the British and conquering their territory.

With the durbar's intention clear, and with her two trusted leaders now in position to carry out this policy, the stage was set for the inevitable disaster. The army leadership at the upper level had no confidence in the two appointees, and at the regimental level, the leaders were in complete disarray. There had been no large-scale exercises or training for five years, since the rule of Nau Nihal Singh who was killed in 1840. All that the troops could now count on was their high morale. With this one positive attribute in hand, the Sikh army plunged into war with the British.

Gulab Singh had tactfully opted out and was at his base at

Jammu. Lal Singh and Tej Singh had, at the very beginning, been in touch with the British political agents Major Broadfoot and Captain Nicholson at Ferozepur. Prior to hostilities commencing, they had sent a message to General Litter about the fact that they were not going to attack his small force at Ferozepur. Through his confidential agent, Shamsuddin, Lal Singh sent the British C-in-C Gouch a full report on the eve of battle of Sobraon and after the Battle of Ferozeshahar, 'on the position of and nature of the entrenchments and an account of disposition of troops and guns'.[7] That consistent and regular reports were communicated to the British is borne out by the accuracy of the report of decisions taken by the Council of Lahore, which were regularly sent by the political agent Major Broadfoot to the Governor-General.

Captain Peter Nicholson, Major Broadfoot's political assistant at Ferozepur during this period, wrote that at the very beginning: 'Lal Singh had already, in a letter, requested the British to consider him and the Bibi Saheba (Maharani Jindan) as their friends and to cut up the *Burchas* (ruffians of the army) for them. So, there was no point in Lal Singh and Tej Singh compromising themselves by destroying Littler's small force at Ferozepur.' Nicholson, according to contemporary authorities, had also received a letter from Lal Singh, asking what he should best do.

THE LAST HEIR DALIP SINGH

MAHARAJA DALIP SINGH was only ten when his Kingdom was annexed. In those ten years he had seen his mother grossly insulted by low upstarts, exploited by the ambitious, and misused by men of lust; he had seen his relations and friends murdered before his eyes, and he had also seen the best of men behave in the most disgraceful manner. He was seated on the throne and had his feet kissed in public by men who had no hesitation in calling him a bastard when they wanted to. He wore the world's greatest diamond on his arm but was denied expenses to maintain himself and his mother with dignity.

The process of segregating Dalip Singh from his people had begun even before the formalities of the annexation were complete. Just a week after the second Anglo-Sikh War ended, on 6 April 1849, a doctor, John Spencer Login of the Bengal Army Medical Service was appointed his guardian. Dalhousie had become the EIC Governor-General in January in 1848. It was his expansionist policies and diabolical plotting that had helped the British annex the Punjab. He thought of himself as a modernist, who would change India but he had no hesitation in taking the Kohinoor diamond from the minor ruler, according to the traditional practise of war that allowed loot. The treasury of Dalip Singh was considered war booty and Dalip Singh was forced to hand over the diamond to the British in 1848. It was, after all, war booty and old-fashioned plunder imperialism (D C Kinsey 2009, p392).

The Process of Exile

After that Dalhousie plotted to move the minor ruler out of the Punjab. Eleven months later, on 19 February 1850, Dalip Singh arrived at the small town of Fatehgarh on the river Ganges, in what is today the district of Farukhabad in Uttar Pradesh where he would spend the next four years. The excuse used by Dalhousie was that information had reached the government (EIC government) that an attempt would be made to abduct Dalip Singh from Lahore and take him to the hills, from where a fresh attempt would be made to rally the Sikhs in the Punjab in another attempt at Sikh revival.

This story was planted, knowing full well that it was pure fiction, in order to remove him from Punjab. With no Sikh army left at Lahore and with the Sardars and hill chiefs by now subservient to British authority, and with the British army now at Lahore in full force, Dalhousie's conspiracy theory seemed if anything childish, nevertheless it was used to ensure that Dalip Singh was banished from Lahore. The clever British did not use the word exile formally. However, Dalip Singh, a possible Sikh ruler, was effectively moved far far away – not only from his Punjab, but from his country, India, as well.

Assuming that the news of Dalip Singh being moved out of the Punjab would leak out and that there would be a reaction of sorts to his removal from the State, military precautions were taken to defend Lahore from the Sikhs. Imagine what the story would have been if Dalip Singh had been even the titular ruler of the Sikhs (even in an annexed Punjab) in 1857.

In retrospect, the overall plan behind his removal from the Punjab, appears to be not only to separate Dalip Singh from his mother but also isolate the eleven-year-old from his people and the events of the State, and then convert him to Christianity, after which he was to be sent to England. Of the family, only the late Maharaja Sher Singh's Rajput lady of his harem, Rani Dukhnoo of Kangra,[1] and her son Sheo Deo Singh, who was then six-year-old, but who could also be a claimant to the throne, were sent into exile along with Dalip Singh. Basically, the Brits were ensuring that there were no claimants to the throne anywhere nearby, if the rebellious Sikhs ever rose in revolt again.

Suitable accommodation was found in Fatehgarh, the cantonment area of Farrukhabad. A property which lay on the Ganges, surrounded by a park with a number of outhouses was bought for him out of his own allowances and was renovated; his captors were such misers. This had once belonged to a local Nawab and was now with the East India Company. The accommodation was sumptuous. It was partly damaged during the revolt of 1857, and today forms a part of the Rajput Regiment's Centre at Fatehgarh.

Life in Dalip Singh's new surroundings was forged into a set routine. A ride early in the morning 'escorted by an escort of fierce looking Sikhs jostling behind, followed by a detachment of the Body Guard in scarlet uniforms and troopers of the famous regiment Skinner's Horse, otherwise known as "canaries" in saffron'.[2] This was followed by studies under his new tutor Walter Guise, which included English, history, general knowledge and sciences.

He was an average student as Dr Login had assessed him. In a letter to Login, who was in Calcutta on holiday, Dalip Singh wrote: 'We are all well here, captain Campbell presided at our examination, and I got twenty marks; but Shahzada (his nephew) got only ten'.[3] The afternoons were spent in play and his favourite sport was fishing and hunting, out in the country.

At six o'clock, he routinely met with those of his staff members who had accompanied him into exile and spent an hour or so with them. These included Dewan Ajodha Prasad, his Secretary, his Persian tutor Zahoor-Deen, Hakim Jaikishan, his doctor and his *purohit* Golab Rai, amongst others. All of them were soon to be sent back to Lahore, including his old faithful personal servant Main Kheema, who was replaced by Bhajan Lal who had been engaged by Dr Login.

Conversion to Christianity

Bhajan Lal was the son of a wealthy Presbyterian merchant of Farukhabad, and though a Brahmin, he studied in the American Presbyterian Mission, while still observing the rules of Hinduism he had acquired more than Christianity. 'Why he should accept to be a servant when he was from a well-to-do family is fairly obvious: to educate Dalip Singh, as he put it, in the beliefs of the firangis. Bhajan Lal now began to read the Bible to the twelve-year-old Dalip Singh. In a second letter to Dr Login during the same holiday, he writes: "You will be surprised to learn of my determination to embrace the Christian religion. I have long doubted the truth of the one I was brought up in and convinced of the truth of the religion of the Bible which I have made, Bhajan Lal read portion of it to me."'[4]

Dalhousie's cunning knew no limits. He pretended to be outraged as it would be assumed in India that the (still EIC) government had brought about this conversion. So Dalhousie ordered an enquiry to find out if Dalip Singh had been coerced into this decision by someone at Fatehgarh, or whether it truly was a calling from his inner self. The enquiry duly over, and Dalhousie duly convinced that it was indeed a decision of Dalip Singh's *inner self*, permission was given for him to be converted. He now wrote to Dalip Singh:

> My dear Maharaja,
> I have received with the most lively satisfaction in letter in which you express your desire to be at once baptised, and to be admitted as a member of the Church of Christ. When you at first showed an inclination to believe in truths which you found declared in the word of God, I advised you not to act hastily, to continue in your study of Bible, and to test by time the strength and sincerity of your belief.
> You have followed my advice, and I have learnt with real pleasure from the statement of the Archdeacon and Mr Jay that they have found you quite fit to receive baptism you desire to obtain. I, on my part, most readily assent to your wish and I thank God and a belief in, the truth of our holy religion, and that you may show to your countrymen in India an example of a pure and blameless life, such as befits a Christian prince.
> I beg your highness to believe in the strength and sincerity of the regard in which I shall ever feel towards you, and to remain, now and always, your Highness's sincere and affectionate friend.[5]

The Kohinoor had already not only changed hand but changed country. It became a part of Victoria's jewellery. In 1851, it went on display at the Great Exhibition in London. Dalhousie was now delighted and put in motion the third step, which was to send Dalip Singh to England. As part of his overall plan, which he had confided to Login at the very beginning, and which Login in turn had confided to his wife in a letter from Lahore, 'I cannot put Bible in his hands yet' after receiving a letter from Dalhousie which stated that, 'If Duleep Singh is to go to England, let him be quietly baptised before he goes as and by his own name of Duleep Singh'.[6]

Dalip Singh was baptised on 8 March 1853 by the Reverend William Jay, the cantonment Chaplin in the Fatehgarh Church, in the presence of about twenty officers and an equal number of his own staff from the Punjab. At the beginning of 1854 Dalip Singh was given the requisite approval to visit England.

In England

In April 1854, Dalip Singh set off for Calcutta, halting en route at Lucknow and Benaras where a Pandit, Nilkanth Goreh (christianised as Nehemiah), one of the first Brahmins to have been converted to Christianity, and who was now working as a missionary amongst the people, was added to the party. Bhajan Lal had been held back by his family and Pandit Goreh was to be his replacement. In Calcutta, Dalhousie met Dalip Singh and he gave him a parting gift of a beautifully-bound Bible.

Dalip Singh sailed for England on 19 April 1854. He reached England in the mid-summer of 1854. On the way they had passed Malta and Gibraltar where he was given a twenty-one-gun salute. On reaching Southampton, he was taken straight to London, and put up in Mrs Claridge's hotel, The Mivert, in Brook Street.

Soon, a summon arrived from the Buckingham Palace for Dalip Singh to meet the Queen. This meeting between the thirty-five year old Victoria and the fifteen-year old Dalip Singh took place on 1 July 1854; as the Queen recorded in her journal: 'After luncheon, to which Mama came, we received the young Maharaja Dalip Singh, the son of Ranjit Singh, who was deposed by us after annexation of the Punjab. He has been carefully brought up, chiefly in the hills, and was baptised last year, so that he is a Christian. He is extremely handsome and speaks English perfectly and has a pretty graceful and dignified manner. He was beautifully dressed and covered with diamonds. The "Koh-i-noor" belonged to and was once worn by him. I always feel so much for these poor deposed Indian princes.'[7] A sense of wrongdoing somewhere perhaps.

European Prince Dalip Singh

The queen was so impressed with him that she there and then commissioned the court painter, Franz Xavier Winterhalter, her favourite artist, to paint his portrait. This relationship between the two weathered many storms, but Queen Victoria remained his friend and supporter to his very last day. She also ordered, despite local rumblings, that in protocol, in the order of precedence, his would be the same as that of an European prince, and Dalip Singh would be addressed as 'Your Serene Highness'. To this, there were murmurs in certain quarters in England, but the Queen refused to budge.

She then wrote to Lord Dalhousie:

> The Queen wishes to tell Lord Dalhousie how much interested and pleased we have been in making the acquaintance of your Maharaja Dalip Singh. It is not without pain and sympathy that the Queen sees this young Prince, once destined to so high and powerful position and now reduced to a so-dependent one by our arms; his youth, amiable character, and striking good looks; as well as being a Christian, the first of his high rank who has embraced our faith, must incline everyone favourably towards him, and it will be a pleasure to us to do all we can to help him and to befriend and protect him.[8]

On 21 August 1854, the Queen went to her estate, Osborne, on the Isle of Wight, and Dalip Singh was invited to stay for a week. Prince Albert and the royal children too became just as fond of him during this visit and from then on, he became an integral part of the royal family's social calendar. The Queen now tried her hand at match-making and suggested that he marry the exiled Raja of Coorg's daughter, who was also her goddaughter, Princess Gouramma. Dalip Singh politely declined, saying that Gouramma was his friend but he did not wish to marry till he was twenty-one or two and until he had seen the world.

Being befriended by various people in England and with the queen's warm support, Dalip Singh took a liking to England and decided that for the present, he would like to live there for some time. Dr Login was able to get him Mulgrave Castle in Yorkshire, which was to be his first rented home and which got him involved in English country life and shooting. He next rented the estate of Lord Breadalbane at Auchlyne on Loch Tay. By now, he had also decided that despite his closeness to Sir John and Lady Login, he should break free of their influence over him and accepted the advice of Dr Login, who was surprisingly of the same opinion, to meet Colonel Oliphant, an ex-chairman of the Board of Directors of the East India Company, who was prepared to look after Dalip Singh's affairs. By 1857, the ruler of the valiant Sikhs, Dalip Singh had become completely English and soon Victoria also assumed the role of Empress of India. Crown control and the Raj rule was well on its way and India was now England's colony.

Dalip Singh Gets Married

Meanwhile, Dalip Singh decided to bring his mother, Jindan to England. His request was accepted by the government. For this purpose, for the first time after seven years, the young man visited India in early February 1861. He returned to England in early summer of the same year along with Rani Jindan Kaur. However, after only two years of stay in England Rani Jindan suddenly died on 1 August 1863.

On his way to India, with the dead body of his mother, Dalip Singh happened to stop at Cairo. There he went to a

Presbyterian Mission where he saw a small fifteen-year-old teacher giving lessons to a large, but disciplined class, and decided she was just the girl for him. Her name was Bamba Müller, she was the daughter of a German banker and an Abyssinian slave. The 25-year-old Maharaja proposed to her through an interpreter, as she knew no English and received her consent. Then, after giving the mission the task of preparing her as a suitable bride, saying: 'I think it desirable that she could learn English and music, and to give her own orders', he[9] informed the mission that he would be back from India in six months, when he would marry her and take her back to England.

Shortly after his mother's cremation in Nasik, Dalip Singh returned to Cairo and called on the British Consul, Robert Colquhoun on 28 April 1864, to inform him that he intended to get married and he requested him to publish the news about his marriage. Queen Victoria, when she heard the news, wondered why the maharaja had not taken her into confidence. Perhaps, by now Dalip Singh knew all the stories of his own plebian origin and chose to take a commoner wife. Dalip Singh was married on 7 June 1864.

At the beginning of August 1865 Dalip Singh took his pregnant wife to Auchlyne on Loch Tay. No Sooner had they arrived that Bamba gave birth to a boy who lived for just two days and was buried under a block of polished granite opposite the church at Taymouth. Dalip Singh took his wife on holiday to Egypt after the trauma of losing her newborn son. On his return, they settled down in Elveden which was in the centre of England's sporting country.[10]

Bamba's second son was born in June next year and a small christening ceremony was held at Elveden. Eight months later, the queen commanded them to Windsor for a second christening, at which she would be the Godmother. The boy was christened Victor Albert by Victoria. Victor Albert was followed by Frederick Victor born in 1868, Bamba Sofia Jindan in 1869, Catherine Hilda in 1871, Sophia Alexandra in 1876, and Edward Albert Alexander in 1879.

Reconversion to Sikhism

By now Dalip Singh, with growing responsibilities, knew exactly where he stood vis-à-vis the English. He started a long-drawn-out dispute with the India Office about more money and possession of his private estates in India. A little money was conceded, but the government of British Indian refused to concede what he wanted, including the private property owned by his forefathers. Though Queen Victoria took up his cause on a number of occasions with successive governments, nothing was forthcoming in cash or kind, which drove Dalip Singh to despair and bitterness.

It was now that the thought of the prophecy regarding him, told to him by his mother Jindan, came to his mind. The Maharaja wrote a series of letters to the *Time* and other papers staking his claim, and highlighting the injustice done to him, hoping that the papers, as well as the people, would support him. As no assistance seemed forthcoming from any quarter, Dalip Singh, by now frustrated and disillusioned, decided to become a Sikh again and to follow the prophecy. He wrote to the Queen's Secretary, Sir Henry Ponsonby, declaring his intention of returning to the 'faith of his ancestors'. Dalip Singh then wrote to the Queen:

> … as your Majesty is the only true and disinterested friend I possess in the world, I did not like that you my Sovereign should hear from any other source in the first instance but myself of the possibility of my re-embracing the faith of my ancestors, though I mentioned it to Sir Henry Ponsonby.

> I have sent for Bhaee or Brother to come with a copy of the Holy Book of the Sikhs to teach me to read it. ... Shortly after I ascended to the throne of the Punjab, it was found written in a book of Sikh prophecies called *Sakheean* that a man of my name would be born who, after becoming entirely dispossessed of all he inherited and residing alone for a long period in a foreign country, would return to be the eleventh gooroo or teacher of the Khalsa or the pure and that his prosperity then would exceed that of his ancestors. He would also establish a new faith.
>
> ... While discussing the prophecy with my mother, I jeeringly remarked, 'but mother, how can all this come to pass if I do not return to India at all'. She replied, 'Mark my words my child, perhaps I may not live to see the day but whenever the right moment arrives, circumstances will so shape themselves such that thou wilt be compelled to quit England against thy will'.
>
> Under these circumstances, my Sovereign, I do not believe and indeed my Sovereign I do not now particularly care, that justice will ever be done to me, but I do now believe that my destiny, whatever that may be, will be fulfilled.[11]

On 25 March 1886, Dalip Singh released to the English press, the text of an open letter to be published in their columns. It said:

> My dear countrymen,
>
> It was not my intention ever to return to India, but Satgooroo, who governs all destiny, and is more powerful than I, his erring creature, has caused circumstances to be so brought about, that against my will, I am compelled

to quit England, in order to occupy a humble sphere in India. I submit to his will, being persuaded that whatever is for the best will happen.

I now, therefore, beg forgiveness of you, Khalsajee, or Pure, for having forsaken the faith of my ancestors for a foreign religion; but I was very young when I embraced Christianity.

It is my fond desire on reaching Bombay to take the *Pahul* again, and I sincerely hope for your prayers to the Sutgooroo on that solemn occasion. But in returning to the faith of my ancestors, you must clearly understand, Khalsajee, that I have no intention of conforming to the errors introduced into Sikhism by those who were not true Sikhs – such, for instance, as wretched caste observations or abstinence from meats and drinks, which Sutgooroo has ordained should be received with thankfulness by all mankind – but to worship the pure and beautiful tenets of Baba Nanak and obey the commands of Guru Gobind Singh.

I am compelled to write this to you because I am not permitted to visit you in the Punjab, as I had much hoped to do. Truly a noble reward for my unwavering loyalty to the Empress of India. But Satgooroo's will be done.

With *Wah Gooroojee de Fateh*, I remain, my beloved countrymen,

Your own flesh and blood. Duleep Singh.[12]

Attempts to Return to India

On the morning of 31 March 1886, the Maharaja's party, comprising a reluctant and ailing Maharani, his six children, a Sikh attendant, a native servant, an European nurse and an *ayah* embarked on the P&O Verona, bound for Bombay. His last letter written on board ship, before sailing, was to an aging

Queen Victoria, in which he thanked her for all that she had done for him and his family and then bid her goodbye.

In British India, rumours of the 48-year-old Dalip Singh's return were rife and the government soon entered into consultations at all levels to assess the reaction amongst the Sikhs to his arrival, particularly so after his open latter. Government House asked Colonel Hennessy of the 15th Sikhs, for his opinion. Hennessy wrote back: 'In regard to Duleep Singh's influence over the Sikhs, he would indeed be a bold man who could say he had no fear of it in his own regiment. I most devoutly trust the subject will not be put to the test in my day. The spirit of the Sikhs is not dead. And they are full of national fire. I should tremble in my shoes were the gentleman to arrive at our borders with Russians. The British government should hold him fast and secure in England in my opinion.'[13]

With similar views coming from all sources, the then Viceroy, Lord Dufferin, decided that Dalip Singh should be detained enroute. He was to be arrested under Regulation 111 of 1818. On 15 April 1886, the order went out from Shimla to Aden, where he was expected to arrive by then. Delayed by headwinds, the Verona reached Aden on 21 April. Brigadier Hogg, the Resident, went on board and informed the Maharaja that by the order of the Government of India, he could not go further. Dalip Singh, however, refused to leave the ship till he was arrested. This the Resident did by tapping him symbolically on the shoulder. Passengers and crew then gave a loud and sympathetic cheer as he and his family were taken into captivity.

Now followed a flurry of telegrams between Aden, Shimla (the winter capital of the Raj) and London and finally Dalip Singh, by now highly frustrated, wired the Viceroy, 'I desire to take advantage of my cousin's presence here to be re-initiated into Sikhism. Kindly telegraph the Resident, saying I may go through the ceremony in his presence'.[14] After due consultations with the Lieutenant-Governor in the Punjab, whose opinion was that 'refusal might be misunderstood', permission to reconvert was given to Dalip Singh, but the Resident was told to stay away. Dalip Singh returned to the Sikh faith by taking *Pahul* on 25 May 1886. The Panj Piyaras, mandatory on such occasion, were composed of Sikhs brought in for the ceremony from the neighbouring ships in the harbour of Aden.

Dalip Singh Woos the French, Russians and Others

His failed efforts to return to India made Dalip Singh very bitter and he began to describe himself as 'a determined foe of the British'. Dalip Singh had reached the end of his tethers and was set to take on the Raj establishment. To start with, he wrote to Queen Victoria's Secretary, Sir Henry Ponsonby: 'I return to Paris, being unable to get justice. Resigned stipend, thus ending Annexation Treaty, and getting rid of all dealings with the most tyrannical government in the world, (the) Indian administration.'[15] In Russia, Tsar Alexander III ruled. France no longer had a King; it was ruled by a government headed by a President, Marie François Sadi Carnot, who was not really interested in antagonising the British.

In Aden, on 3 June Dalip Singh boarded the SS Natal, bound for Marseilles in France. Here he tried to win the support of the French government but did not make any headway. Unfazed, but disappointed by the negative behavior of the French, Dalip Singh now entered discussions with a number of revolutionary groups, active in Paris. The venue of these meetings was the Reynolds Bar on Rue Royale. The diverse groups included the Irish Fenians, whose leaders were the Casey brothers (who were fighting for freedom from the English), Patrick and James. They took him under their wing and printed manifestos and proclamations etc. Among

Dalip Singh's friends in Paris were also their fraternal Irish-Americans, English detectives, journalists, spies and Russians with influence in the Tsar's court. The Namdhari Sikh leaders from India were already in touch with the Russians, wanting their support against the English.

During his Paris sojourn, Dalip Singh's proclamations and letters to newspapers were signed by him, initially as 'Maharaja of the Sikhs under the Treaty of Bhyrowal with Great Britain, 1846'. And finally, as 'Both Sovereign and Guru of the Sikh nation'.[16]

A few years earlier, Dalip Singh had met and was enchanted by a worker at Cox's Hotel in west London. Her name was Ada Wetherill. The young woman had become the Maharaja's lover. Dalip Singh now summoned the nineteen-year-old Ada Wetherill to Paris to accompany him to Russia and left Paris by train on 21 March 1887, accompanied by Ada, who was now expecting a child, and his ADC, Aroor Singh. His wife Bamba had been very ill after so many frequent childbirths. On 18 September 1887 Maharani Bamba died in Aden following renal complications and was buried in Elveden in the UK.

In Moscow, the Russians showed no interest in the Maharaja. So, Dalip Singh first moved to a cheap hotel, and then left Moscow to live in Kiev at the Hotel de France. While in Kiev, he toyed with the idea of joining the Russian Orthodox Church, which he thought may endear him to the Russian establishment. He wrote to his cousin Gurbachan Singh who was initially horrified and hastened to write back:

> As to your Majesty's joining the Russian faith, we beg to say that it would produce a very bad effect among the Indians and more particularly with Sikhs who believe in you as their Guroo.... According to their idea, you became Christian in accordance with the prophecy... and not on your own accord. Already the English papers in

> Punjab are giving out that you are not Sikh. If you ever take Russian Orthodox baptism, they will spread the news at once and the people will not trust us.[17]

Dalip Singh returned to Paris at the beginning of November 1888. The purpose of his return was to sell his jewellery, left with an agent in Paris before leaving for Russia, to raise money to live on in Paris. From here, he once again wrote to Victoria. Not holding her responsible for his personal matters being held up by various governments 'as she was a constitutional monarch', Dalip Singh then went on to say: 'My diamond, the Koh-i-noor, I understand, is entirely at your own personal disposal. Therefore, believing your Majesty to be "the most religious lady" that your subject pray for every Sunday, I do not hesitate to ask that this gem be restored to me, or else that a fair price be paid for it to me out of your privy purse.'[18]

Dalip Singh Paralysed, Pardoned, Dies

On 21 May 1989, Dalip Singh married Ada, pregnant with his second child. Ada's second child, a girl, was born on 25 October 1889 and was christened Princess Ada Irene Halen Bergl Dalip Singh.

At the beginning of 1890, Dalip Singh had a stroke in his hotel room in Paris which affected his left leg and side, and left half of his face paralysed. What had happened with Maharaja Ranjit Singh had struck him too. His son, Prince Victor, visited him on two occasions in Paris and during the second visit found that Dalip Singh, by now lonely and depressed after his stroke, had matured considerably. He wrote a long letter to Queen Victoria, asking her to pardon him for all he had done against her: 'May it please your majesty, My son Victor is writing this letter from my dictation – I have been struck down by the hand of God and am in consequence quite unable to write myself – I have been disappointed in everyone in whom I have been led to believe and now my one desire is to die at peace with all men. I, therefore, pray your majesty to pardon me for all I have done against you and your government and I throw myself entirely on your clemency.'[19]

Maharaja's letter was answered by Lord Cross on behalf of Victoria, conveying to him the grant of pardon by the Queen:

'I am now commanded to inform you that, on the understanding that henceforward your Highness will remain obedient to the Queen-Empress of India and will regulate your movements in conformity with instructions that may be issued to you by her Majesty's Government. Her Majesty, on the advice of Her Ministers, has been graciously pleased to accord you the pardon you have sought.'[20] Victoria had really been fond of Dalip Singh.

The Maharaja arrived in England on 26 August 1890 and settled down at No 6 Clifton Gardens, Folkestone which Victor had rented for him. After a month, however, he returned to France for a cure, to Aix-la-Chapelle for curative baths and then decided to stay the winter in Paris.

On 24 April 1893, though ill and weak, Dalip Singh again crossed over to England to visit his youngest son, Edward, who was now seriously ill. He stayed in England a week and then returned to France. The very next day, the thirteen-year-old Edward, suffering from pleuro-pneumonia died. Six months later, on 22 October 1893, the last Maharaja of Lahore, Dalip Singh, died in his small hotel room in Paris. He was fifty-five-years old.

The funeral took place on 29 October 1893 at Elveden. Queen Victoria, now 84, had outlived her handsome Maharaja and sent her Lord in Waiting, Lord Camoys to stand in for her. Wreaths from old friends lay all around. Many friends from France and England attended. On the plate of the coffin was engraved 'Duleep Singh, Maharaja of Lahore Born on

4 September 1838. Died 22 October 1893'.

There is no record of Dalip Singh's conversion to Christianity again. But his last rites were performed as a practicing Protestant and he was buried close to the Elveden Chapel. All his children remained Christians till the day of their death.

Of Dalip Singh's nine Children, four sons, of whom two died young and five daughters, Prince Victor and Princesses Bamba Sofia and Irene were married. They, however, had no children.The residence Elveden was sold by Dalip Singh's trustees to the Guinness family in 1894 for 159,000 pounds sterling. It remains today as part of the same trust.

Ranjit Singh's Sikh Empire

The Kingdom of Lahore, which was created by Maharaja Ranjit Singh in 1801, ended in 1849 with the annexation of the Punjab by the British. Though there is continuing dispute among historians over his paternity, with the death of Dalip Singh's nine children, the last of who died in 1957, ended the Sikh dynasty of the Lahore Durbar.

After the revolt of 1857, the last Moghul Emperor, Bahadur Shah Zafar was transported to Burma where he lived in a bamboo hut with two companions. When he died, he was buried in an unmarked grave. At Lahore too, Princess Bamba Sofia, Maharaja Dalip Singh's activist daughter, was buried in a two square piece of ground in the 'Goren ka Kabristan', with no family or friends from the former Lahore Durbar present. Dalip Singh, if history accepts him as Ranjit Singh's youngest son, is buried in an English graveyard. Was it a coincidence that none of Dalip Singh's children had any children, with the tenuous lineage fading out of history? Or was it the *Hukum* (directive) of Guru Gobind Singh, the tenth Guru, who had said that if anyone built a memorial to the Guru, his dynasty and his family would end?

This speculation will go on forever, but the name of Ranjit Singh, the great Maharaja of Lahore will continue to inspire generations. Ranjit Singh, an illiterate man, like Napoleon, had built and ruled a kingdom larger than what is today Pakistan, before he had reached the age of twenty-one.

He was the one who created modern-day Punjab as we know it today, both on the west, the Pakistani Punjab and on the east, the Indian Punjab, uniting all the fiefdoms between the Indus and the Yamuna rivers and many beyond the Khyber. And he was the one who successfully put a stop to foreign invasions into India through the passes in the Hindukush ranges.

GLOSSARY

Cis-Sutlej area and States—The Cis-Sutlej States were a group of States in the modern Punjab and Haryana States of northwestern India during the 19th century, lying between the Sutlej river on the north, the Himalayas on the east, the Yamuna river and Delhi district on the south, and Sirsa district on the west. These States included Kaithal, Patiala, Jind, Thanesar, Faridkot and Malerkotla.

These small States were under the suzerainty of the Scindia dynasty. The Mughals had been defeated by the Marathas, so even Delhi district was with the Marathas. Small Punjabi kingdoms of the Cis-Sutlej States paid tributes to the Marathas, until the Second Anglo-Maratha War of 1803–1805, after which the Marathas lost this territory to the British. When this war ended, Arthur Wellesley, the Duke of Wellington who was then the Governor-General of territories captured and taken by the East India Company through various means, drafted a treaty granting *independence* to the Sikh clans east of the Sutlej river in exchange for their allegiance to the British General, Gerard Lake. At the end of this war, the frontier of British India (or rather EIC's) was extended to the Yamuna river, that is to territories east of the Yamuna. East of the Sutlej was Sikh.

An 1809 agreement with Ranjit Singh, the ruler of the Sikhs west of the Sutlej, brought these States under the aegis of Sikh dominion.

Before 1846 the greater part of this territory was relatively independent, the chiefs being subject to supervision from a political officer stationed at Umballa (now Ambala), and called, the agent of the British Governor-General of India for the Cis-Sutlej States. After the First Anglo-Sikh War, the full administration of the territory became vested in this Agent. A number of states were confiscated or acquired by Britain under the *Doctrine of Lapse.*

In 1849, when the entire Punjab was annexed by the British and attached to their India holdings, the Cis-Sutlej States comprising the districts of Ambala, Ferozepore, Lūdhiana, Thanesar and Simla, was incorporated with the new Punjab Province. These States, because they were once held by the Marathas of Malwa or the Deccan, are also called Malwa of Punjab. Brides from this region for the Sikhs farther west were called (Mai, Mother from) Malwani.

*Malwa Punjab**—*(Holkar ran from his Central Indian citadel, across Rajasthan into Haryana and Punjab.)*—This was during the second Anglo-Maratha war, when Ranjit Singh mediated between the Marathas and the English.

Poorabias—People of the East (of Punjab).

Gurkhas—Ethnic Nepali soldiers.

Khatri—Khatri is a caste, originally found in South Asia. Apart from India, they are also found in Afghanistan and Pakistan. Afghan Hindus and Sikhs are predominantly of Khatri and Arora origin.

Jats—These are a community of traditionally non-elite, non-Brahmin, non- Kshatriya tillers and herders in Northern India and Pakistan.

Napoleon's Generals who served Ranjit Singh:

Avitabile—General Paolo Crescenzo Martino Avitabile Hindko, known in the region as Abu Tabela (25 October 1791 – 28 March 1850) was an Italian soldier from Naples. He joined Ranjit Singh's army in the Punjab in 1827, and later also received various civilian appointments. In 1829 he was made administrator of Wazirabad and in 1837 he succeeded Hari Singh Nalwa as governor of Peshawar.

---

* https://en.wikipedia.org/wiki/Malwa_(Punjab)

He remained in the Punjab until the assassination of Sher Singh in 1843, after which he retired to Italy, where his rank as a general was confirmed and he was knighted.

Allard—General Jean-François Allard (1785–1839) was a French soldier and adventurer. Allard served in Napoleon Bonaparte's army, where he was twice injured. He was awarded the Légion d' Honneur. After the Battle of Waterloo, Allard drifted, going to Persia and then coming south to the Punjab. In 1822 he entered the service of Maharaja Ranjit Singh. He was commissioned to raise a corps of dragoons and lancers. On completion of this task, Allard was awarded the rank of General, and became the leader of the European officer corps in the Maharaja's service. Allard was a charming and gentle man, very different from some of the other European mercenaries in the Punjab. He made the effort to learn Persian and is said to have composed poetry in Persian. He was an amateur numismatist, and contributed greatly to the early study of Ancient Indian coins.

Court—Claude Auguste Court (24 September 1793 – January 1880) was a French soldier and mercenary. In 1813, he joined the French army. After Napoleon's defeat in the Waterloo in 1815 he was dismissed from service. He left France in 1818 for Baghdad and joined the Persian forces which were being trained at Kermanshah by a handful of ex-officers of Napoleon's army including by Ventura. While in Persia, Court met Paolo Avitabile, another Neapolitan adventurer, and together they travelled on to Lahore, reaching there in early 1827. He was hired by Maharaja Ranjit Singh in 1827 to organise and train the Khalsa army's artillery. He was promoted to the rank of General, and served as one of the leading European officers in the Punjab army. A Ranjit Singh gave Court employment in the artillery befitting his talents and scientific attainments. Court was responsible for the training of artillerymen, the organisation of batteries and the establishment of arsenals and magazines on European lines. The Maharaja had his own foundries for casting guns and for the manufacture of shells. Court supervised these in collaboration with Sardar Lehna Singh Majithia.

After Maharaja Sher Singh's assassination in September 1843, he fled to Firozpur, in British territory, and, ultimately securing his discharge from the Sikh army, proceeded with his Punjabi wife, Fezli Azam Joo and the children to France in 1844. He purchased an estate in the countryside and a residence in the city of Paris where he lived until his death in 1880. A very useful overview of Court's life in India is found in Jean-Marie Lafont's book *Indika: Essays in Indo-French Relations*, 1630-1976 [New Delhi, 2000]. Lafont presents an enormous amount of new information of the 'French Generals' serving in Lahore in the 1820s-40s.

Court was one of the first Europeans to become interested in the coins of South Asia, which he collected from 1829. Part of the collection was described in a work called the *Revue Numismatique in 1839* and Court talks of his coin collection in his valuable Memoires published in Paris in 1856-57. Court died in Paris in January 1880 leaving his heirs his rich coin collection. Almost nothing of its fate was known until three albums came to light in an English book sale. They contained 627 coin rubbings, allowing many of Court's coins to be identified. These had been bought by a coin collector in India, none other than the Scottish explorer Alexander Cunningham, whose collection was acquired by the British Museum in 1888-94.

Ventura—General Jean-Baptiste (Giovanni Battista) Ventura (25 May 1794–3 April 1858) was an Italian soldier, mercenary in India, general in Maharaja Ranjit Singh's Sarkar-i-Khalsa, and early archaeologist of the Punjab region of the Sikh Empire.

At first he was a volunteer in the militia of the Kingdom of Italy, later serving with Napoleon's imperial army. After Napoleon's abdication and the dissolution of the French Army of Italy in April 1814, he sought greener pastures. Having learned that Persia was seeking the services of European soldiers, he obtained a commission as an officer and helped train the Shah's army with European military methods. On the death of the Shah in 1822, Ventura offered his services to his successor. However, there were a number of English officers in the new ruler's army who were decidedly hostile to the French; they considered Ventura to be French because he had fought under Napoleon. As a result of their political intrigues, Ventura was dismissed. He traveled east, ending up in Lahore alongside Jean-François Allard in 1822. They took service with Ranjit Singh, as the Maharaja was encouraging veterans from erstwhile Napoleon's army in his ongoing bid to modernise his Sikh army like the European ones. In March of the following year both Allard and Ventura commanded the Maharaja's troops in the Battle of Nowshera, where they defeated the Afghan army and captured Peshawar. Following a rebellion in Afghanistan, Ventura commanded several difficult campaigns and greatly expanded the boundaries of the kingdom of Lahore. Along with Jean-Francois Allard, Paolo Avitabile and Claude Auguste Court, Ventura formed a group of European officers responsible for modernising the Sikh army and training and commanding the Fauj-i-Khas, the European-model brigade of which Ventura was the commander. Ventura was highly esteemed by the Maharaja, and in addition to the rank of General he was appointed kazi (i.e., Supreme Judge), and Governor of Lahore. He quickly rose through the ranks of the court and became the de facto Commander-in-Chief of the Darbar forces. In 1830 he was the first ever to explore a stupa, that of Manikyala, where he recovered numerous coins and relics, some of which are now on display at the British Museum. He spent his spare time in Peshawar exhuming Bactrian and Greek and Kushan coins from Hindu temples and Buddhist stupas in the Khyber Pass, making numerous excavations then sending the findings on to the Asiatic Society of Bengal in Calcutta. These coins were taken as evidence of Alexander's march through Afghanistan and the Sindh-Punjab region of ancient India.

Ventura served under Ranjit Singh and his successors Kharak Singh, Nau Nihal Singh, and Sher Singh. Upon Maharaja Sher Singh's assassination in September 1843, he left the Punjab.

The list of foreign Generals goes something like this:
Jarnail Jean-Bapiste Ventura
Jarnail Claude Augustus Courte
Jarnail Jean-Francois Allard

Jarnail Pablo Di Avitable
Jarnail Oms
Jarnail Alexander Gardener
Jarnail Joshiah Harlan
Jarnail Honignberger
Kolonel Henry Steinbach
Jarnail Charles Van Cordant

Maharaja, Raja—King, in hierarchical order.

Maharani, Rani—Queen, in hierarchical order.

Raj Tilak—A vermilion or sandalwood paste mark on the forehead, in recognition as ruler.

Gaddi—Seat of power. Throne.

Sati—A woman who immolates herself on the husband's funeral pyre, according to Hindu and Sikh rites.

Dharma—Duty, as in the Bhagavat Gita, opposed to *Karma,* doing, action.

Avataar—Incarnation.

Advaitya—The formless form of worship; it bases worship in scriptures rather than idol worship.

Baani—Words, the Guru's words.

Panja Sahib—Is a famous Gurdwara located in Hasan Abdal, Pakistan. The shrine is considered to be particularly important as the handprint of the founder of Sikhism, Guru Nanak, is believed to be imprinted on a boulder at the Gurdwara.

Akalpurkh—The timeless God.

Khalsa Panth—The way of the Khalsa or Pure.

Kaliyug—The Kaliyuga, in Hinduism, is the fourth and worst of the four yugas in a Yuga Cycle, preceded by Dvapara Yuga. Followed by the next cycle's Krita Yuga. It is believed to be the present age, which is full of conflict and sin, vice and misery.

Samadhi—Samadhi is a state of profound and utterly absorptive contemplation of the Absolute that is undisturbed by desire, anger, or any other ego-generated thought or emotion. It is a state of joyful calm.

Ardās—The Ardās is a set prayer in Sikhism. It is a part of worship service in a Gurdwara, and a part of the daily rituals.

Bhaktas—Devotees.

Sanyasi, Sanyasin—Hermits, ascetics, monks in Hinduism; male and female.

Purohit—Priest.

Sadhu—A mendicant, a monk.

Fakir—A Muslim mendicant.

Mullah—A Muslim, learned in Islamic theology and sacred law.

Mufti—In Shia Islam, a Mufti is an Islamic jurist qualified to issue a nonbinding opinion (fatwa) on a point of Islamic law (sharia).

Ulema—A body of Muslim scholars who are recognised as having specialist knowledge of Islamic law and theology.

Ghazi—A Muslim fighter against non-Muslims.

Mujahid—Struggler or striver (for justice, right conduct, Godly rule, etc or doer of jihād), an Arabic term that broadly refers to Islamic guerrillas who engage in jihad. Interpreted in a jurisprudence of Islam as the fighter on behalf of God, religion or the community (ummah).

Jihad—A holy war for religious supremacy.

Sharia – Shariat—is a religious law forming part of the Islamic tradition. It is derived from the religious precepts of Islam and is based on the sacred scriptures of Islam, particularly the Quran and the Hadith. Shariat is the rule of these laws, by these laws.

Naqshbandi—The Naqshbandi, also known as Naqshbandiyah, Neqshebendi and Nakşibendi is a major Sunni order of Sufism.

Goren ka Kabristan—Graveyard of the Whitemen.

Mlechcha—The Untouchables.

Firangi—The foreigner.

Yunani—The Greeks; the Greek-Arabic system of medicine.

Hakim—A physician practicing the Arabic system of medicine.

Vaid—A physician practicing the Ayurvedic system of medicine.

Do Ab, Doab—Land, area between two rivers.

Misl—Misl is a term used to refer to major Sikh confederacies that sought to expand Sikh rule across the Panjab in the eighteenth century, leading to significant weakening of the Mughal rule across the region. There were 12 major misls.

Misldars—Leader of the misl or chieftain.

Jaagir—Landholding.

Zamindar, Jaagirdar—Owner of land.

Haveli—A large homestead; mostly that of the chieftain.

Baradari—balcony.

Diwan, Dewan—A hereditary title of chief minister.

Nazim—A governor, administrator, manager.

Najibs—A Nobleman, courtier.

Loya jirga, Panchayat—A village council; a council in the Khalsa armed forces after Ranjit Singh.

Baishakh, Baisakhi Day—New Years Day according to the Indian and Islamic calendars, in April.

Ayahs—Children's nursemaids.

Zenana—Women's quarters.

Purdah—Veil, covering face and body.

Howdah—Decorations and decorated seats on an elephant.

Mohur—A gold coin, of about 11 gm weight.

Kos—1.8 kms.

1 Yard—0.9144 meter.

Sarai—A caravanserai, inn.

Laila-Majnu—Characters from a famous eighteen century ballad.

Palki—Palanquin.

Khooni Darwaza—A gateway for murder. Most Mughal cities had one, where people beheaded, murdered, were displayed.

Kukri—A curved knife Gurkhas traditionally use.

REFERENCES

Sikh Consolidation and the Martyr Gurus

1. *Guru Granth Sahib*, Rag Bhairov, p-1136.

2. H M L Lawrence, *Adventure of an officer in the Punjab,* two volumes, Patiala, Punjabi University Languages Department, vol-I, 1970, pp-30-31.

3. Sir Lepel Griffin, *Rulers of India: Ranjit Singh*, Oxford, London, 1892, p-42.

4. Kartar Singh Duggal, *Maharaja Ranjit Singh: The Last to Lay Arms*, Abhinav Publications, New Delhi, 2001, p-18.

5. Ibid, pp-19-21.

6. Patwant Singh, Jyoti Rai, *Empire of the Sikhs: The Life and Times of Maharaja Ranjit Singh*, Hay House Publishers (India) Pvt. Ltd, Vasant Kunj, New Delhi, 2008, p-48.

7. *Tuzuk-i-Jahangiri* (Memoirs of Jehangir), Alexander Rogers (trans), Henry Beveridge (ed), Munshiram Manoharlal, Delhi, 1968 pp-72-73.

8. Max Arthur Macauliffe, *The Sikh Religion: Its Gurus, Sacred Writings and Authors* (Six volumes), Oxford University Press, London, vol-3 (first published 1909), reprint 1995, p-14.

9. Ibid, p-99.

10. Ibid.

11. Kartar Singh Duggal, *Maharaja Ranjit Singh:The Last to Lay Arms*, Abhinav Publications, New Delhi, 2001, p-23.

12. Hari Ram Gupta, *History of the Sikh: 1469-1708,* vol-I, Munshiram Manoharlal, Delhi, pp-161-162.

13. Indubhushan Banerjee, *Evolution of the Khalsa: Foundation of the Sikh Panth* (two volumes), A Mukherjee & Co, Calcutta, vol-I (first published in 1946) reprint 1972, p-14.

14. Max Arthur Macauliffe, *The Sikh Religion: Its Gurus, Sacred writings and Authors* (Six volumes), Oxford University Press, London, vol-4 (first published in 1909) reprint 1995, p-305.

15. Patwant Singh-Jyoti Rai, *Empire of the Sikhs: The Life and Times of Maharaja Ranjit Singh*, Hay House publishers (India) Pvt Ltd, New Delhi, 2008, p-57.

16. Ibid.

17. Saqi Mustad Khan, *Maasir-i-Alamgir (A History of the Emperor Aurangzeb-Alamgir, 1650-1707)* Jadunath Sarkar (trans) Munshiram Manoharlal, Delhi, (first published 1947) reprint 1986, pp-51-52.

18. Kartar Singh Duggal, *Maharaja Ranjit Singh: The Last to Lay Arms,* Abhinav Publications, New Delhi, 2001, pp-28-29.

19. Ibid, p-29.

20. Duncan Greenlees, the *Gospel of the Guru Granth Sahib*, Theosophical Publishing House, Madras, 1952, p-87.

Gobind Singh Welds the Sikh into a Nation

1. Edmund Candler, the *Mantle of the East,* William Blackwood & Sons, London, 1910, pp-120-121.

2. Kartar Singh Duggal, *Maharaja Ranjit Singh: The Last to Lay Arms*, Abhinav Publications, New Delhi, 2001, p-31.

3. Ibid.

4. Harbans Singh, *Guru Gobind Singh*, Sterling Publishers, Delhi, 1979 pp-46-47.

5. Dilip Singh, *Guru Gobind Singh and Khalsa Discipline,* Singh Brothers, Amritsar, 1992.

6. Harbans Singh, *Guru Gobind Singh*, Sterling Publishers, Delhi, 1979, p-58.

7. Kartar Singh Duggal, *Maharaja Ranjit Singh: The Last to Lay Arms*, Abhinav Publications, New Delhi, 2001,pp-34-34.

Gobind Singh Prepared Ground for Sikh Kingdom

1. Khafi Khan, Muntakhab-ul-Lubab, in H M Elliot and J Dowson (eds), *The History of India as told by Its Own Historians*, Vol-7, Kitab Mahal, Allahabad, reprint, 1972, p-415.

2. Kartar Singh Duggal, *Maharaja Ranjit Singh: The Last to Lay Arms,* Abhinav Publications, New Delhi, 2001, p-41.

3. *Akhbar-i-Darbar-i-Mualla: Mughal Court News Relating to the Punjab, A. D. 1707-1718, Punjab Past and Present*, Patiala, Panjabi University, October 1984, p-141.

4. Patwant Singh, Jyoti M Rai, *Empire Of The Sikhs: The Life and Times of Maharaja Ranjit Singh,* Hay House Publishers (India) Pvt Ltd, New Delhi, 2008, pp-80-81.

5. The figures here and also in earlier paragraphs are taken from Bhagat Singh's, *A History of Sikh misls*, Punjabi University, Patiala, 1993, p-53.

6. Kartar Singh Duggal, *Maharaja Ranjit Singh: The Last to Lay Arms,* Abhinav Publications, New Delhi, 2001, p-46.

7. Sir Lepel Griffin, KC 31, *Rulers of India: Ranjit Singh*, Edited by Sir William Wilson Hunter, Oxford University Press, New York 1892, p-83.

The State of Punjab and Rise of Ranjit Singh

1. Khushwant Singh, *Ranjit Singh: Maharaja of the Punjab*, George Allen & Unwin Ltd, London, 1962, p-23.

2. Sir Lepel Griffin, *Rulers of India: Ranjit Singh,* Sir William Wilson Hunter, (Editor), Oxford University Press, New York, 1892, pp-88-89.

3. Kartar Singh Duggal, *Maharaja Ranjit Singh: The Last to Lay Arms*, Abhinav Publication, New Delhi, 2001, p-50.

4. Major G Smyth, *A History of the Reigning Family of Lahore* (first published in 1847), Nirmal Publishers & Distributors, New Delhi, reprint 1987, p-14.

5. Hari Ram Gupta, *History of the Sikhs* (five volumes) Munshiram Manoharlal, New Delhi, vol-5, p-10.

6. Sir Lepel Griffin, *Rulers of India: Ranjit Singh,* Sir William Wilson Hunter (Ed) Oxford University Press, New York, 1892, p-98.

7. Ibid, pp 79-80.

8. Bikrama Jit Hasrat, *Life and Time of Ranjit Singh: A Saga of Benevolent Despotism*, V V Research Institute Book Agency, Hoshiarpur, 1977, p-35.

The Maharaja

1. Khushwant Singh, *Ranjit Singh: Maharaja of the Punjab,* George Allen & Unwin Ltd, London, 1962, p-33.

2. Ibid.

3. Hari Ram Gupta, *History of the Sikhs* (five volumes), Munshiram Manoharlal, Delhi, vol-5, p-16.

4. Khushwant Singh, *Ranjit Singh: Maharaja of the Punjab,* George Allen & Unwin Ltd, London, 1962, p-14.

5. Hari Ram Gupta, *History of the Sikhs* (five volumes) Munshiram Manoharlal, Delhi, vol 5, 1991, p-22.

6. Patwant Singh, Jyoti M Rai, *Empire of the Sikhs: The Life and Times of Maharaja Ranjit Singh,* Hay House Publishers (India) Pvt Ltd, New Delhi, 2008, p-123.

7. General Sir John J H Gordon, *The Sikhs* (first published in 1904), Punjab University Languages Department, Chandigarh, reprint 1988, pp-86-87.

8. Harbans Singh, *Guru Gobind Singh*, Sterling Publishers, Delhi, 1979, pp-46-46.

A Sovereign and Secular Ruler

1. Baron Charles von Hügel, *Kashmir and the Punjab* (first published in 1845), Light & Life publishers, Jammu, reprint 1972, p-288.

2. Lala Sohan Lal Suri, *Umdat-Ut-Tawarikh*, Daftar III, Parts (I-IV), first published in 1889, S Chand & Co, Delhi, reprint 1961, pp-XVIII and XIX.

3. Fauja Singh and A C Arora, *Maharaja Ranjit Singh: Politics, Society and Economy*, Punjabi University, Patiala, 1984, p-316.

4. Patwant Singh, Jyoti M Rai, *Empire of the Sikhs: The Life and Times of Maharaja Ranjit Singh,* Hay House publishers (India) Pvt. Ltd., New Delhi, 2008, p-127.

5. Alexander Burns, *Travels into Bokhara,* vol-I of 3 vols, Oxford University Press, London, 1973.

6. Fauja Singh Bajwa, *Military System of the Sikhs: During the Period 1799-1849,* Motilal Banarsidass, Delhi/Varanasi/Patna, 1964.

7. Amrinder Singh, *The Last Sunset: The Rise and Fall of Lahore Durbar,* Roli Books Pvt Ltd, New Delhi, 2011, p-22-23.

8. Kartar Singh Duggal, *Maharaja Ranjit Singh:The Last to Lay Arms,* Abhinav Publications, New Delhi, 2001 pp-57-58.

9. Sir Lepel Griffin, *Rulers of India: Ranjit Singh,* (Ed. Sir William Wilson Hunter), Oxford University Press, New York, 1892, p-115.

10. Patwant Singh, Jyoti M Rai, *Empire of the Sikhs: Maharaja Ranjit Singh,* Hay House Publishers, (India) Pvt Ltd, New Delhi, 2008, p-178.

11. Sir Lepel Griffin, *The Punjab Chiefs,* Civil and Military Press, Lahore, vol-I, 1890, reprint 1909, p-260.

12. Patwant Singh, Jyoti M Rai, *Empire of the Sikhs: The Life and Times of Maharaja Ranjit Singh,* Hay House Publishers (India) Pvt. Ltd, New Delhi, 2008, p-180-181.

13. S R Kohli, *Land Revenue Administration under the Sikhs* in the *Journal of the Punjab Historical Society, 1918.*

14. Khushwant Singh, *Ranjit Singh: Maharaja of the Punjab,* George Allen & Unwin Ltd, London, 1962, p-50.

15. Patwant Singh, Jyoti Rai, *Empire of the Sikhs: The Life and the Times of Maharaja Ranjit Singh* Hay House Publishers (India) Pvt Ltd, New Delhi, 2008 pp-181-182.

16. Ibid, p-182.

17. Jean Marie Lafont, *Maharaja Ranjit Singh: Lord of the Five Rivers*, Oxford University Press, New Delhi, 2002, p-87.

18. Ibid, pp-91-92.

19. Ibid, pp-92-93.

20. Ibid, p-97.

21. Ibid, pp-98-99.

22. Ibid, p-101.

The British and Ranjit Singh

1. Philip Woodruff, *The Men who Ruled India*, Jonathan Cape, Vol 1, The Founders, London, 1953, p-200.

2. Thompson Edward, *The Life of Charles, Lord Metcalfe,* Faber and Faber, London, 1937, p-75.

3. Kartar Singh Duggal, *Maharaja Ranjit Singh: The Last to Lay Arms,* Abhinav Publications, New Delhi, 2001, p-70.

4. Khushwant Singh, *Ranjit Singh: Maharajah of the Punjab,* George Allen & Unwin Ltd, London, 1962, p-92.

5. Ibid, p-93.

6. Ibid, p-93.

7. Joseph Davey Cunningham, *A History of the Sikhs: From the Origins of the Nation to the Battles of the Sutlej* (first published 1849, S Chand & Co., Delhi, reprint, 1966, Appendix xxv, p-352.

8. Khushwant Singh, *Ranjit Singh: Maharaja of the Punjab*, George Allen & Unwin Ltd., London, 1962, p-94.

9. Ibid.

10. K K Khullar, *Maharaja Ranjit Singh,* Prominent Printers, Delhi, 1980, p-154.

Conquests and the Kohinoor

1. Hari Ram Gupta, *History of the Sikhs* (five volumes), Munshiram Manoharlal, Delhi Vol-5, p-102.

2. Dr J S Grewal, from the *Treaty of Amritsar to the Conquest of Multan: The Evidence of Umdat-ut-Tawarikh* in Fauja Singh and A C Arora, *Maharaja Ranjit Singh: Politics, Society and Economy*, Punjabi University, Patiala, 1984, pp-15-16.

3. Patwant Singh, *The Sikhs*, John Murry, London, 1999, p-119.

4. Jean Marie Lafont, *Maharaja Ranjit Singh: Lord of the Five Rivers*, Oxford University Press, New Delhi, 2002, p-48.

5. Iradi Amini, *Koh-i-Noor*, Roli Books, Delhi, 1994, p-27.

6. Sir Lepel Griffin, Rulers of India: *Ranjit Singh*, Oxford University Press, London, 1892, pp-100-101.

7. Ibid, p-101.

8. Under the liberal government of Maharaja Ranit Singh Bahadur over the region of Peshawar, in the (VS) year 1891 (A.D. 1834).

Leili and The Capture of Peshawar

1. *Gazeetteer of the Peshawar District* 1897-98, Sang-e-Meel Publications, Lahore 1989, p-73.

2. Dr Ahmad Hasan Dani, *Peshawar: Historic City of the Frontier*, Sang-e-Meel Publications, Lahore, 1995, P-15, quoted in Patwant Singh, Jyoti M Rai, *Empire of the Sikhs: The Life and Times of Maharaja Ranjit Singh*, Hay House Publishers (India) Pvt Ltd, New Delhi, 2008, p-168.

3. Kartar Singh Duggal, *Maharaja Ranjit Singh: The Last to Lay Arms*, Abhinav Publications, New Delhi, 2001, p-96.

4. Ibid.

Conquest of Multan

1. Kartar Singh Duggal, *Maharaja Ranjit Singh: The Last to Lay Arms,* Abhinav Publications, New Delhi, p-82.

2. Sir Lepel Griffin, *Rulers of India: Ranjit Singh*, Oxford University Press, London, 1892, p-185.

3. Khushwant Singh, *Ranjit Singh: Maharaja of the Punjab,* George Allen & Unwin Ltd, London, 1962, p-125.

4. Kartar Singh Duggal, *Maharaja Ranjit Singh: The Last to Lay Arms* Abhinav Publications, New Delhi, 2001, p-84.

5. W G Archer, *Paintings of the Sikhs*, Her Majesty's Stationery Office, London, 1966, p-9.

Afghan Invasions and The Punjab

1. Hari Ram Gupta, *History of the Sikhs* (five volumes), Munshiram Manoharlal, Delhi, vol – 5, 1991, p-14.

2. Patwant Singh, Jyoti M Rai, *Empire of the Sikhs: The Life and Time of Maharaja Ranjit Singh,* Hay House Publishers (India) Pvt Ltd, New Delhi, 2008, p-83.

A Sensualist

1. Fakir Syed Waheeduddin, *The Real Ranjit Singh* (first published in 1965), Punjabi University reprint, Patiala, 1981, pp-170-172.

2. Sir Lepel Griffin, *Rulers of India: Ranjit Singh,* Oxford University Press, London, 1892, p-105.

3. W G Osborne, *Court and the Camp of Ranjit Singh,* Henry Colburn Publisher, London, 1840, pp-189-192.

4. Sir Lepel Griffin, *Rulers of India: Ranjit Singh,* Oxford University Press, London, 1892, p-106.

5. Ibid.

6. Fakir Syed Waheeduddin, *The Real Ranjit Singh* (first published 1965) Punjabi University, Patiala, reprint 1981, p-169.

7. Fakir Syed Waheeduddin, *The Real Ranjit Singh,* (first published in 1965), Punjabi University, Patiala, reprint 1981.

8. Lala Sohan Lala Suri, *Umdat-ut-Tawarikh,* Daftar III, Part I-V (first published in 1889), S. Chand & Co., Delhi, reprint 1961.

9. Syed Muhammad Latif, *Lahore: Its History, Architectural Remains and Antiquities* (first published in 1892), Sang-e-Meel publications Lahore, reprint 1994, pp-249-250.

10. W G Osborne, *Court and Camp of Ranjit Singh,* Henry Colburn, Publisher, London, 1840, pp-85-86.

11. Hari Ram Gupta, *History of Sikhs: The Sikh Lion of Lahore Maharaja Ranjit Singh, 1799-1839,* (five volumes), vol-5, Munshiram Manoharlal, Delhi pp-537-538.

12. Fakir Syed Waheeduddin, *The Real Ranjit Singh* (first published 1965), Punjabi University, Patiala, reprint 1981, p-165.

13. Sir Lepel Griffin, *Rulers of India: Ranjit Singh,* Oxford University Press, London, 1892, p-107.

14. Ibid, pp-107-108.

15. Syed Muhammad Latif, *History of the Punjab* (first Published 1891), Kalyani publishers, New Delhi, reprint 1989, p-423.

16. Ibid.

17. Sir Lepel Griffin, *Rulers of India: Ranjit Singh,* Oxford University Press, London, 1892, p-109.

18. Ibid, p-110.

Foreigners at the Lahore Durbar

1. S S Thorburn, *The Punjab in Peace and War* (first published in 1883), Punjab University Language Department, Chandigarh, reprint 1989, p-4.

2. Major Hugh Pearse (ed), *Soldier and Traveller: Memoirs of Alexander Gardner*, William Blackwood and Sons, Edinburg, London, 1898.

3. Sir Lepel Griffin, *Rulers of India: Ranjit Singh*, Oxford University Press, London, p-134-135.

4. Ibid, p-135.

5. Ibid, p-136.

6. W G Osborne, *Court and Camp of Ranjit Singh*, Henry Colburn, Publisher, London, 1840, pp-142-145.

7. Kartar Singh Duggal, *Maharaja Ranjit Singh: The Last to Lay Arms*, Abhinav publications, New Delhi, 2001, p-85.

8. Ibid, p-87.

9. Ibid, p-88.

10. Ibid, p-89.

11. Ibid, p-89.

12. Andrew Preziosi, *The First Sikh War 1845-1846: Order of the Battle Book*, Khyber Pass Games and Books, Miami, 2004.

13. Joseph Davy Cunningham, *A History of the Sikhs: From the Origins of the Nation to the Battle of the Sutlej* (first published 1849),

S Chand & Co., Delhi, reprint 1966, p-153.

14. Hari Ram Gupta, *History of the Sikhs from Nadir Shah's Invasion to the Rise of Ranjit Singh 1739-1799*, Minerva Book Shop, Simla, vol-5, 1952.

The Last Battle

1. Kartar Singh Duggal, *Maharaja Ranjit Singh: The Last to Lay Arms*, Abhinav Publications, New Delhi, 2001, p-180.

2. Khushwant Singh, *Ranjit Singh: Maharajah of the Punjab,* George Allen & Unwin Ltd, London, 1962, p-218.

3. Henry Steinbach, *The Country of the Sikhs* (first published 1846), KLM Book House, New Delhi, reprint 1978, p-14.

4. General Sir John J H Gordon, KCB, *The Sikhs* (first published 1904), Punjab University Language Department, Chandigarh, reprint 1988, pp 116-17.

5. Khushwant Singh, *Ranjit Singh: Maharaja of the Punjab,* George Allen & Unwin Ltd, London, 1962, p-222.

6. Ibid.

7. *Lahore Akhbar*, June 1839, quoted in Ibid, p-223.

8. John Martin Honigberger, *Thirty-Five Years in the East*, p-102 (first Published in 1852), reprint, Forgotten Books, 218, quoted in Ibid.

9. Honigberger, *Thirty-Five Years in the East*, pp-103-4, quoted in Ibid, p-224.

10. Joseph Davy Cunningham, *A history of the Sikhs: From the Origins of the Nation to the Battles of the Sutlej* (first Published 1849), S. Chand & Co, Delhi, reprint 1966, p-200.

The Worm Within

1. Major Evans Bell, *The Annexation of the Punjab and Maharajah Duleep Singh* (first published 1882) Nirmal Publisher & Distributors, New Delhi, reprint 1986, pp-9-10.

2. Barbara W Touchman, *Sand against the Wind: Stilwell and the American Experience in China 1911-45,* Lowe and Brydone, London, 1971, p-436.

3. Donald Featherstone, *At Them With the Bayonet:* The first Sikh War, Jarrolds, London, 1968, p-X.

4. Syed Muhammad Latif, *History of the Punjab from the Remotest Antiquities to the Present Time,* Calcutta Central Press Co, Calcutta, 1891.

5. Syed Muhammad Latif, *History of the Punjab* (first published 1891), Kalyani publishers, New Delhi, reprint 1989, p-498.

6. Bikrama Jit Hasrat, *Life and Times of Ranjit Singh: A Saga of Benevolent Despotism,* V V Research Institute Book Agency, Hoshiarpur, 1977, p-217.

7. Fauja Singh, *Maharaja Kharak Singh,* Punjabi University, Patiala, 1977, p-XLIV.

8. Major G Carmichael Smyth, *A History of the Reigning Family of Lahore,* (first published in 1847.), Gyan Books Private Ltd., Delhi, reprint.

9. Amrinder Singh, the *Last Sunset: The Rise and fall of the Lahore Durbar,* Roli Books, New Delhi, 2010, p-50.

10. Major G C Smyth, *A History of the Reigning Family of Lahore* (first published 1847), Nirmal Publishers & Distributors, New Delhi, reprint 1987, p-36.

11. Quoted in Ibid, p-36.

12. Syed Muhammad Latif, *History of the Punjab* (first published 1891) Kalyani Publishers, New Delhi, reprint 1989, p-502

13. Major G C Smyth, *A History of the Reigning Family of Lahore* (first published 1847) Nirmal publishers & Distributors, New Delhi, reprint 1987, p-38.

14. Syed Muhammad Latif, *History of the Punjab* (first published 1891), Kalyani Publishers, New Delhi, reprint 1989, p-505-506.

15. Ibid, p-506.

16. Ibid.

17. Major Hugh Pearse, *Soldier and Traveller: Memoirs of Alexander Gardner,* quoted in Amrinder Singh's *The Last Sunset: The Rise & Fall of the Lahore Durbar*, Roli Books, New Delhi, 2010, p-55.

18. Amrinder Singh *The Last Sunset: The Rise & Fall of the Lahore Durbar*, Roli Books, New Delhi, 2010, p-57.

19. Major Hugh Pearse, *Soldier and Traveller: Memoirs of Alexander Gardner,* Appendix-XXXIX, quoted in Ibid, p-58.

20. Quoted in Harbans Singh, *The Heritage of the Sikhs*, Manohar publications, New Delhi, 1985, p-199.

21. Bikrama Jit Hasrat, *Life and Times of Ranjit Singh: A Saga of Benevolent Despotism,* V V Research Institute Book Agency, Hoshiarpur, 1977, p-217.

22. Michael Alexander and Sushila Anand, *Queen Victoria's Maharaja: Duleep Singh* 1838-93, Weidenfeld and Nicolson, London, 1980, p-2.

23. C H Payne, *A Short History of the Sikhs,* Thomas Nelson & Sons, London 1915, p-146.

The First Anglo-Sikh War

1. Bikrama Jit Hasrat, *The Punjab Papers* (1836-1849), V V Research Institute Book Agency, Hoshiarpur, 1970, p-72.

2. Dewan Ajudhia Parshad, *Waqai Jang-i-Sikhan (Events of the first Anglo-Sikh War – 1845-46),* Punjab Itihas Prakashan, Chandigarh, 1975, pp-11-12.

3. Patwant Singh, *The Sikhs*, John Murry, London, 1999, p-153.

4. Ibid.

5. Sita Ram Kohli, *Sunset of the Sikh Empire*, Orient Longman, New Delhi, 1967, p-103

6. Joseph Davey Cunningham, *A History of the Sikhs: From the Origins of the Nation to the Battles of the Sutlej* (first published in 1849, S. Chand & Co, Delhi, reprint 1966, pp-257- 58.

7. Khushwant Singh, *The Fall of the Kingdom of the Punjab,* Penguin Books, Gurgaon, 2014, p-103.

8. George Bruce, *Six Battles for India: The Anglo-Sikh Wars, 1845-46, 1848-49*, Arthur Barker Ltd, London, 1969.

9. Khushwant Singh, *The Fall of the Kingdom of the Punjab,* Penguin Books, Gurgaon, 2014, pp-104-105.

10. George Bruce, *Six Battles for India: The Anglo-Sikh Wars, 1845-46, 1848-49*, Arthur Barker Ltd, London, 1969, quoted in Amrinder Singh's *The Last Sunset*, Roli Books, New Delhi, 2010, p-66.

11. Khushwant Singh, *The Fall of the Kingdom of the Punjab,* Penguin Books, Gurgaon, 2014, p-106.

12. George Bruce, *Six Battles for India: The Anglo-Sikh Wars 1845-46, 1848-49,* Arthur Barker Ltd, London, 1969, quoted in Amrinder Singh's *The Last Sunset*, Roli Books, New Delhi, 2010, p-67-67.

13. Khushwant Singh, *The Fall of the Kingdom of the Punjab,* Penguin Books, Gurgaon, 2014, p-108.

14. Joseph Davey Cunningham, *A History of the Sikhs: From the Origins of the Nation to the Battles of Sutlej* (first published 1849, S. Chand & Co, Delhi, reprint 1966, p-265.

15. Sita Ram Kohli, *Sunset of the Sikh Empire,* Orient Longman, New Delhi, 1967, p-106.

16. Ibid, p-266.

17. Ibid, p-267.

18. Dr W L McGregor, The History of the Sikhs (first published 1846), Rupa, Delhi, reprint 2007, p-120.

19. Donald Fatherstone, *At them with Bayonet: The First Sikh War,* Jarrolds, London, 1968, p-90.

20. Quoted in Khushwant Singh's, *The Fall of the Kingdom of the Punjab, P*enguin Books Gurgaon, 2014, p-110.

21. Khushwant Singh, *The Fall of the Kingdom of the Punjab,* Penguin Books, 2014, Gurgaon, 2014, pp-110-111.

22. Ibid, p-111.

23. Quoted in Ibid.

24. Quoted in Donald Featherstone, *At Them with Bayonet: The First Sikh War,* Jarrolds, London, 1968, pp-97,105.

25. Major G C Smyth, *A History of the Reigning Family of Lahore* (first published 1847), Nirmal Publishers & Distributors, New Delhi, reprint 1987, p-XXVI.

26. Syad Muhammad Latif, *History of the Punjab* (first published 1891), Kalyani Publishers, New Delhi, reprint 1989, p-544.

27. Quoted in Khushwant Singh's, *The Fall of the Kingdom of the Punjab,* Penguin Books, Gurgaon, 2014, p-115.

28. Patwant Singh, Jyoti M Rai, *Empire of the Sikhs: The Life and Times of Maharaja Ranjit Singh,* Hay House Publishers (India) Pvt Ltd, New Delhi, 2008, p-309.

29. H C B Cook, *The Sikh Wars: British Army in the Punjab, 1845-49,* Leo Cooper, London, 1975.

30. Bikrama Jit Hasrat, *Anglo-Sikh Relations, 1799-1849: A Reappraisal of the Rise & Fall of the Sikhs,* V V Research Institute Book Agency, 1968, p-284.

31. Donald Featherstone, *At Them with Bayonet: The First Sikh War,* Jarrolds, London, 1968, pp-134-135.

32. Quoted in Amrinder Singh's, *The Last Sunset: The Rise & Fall of the Lahore Durbar,* Roli Books, New Delhi, 2010, p-150.

33. Quoted in Ibid.

34. Quoted in Ibid.

35. Quoted in Ibid.

36. Quoted in Ibid, p-151.

37. Amrinder Singh, *The Last Sunset: The Rise & Fall of the Lahore Durbar,* Roli Books, New Delhi, 2010, p-151.

38. Ibid, p-152.

British Plan to Annex Punjab in Two Stages

1. Quoted in Khushwant Singh's, *The Fall of the Kingdom of the Punjab,* Penguin Books, Gurgaon, 2014, pp-124-125.

2. Quoted in Ibid, p-126.

3. Quoted in Ibid, pp-126-127.

4. Joseph Davey Cunningham, *A history of the Sikhs: From the Origins of the Nation to the Battles of the Sutlej* (first published 1849), S Chand & Co, Delhi, reprint 1966, p-289.

5. Patwant Singh, Jyoti M Rai, *Empire of the Sikhs: The Life and Times of Maharaja Ranjit Singh,* Hay House Publishers (India) Pvt Ltd., New Delhi, 2008, pp-315-316.

6. Quoted in Khushwant Singh's *The Fall of the Kingdom of the Punjab,* Penguin Books, Gurgaon, 2014, p-134.

7. Ibid.

8. Khushwant Singh, *The Fall of Kingdom of the Punjab,* Penguin Books, Gurgaon, 2014, p-135.

9. Quoted in Ibid, p-136.

10. Quoted Lady Lena Campbell Login, Lady Login's Recollection Quoted in Amrinder Singh's *The Last Sunset*, Roli Books, New Delhi; 2010, p-246.

11. Michael Alexander and Sushila Anand, *Queen Victoria's Maharajah*, quoted in Ibid, p-248.

The Second Anglo-Sikh War

1. Dr W L McGregor, *The History of the Sikhs,* (first published 1846), Rupa, Delhi, reprint-2007, p-256.

2. Papers Relating to the Punjab 1847-1849, Harrison & Son, London, Enclosure 32 in No 38, quoted in Patwant Singh, Jyoti M Rai's, *Empire of the Sikhs: The Life and Times of Maharaja Ranjit Singh,* Hay House Publishers (India) Pvt Ltd, New Delhi, 2008, p-320.

3. Bikrama Jit Hasrat, *Anglo-Sikh Relations, 1799-1849: A reappraisal*

of the Rise & Fall of the Sikhs, V V Research Institute Book Agency, Hoshiarpur, 1968, p-323.

4. Patwant Singh, *The Sikhs*, John Murray, London, 1999, pp-168-169.

5. Bikrama Jit Hasrat, *Anglo-Sikh Relations, 1799-1949: A Reappraisal of the Rise & Fall of the Sikhs*, V V Research Institute Book Agency, Hoshiarpur, 1968, p-328.

6. Ibid, p-332

7. Quoted in Khushwant Singh's *The Fall of the Kingdom of the Punjab,* Penguin Books Gurgaon, 2014, p-169.

8. Quoted in Ibid, p-170.

9. Bikrama Jit Hasrat, *Anglo-Sikh Relations, 1799-1849: A Reappraisal of the Rise & Fall of the Sikhs,* V V Research Institute Book Agency, Hoshiarpur, 1968, pp-335-37.

10. Quoted in Khushwant Singh's *The Fall of the Kingdom of the Punjab,* Penguin Books, Gurgaon, 2014, pp-172-173.

11. S S Thorburn, *The Punjab in Peace and War* (first published 1883), Punjab University Language Department, Chandigarh, reprint 1989, p-142.

12. Ibid, pp-139-40.

13. Quoted in Khushwant Singh's *The Fall of the Kingdom of the Punjab,* Penguin Books, Gurgaon, 2014, p-174.

14. Ibid, p-175.

15. Ibid, p-176.

16. Quoted in Patwant Singh, Jyoti M Rai's *Empire of the Sikhs: The Life and Times of Maharaja Ranjit Singh*, Hay House Publishers (India) Pvt. Ltd., New Delhi, 2008, p-324.

17. Quoted in Amrinder Singh's *The Last Sunset: The Rise & Fall of the Lahore Durbar*, Roli Books, New Delhi, 2017, p-227.

18. https://en.wikipedia.org/wiki/Treaty--of--Lahore

The British Subverted the Sikh State

1. Joseph Davy Cunningham, *A History of the Sikhs: from the Origins of the Nation to the Battles of the Sutlej* (first published 1849) S Chand & Co, Delhi, reprint 1966, p-279.

2. Bikrama Jit Hasrat, *Life and Time of Ranjit Singh: A Saga of Benevolent Despotism* V V Research Institute Book Agency, Hoshiarpur, 1968, p- 251.

3. Ibid.

4. Amarinder Singh, *The Last Sunset: The Rise & Fall of the Lahore Durbar*, Roli Books, New Delhi, 2010, p- 61.

5. H C B Cook, *The Sikh Wars: British Army in the Punjab, 1845-49*, Leo Cooper, 1975, quoted in Amarinder Singh's, *The Last Sunset: Rise & Fall of the Lahore Durbar*, Roli Books, New Delhi, 2010, p-65.

6. Henry Hardinge, Hugh Gouch, and Sir Harry George Wakwlyn Smith, *The War in India: Despatches of Viscount Hardinge, Lord Gouch, Sir Harry Smith… and other documents: comprising the engagements of Mookee, Ferozshah Aliwal and Sobraon*. Smith, London: J. Oliver, 1846, quoted in Ibid, p-65.

7. Donald Featherstone, *At Them with Bayonet: The First Sikh War*, Jarrolds, London, 1968, quoted in Ibid, p- 66.

The Last Heir Dalip Singh

1. Lady Lena Campbell Login, Lady Login's *Recollection: Court Life and Camp Life, 1820-1904,* Smith, Elder, London, 1916. In her

Recollections, Lady Login says that Rani Dukhnoo was of ancient Rajput lineage from the Kangra hills, and had been specially selected for beauty for the harem of Sher Singh (later Maharaja Sher Singh) – Ranjit Singh's adopted son – on his coming to the throne. Thus, the little Sheo Deo Singh was only a few months old when his father was murdered, and Dalip Singh was elected by the Khalsa (Sikh Commonwealth). Quoted in Amrinder Singh's *The Last Sunset: The Rise & Fall of the Lahore Durbar*, Roli Books, New Delhi, 2017, p-339.

2. Michael Alexander and Sushila Anand, *Queen Victoria's Maharajah: Duleep Singh, 1838-93*, Weidenfeld and Nicolson, London, 1980.

3. Ibid.

4. Ibid.

5. Peter Bance, the Duleep Singhs: The Photograph Album of Queen Victoria's Maharaja, Sutton, Stroud, 2004, Quoted in Amrinder Singh's *The Last Sunset*, Roli Books, New Delhi, 2017, p-242.

6. Michael Alexander and Sushila Anand, *Queen Victoria's Maharaja: Duleep Singh*, 1838-93, Weidenfeld and Nicholson, London, 1980, Quoted in Amrinder Singh's *The Last Sunset* p-242.

7. Quoted in Amrinder Singh's *The Last Sunset: The Rise & Fall of the Lahore Durbar*, Roli Books, New Delhi, 2017, p-244.

8. Quoted in Ibid, p-244.

9. Michael Alexander and Sushila Anand, *Queen Victoria's Maharaja*, Quoted in Ibid, p-247.

10. Ibid, p-249.

11. Ibid, p-250.

12. Ibid, p-252.

13. Ibid, pp-252-53.

14. Ibid, p-253.

15. Ibid, p-254.

16. Ibid, p-256.

17. Ibid, p-258.

18. Ibid, p-259.

19. Ibid.

20. Ibid.

ACKNOWLEDGEMENTS

The Publisher and Author gratefully acknowledge all Open Source information available in the worldwide web, Creative Commons sources, Google sources and Google Maps, Wikipedia and Wikimedia for all the relevant textual references, maps and pictures used in this work of non-fiction to facilitate reader understanding of the times, the landscape, the geopolitics and context of that period of history before, during and after Ranjit Singh and the Sikh kingdom. We are also grateful to the Sikh Museum for all the images of various paintings available on their website online.

Cover image: Originally painted on watercolour paper, this painting of Maharaja Ranjit Singh (early 1800s) depicts the Maharaja, with a halo of light around his head as ruler of the Sikh Empire, riding along a landscape of hills with flowers while on a white horse. with gemstones and prestigious attire as well. His trusted soldiers are seen accompanying him.

W G Archer, Paintings of the Sikhs, Her Majesty's Stationery Office, London, 1966.

Availble, courtesy Creative Commons through Sikhexpo bing.com/images.

All maps are British India Maps of the nineteenth century, used here only for reader clarity. None of them are to scale.

Courtesy: Creative Commons.

GALLERY

Guru Nanak

Guru Gobind Singh

Guru Tegh Bahadur

Guru Har Krishan

Guru Arjan

Guru Angad

Guru Amar Das

Guru Hargobind

Guru Ram Das

Guru Har Rai

This is supposedly a photograph of Maharaja Ranjit Singh, with Hari Singh Nalwa, taken some time in the 1830s. It is to be remembered in this context that both, the French and the English, were working still on the permanent imprint of exposure of light. This photograph, if truly Ranjit Singh's, could have been taken by one of his many French and English friends in his staff and visitors to his court.

Maharaja Ranjit Singh listening to Guru Granth Sahib being recited near the Akal Takht and Golden Temple, Amritsar, Punjab, India. *Sikh Museum*

A painting of Maharaja Ranjit Singh at the Maharaja Ranjit Singh Museum in Amritsar. While many foreign artists painted the Durbar scenes, a lot of Indian painters, especially those from Kangra and Kashmir, too contributed to the pictorial records of the times. *sikh museum*

A painting of Maharaja Ranjit Singh in Durbar at Lahore. Can be seen at the Maharaja Ranjit Singh Museum in Amritsar. *sikh museum*

A painting at the Maharaja Ranjit Singh Museum showing the Maharaja meeting the British at a camp site. Note, the two decorated elephants facing in opposite directions, the British had Ranjit Singh to compete with in display of splendour. The Maharaja had a canopy over his head. *sikh museum*

A painting from the Maharaja Ranjit Singh Museum, showing the Maharaja's foreign Generals inspecting his elite troops from the special escorts brigade. *sikh museum*

'Abu Tabela' the name Paolo Avitabile was known by in Afghanistan. He was the Governor of Peshawar and the General who steered Ranjit Singh's North West Frontier and Afghanistan campaign.

Avitabile's portrait by Colesworthy Grant

Book of rubbings of Kushan coins, by Claude Auguste Court, between 1827-1844.

Jean-François Allard, by Joseph-Désiré Court

Ventura, a sketch from Charles Grey's *European Adventurers of Northern India* (Lahore: 1929)

Ranjit Singh's camp in the hills of NWFP, by George Landseer, India, 19th century. Museum no. IS.41:2-1881. Pastel and watercolour

Sikhs and the English engaged in battle, by George Landseer, India, 19th century. Museum no. IS.41:2-1881. Pastel and watercolour

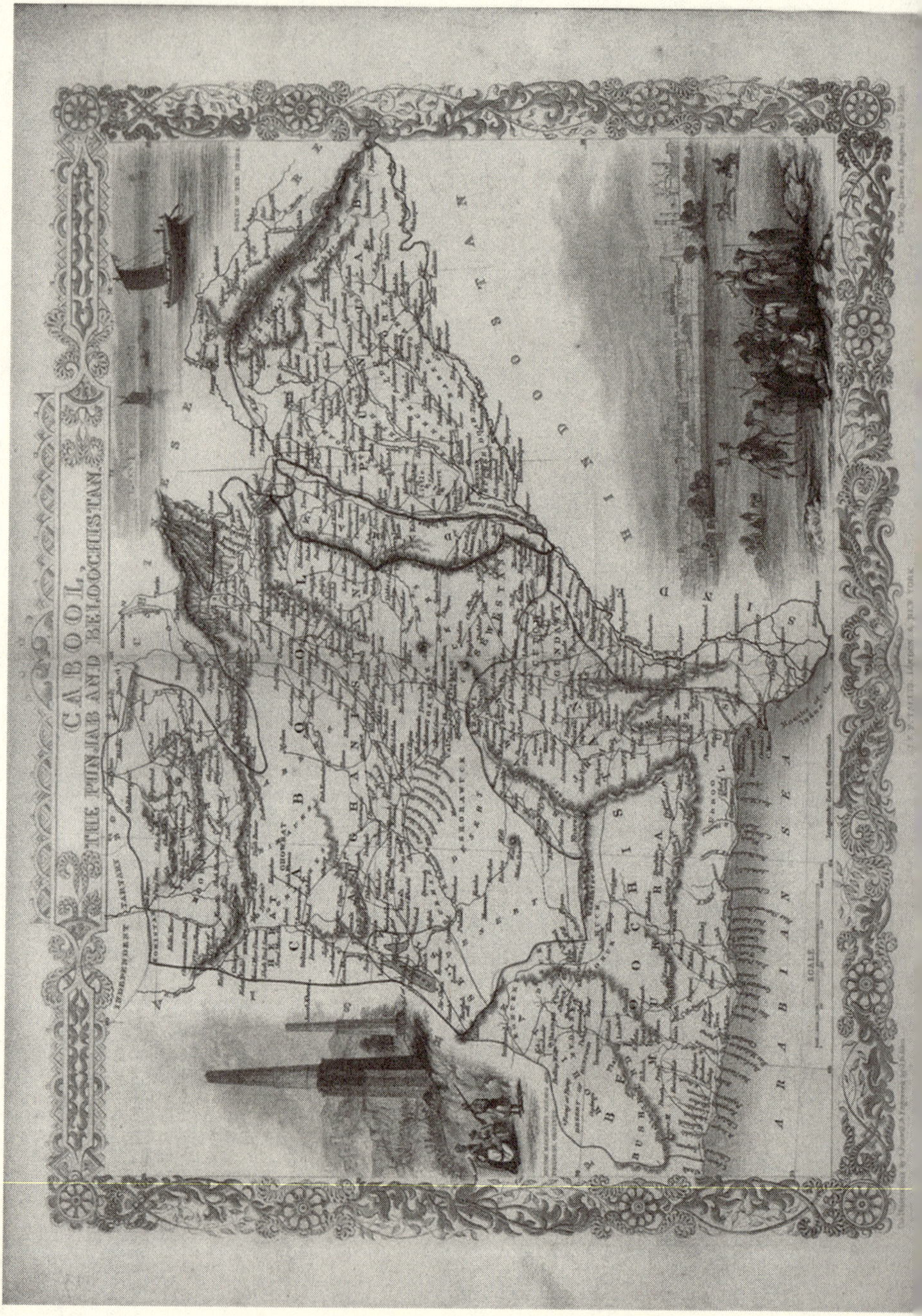

Punjab in the 1800, divided into small principalities

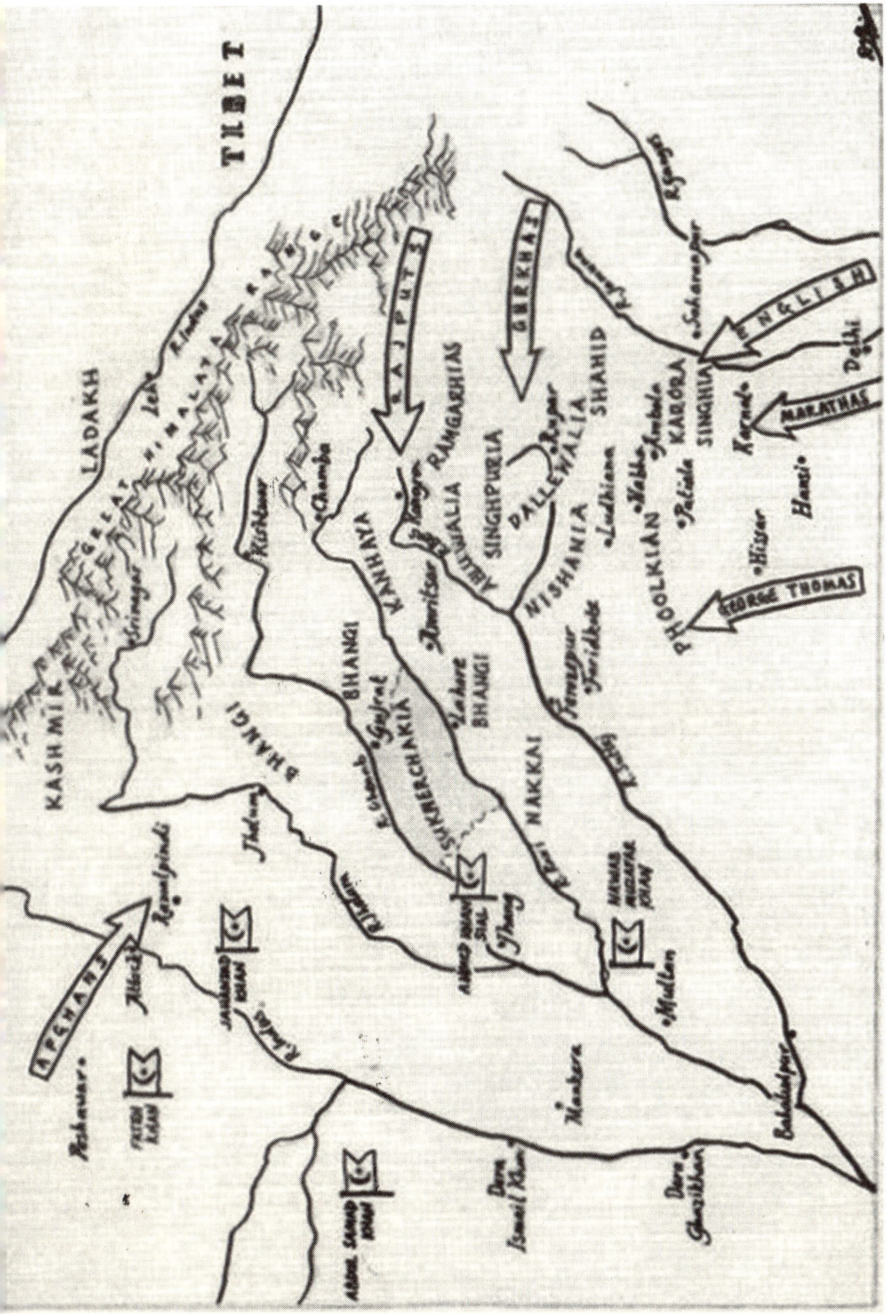

The Sikh Misls in 1780

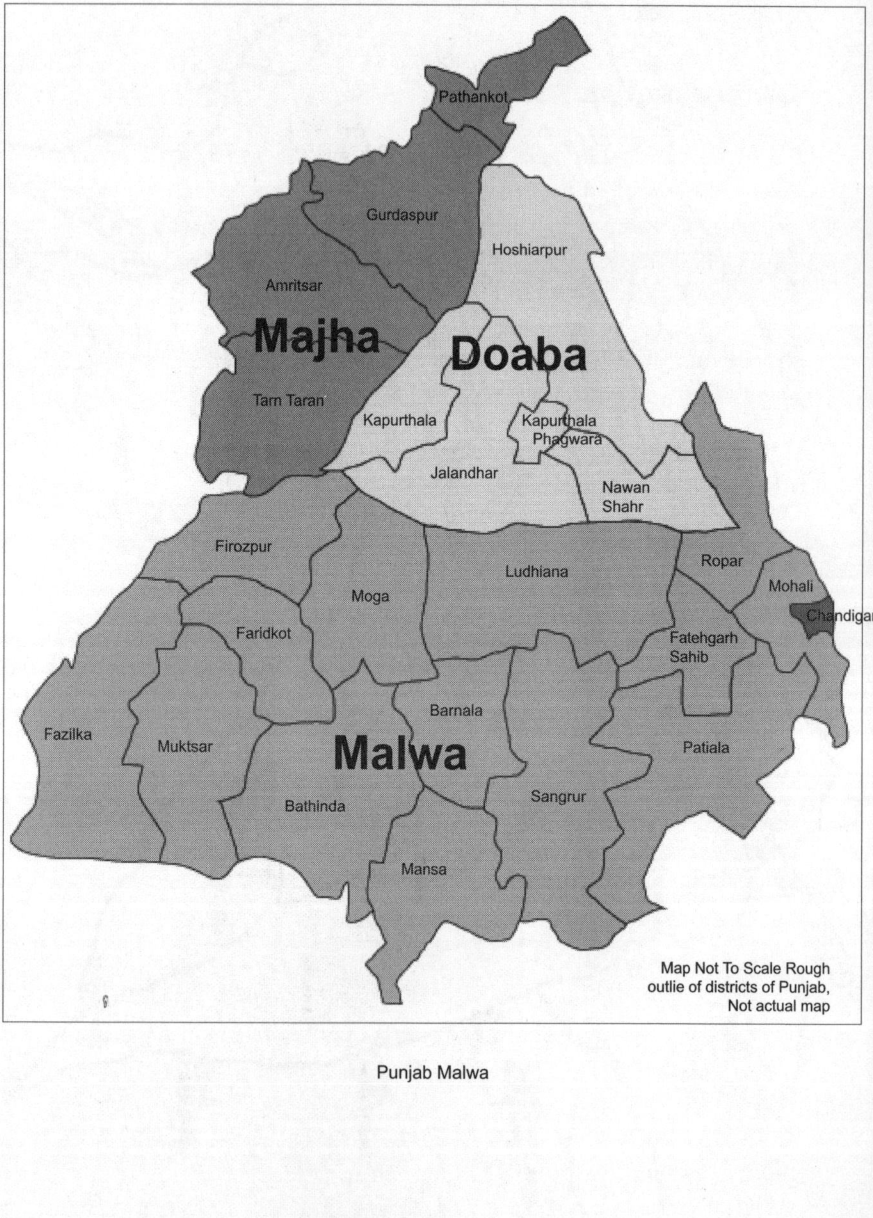

Punjab Malwa

India's Punjab today.

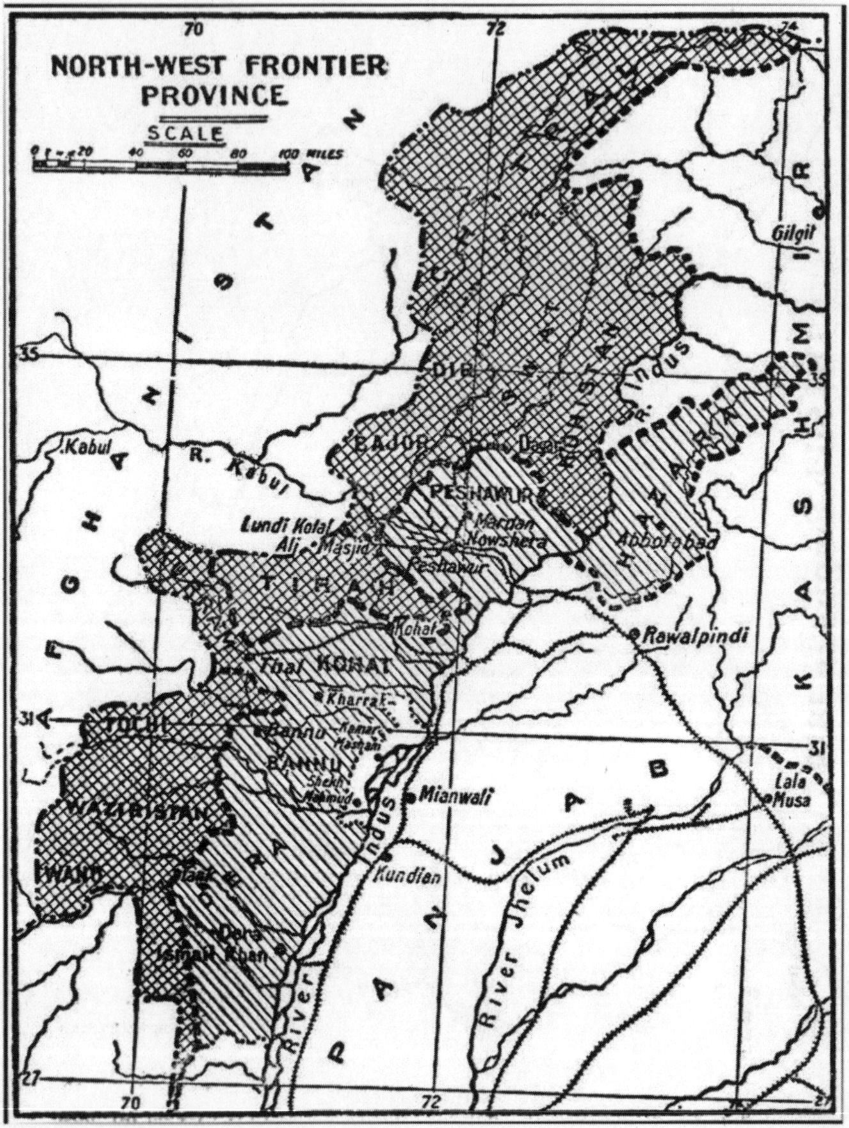

British India NWFP

the sikh empire in 1839

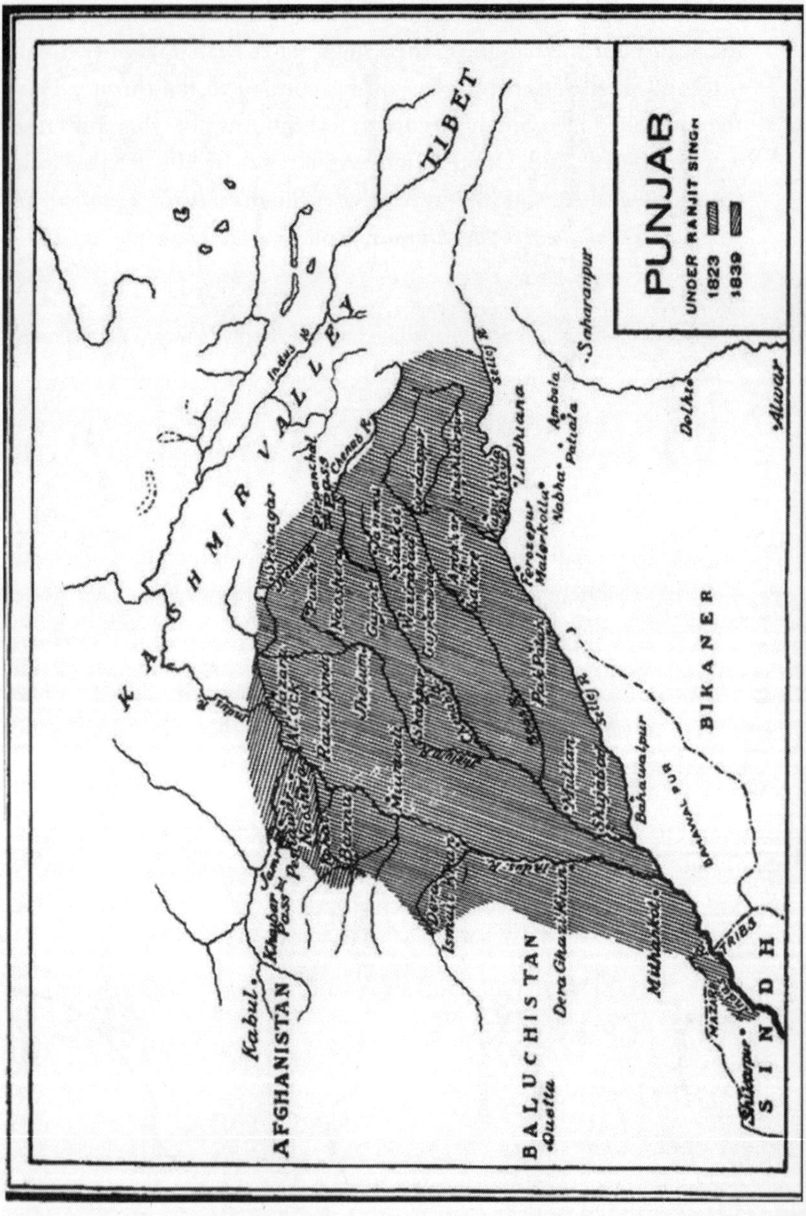
PUNJAB
UNDER RANJIT SINGH
1823
1839
TIBET
KASHMIR VALLEY
AFGHANISTAN
BALUCHISTAN
SINDH
BIKANER
BAHAWALPUR
Kabul
Quetta
Srinagar
Ludhiana
Ferozepur
Saharanpur
Delhi
Alwar
Multan
Bahawalpur
Shikarpur
Mithankot

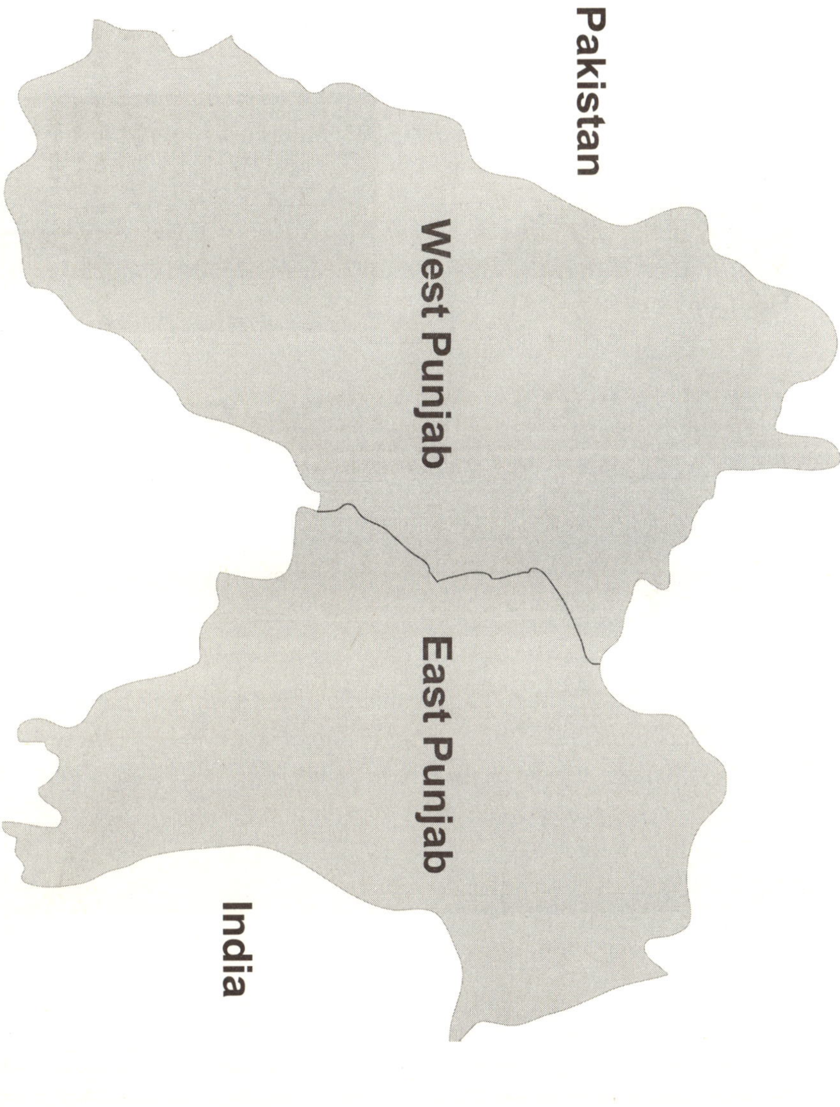
Pakistan
West Punjab
East Punjab
India

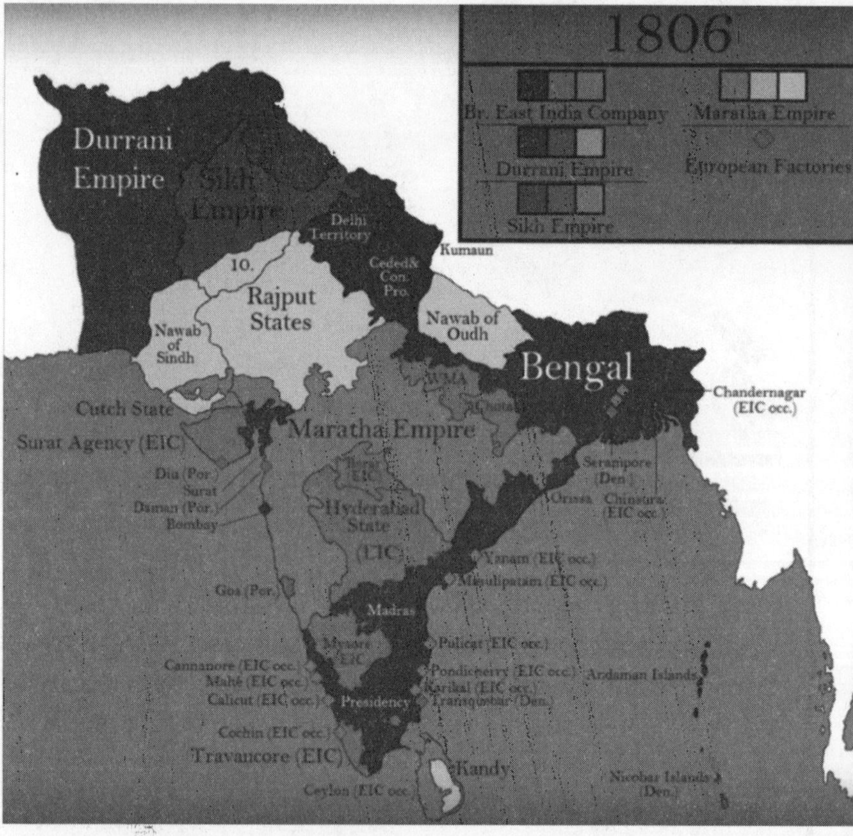
1806
Br. East India Company
Maratha Empire
Durrani Empire
European Factories
Sikh Empire
Durrani Empire
Sikh Empire
Delhi Territory
Kumaun
Ceded& Con. Pro.
10.
Rajput States
Nawab of Oudh
Nawab of Sindh
Bengal
Chandernagar (EIC occ.)
Cutch State
Maratha Empire
Surat Agency (EIC)
Serampore (Den.)
Dia (Por.)
Surat
Daman (Por.)
Bombay
Orissa
Chinsura (EIC occ.)
Hyderabad State (EIC)
Yanam (EIC occ.)
Masulipatam (EIC occ.)
Goa (Por.)
Madras
Mysore EIC
Pulicat (EIC occ.)
Cannanore (EIC occ.)
Mahé (EIC occ.)
Pondicherry (EIC occ.)
Karikal (EIC occ.)
Andaman Islands
Calicut (EIC occ.)
Presidency
Tranquebar (Den.)
Cochin (EIC occ.)
Travancore (EIC)
Kandy
Nicobar Islands (Den.)
Ceylon (EIC occ.)

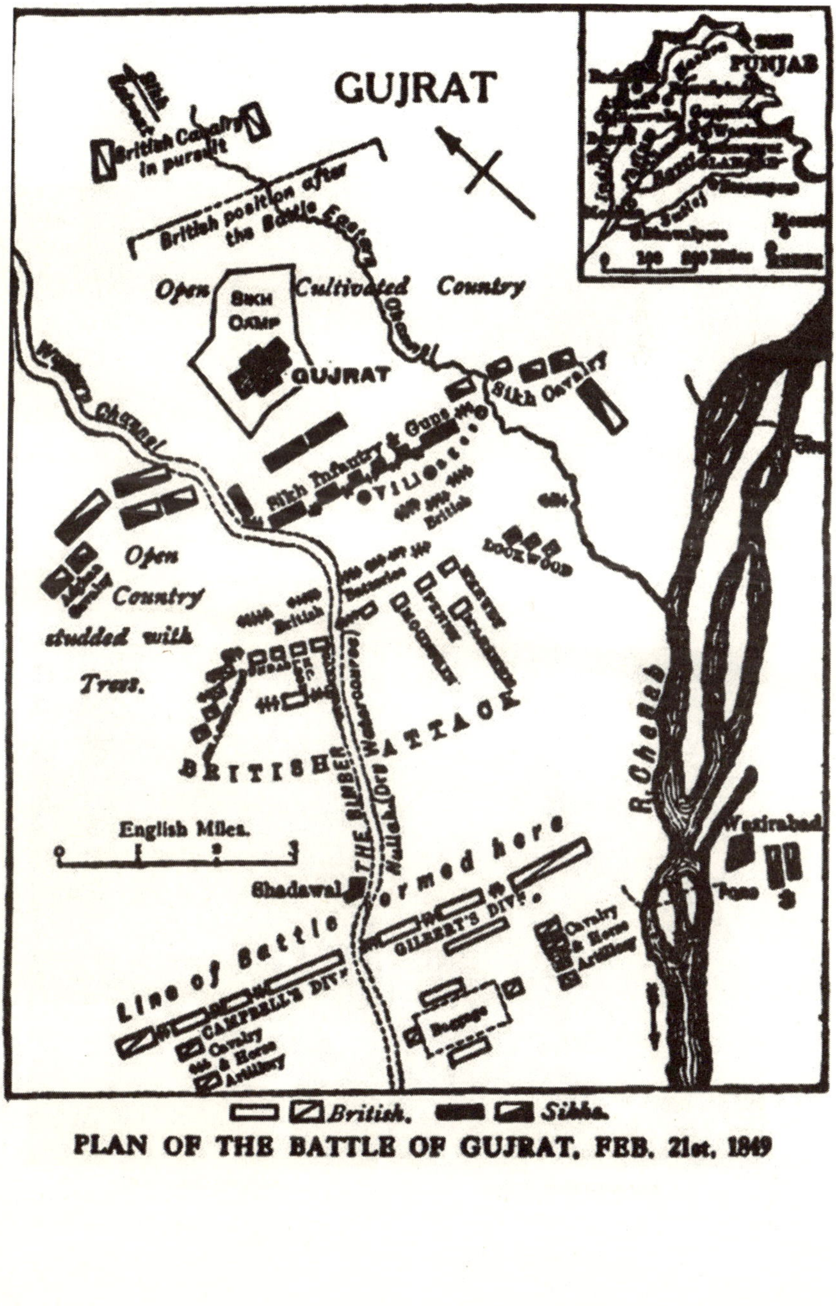

PLAN OF THE BATTLE OF GUJRAT, FEB. 21st, 1849

Maharaja Kharak Singh

Maharaja Nau Nihal Singh

Maharaja Sher Singh

Maharaja Dalip Singh